United in Diversity

Using Multicultural Young Adult Literature in the Classroom

Classroom Practices in Teaching English Vol. 29

Edited by

Jean E. Brown
Saginaw Valley State University

Elaine C. Stephens
Saginaw Valley State University

National Council of Teachers of English
1111 W. Kenyon Road, Urbana, Illinois 61801-1096

Manuscript Editor: Michael Deters, Precision Graphics

Production Editor: Tom Tiller

Interior Design: Doug Burnett

Cover Design: David Droll, Precision Graphics

NCTE Stock Number: 55715-3050

It is the policy of NCTE in its journals and other publications to provide a forum for the open discussion of ideas concerning the content and the teaching of English and the language arts. Publicity accorded to any particular point of view does not imply endorsement by the Executive Committee, the Board of Directors, or the membership at large, except in announcements of policy, where such endorsement is clearly specified.

Library of Congress Catalog Card Number 85-644740

ISBN 0-8141-5571-5
ISSN 0550-5755

This book was typeset in 11/13 Palatino by Precision Graphics of Champaign, IL. Typeface on the cover and spine was Adobe Garamond. The book was printed by Braun-Brumfield, Inc. of Ann Arbor, MI, on 50 lb. acid-free offset.

Classroom Practices in Teaching English

NCTE began publishing the Classroom Practices series in 1963 with *Promising Practices in the Teaching of English*. The following volumes from the

Activities th

Focus on N

How to H N

Ideas for N

Literatur ... by Pa

Process a ... , ar

United ir Cl St

Voices in ec

Classroom Practices in Teaching English

NCTE began publishing the Classroom Practices series in 1963 with *Promising Practices in the Teaching of English*. The following volumes in the series are currently available:

Activities to Promote Critical Thinking (1986), by Jeff Golub, Chair, and the NCTE Committee on Classroom Practices

Focus on Collaborative Learning (1988), by Jeff Golub, Chair, and the NCTE Committee on Classroom Practices

How to Handle the Paper Load (1979), by Gene Stanford, Chair, and the NCTE Committee on Classroom Practices

[illegible] the Working Classroom (1993), by Kent Gill, editor, and the NCTE Committee on Classroom Practices

Literature and Life: Making Connections in the Classroom (1990), edited by Patricia Phelan

Process and Portfolios in Writing Instruction (1993), by Kent Gill, editor, and the NCTE Committee on Classroom Practices

United in Diversity: Using Multicultural Young Adult Literature in the Classroom (1998), edited by Jean E. Brown and Elaine C. Stephens

Voices in English Classrooms: Honoring Diversity and Change (1996), edited by Lenora (Leni) Cook and Helen C. Lodge

We are fortunate to work with numerous gifted and dedicated educators.
We dedicate this book to them.

Acknowledgments

This book is the result of the collective wisdom and experiences of a distinctively talented group of individuals. We feel fortunate to have guided their efforts to fruition. Our deepest appreciation and gratitude go to all of the teachers and teacher educators for their contributions to this volume. Additionally, we are honored to have worked with seven outstanding authors of young adult literature whose generosity of spirit enriched this book and our lives. They are: Joan Bauer, Janet Bode, Eve Bunting, Christopher Paul Curtis, Joyce Hansen, Graham Salisbury, and Deb Vanasse. We are also grateful to their publishers for their help and support.

We thank the members of the NCTE Editorial Board for their thorough and thoughtful reviews of the proposal and manuscript. Perhaps one of the greatest advantages of doing a book for NCTE is the opportunity to work with such a wonderful editorial staff. Special kudos to Marlo Welshons whose help and advice facilitated the early stages of this project; to Zarina Hock whose precision and clear perspective is always helpful; to Pete Feely for his organizational skills and wicked humor; and especially to Tom Tiller whose common sense and uncommon sense of humor make even the most tedious tasks bearable.

We acknowledge and appreciate the Saginaw Valley State University Foundation for its support.

Contents

Foreword

A few months ago I found myself engaged by yet another public discussion in a nearby community about the appropriateness of *The Adventures of Huckleberry Finn* for use in a secondary school English classroom. The arguments appearing in television newscasts, newspaper guest editorials, and school board pronouncements were familiar (centering as they did on the character of Jim and on Twain's use of the racial epithet "nigger" to refer to him), but no less heated for that fact. It mattered not that other citizens in other communities had taken up the same debate earlier. For these parents, teachers, community members, and students, this was a fiery issue, for they were encountering it personally for the first time and were taking the measure of its impact on their own schools and community—indeed, upon their own lives.

In her essay for this volume Janet Bode notes, "This diversity stuff is tricky business," and she's right. Debates about multiculturalism in literature don't proceed, after all, according to the laws of scientific proof. As we examine the personal or cultural significance of *Huckleberry Finn* or any other book, we are not setting up a controlled study that dispassionately isolates the features of the debate and resolves, for all time, whether the work is inflammatory or benign, and furthermore, whether being one way or the other is a good or a bad thing. (I, for one, imagine Twain being delighted by the fuss over his novel.)

Multiculturalism, it seems to me, is mostly about identity. Cultural study invites us to consider whether we will define ourselves by what distinguishes us (skin color, religious belief, or tribal custom) or what unites us (shared feelings, relationships, or notions of truth). And since identities are formed by human perception and judgment, it is no wonder that we are prone to difference and debate as we engage books about personal and cultural identity. We *should* be disagreeing, at least some of the time.

And that points to the first accomplishment of this volume. As I've read through this fine collection of essays on multiculturalism and young adult literature, I've noticed that, despite the civility of the voices in this book, there are some healthy quarrels taking place herein. Should stories for our young people promote cultural assimilation, or should they emphasize individual cultural identity? Should authors be encouraged to write about cultures not their own, or should they confine themselves to "what they know best"—their own culture? And what, in general, should be the role of literature in the examination of cultural issues by our young? Was Louise Rosenblatt right or wrong when she remarked that a literary work "is not primarily a document in the history of language or society . . . [but is rather] a work of art, . . . a mode of living" (287)? Is it appropriate or wise to encourage students to study literary works as remnants of culture rather than simply to embrace them as works of art?

I don't know about you as you begin your way through this book, but if I live in those questions too long, my head starts to throb with the overload. And yet we must live in them, not just for our students, but for ourselves. A refreshing quality in these essays is their honesty in pronouncing that these aren't simply applied questions that relate to teaching practice, but that they are personal questions as well, shaping our own conceptions of self.

A second feature of this collection is that it has reminded me of the significance of change in our lives. The easiest way to conceive of change, of course, is as a temporal commodity. Something is some way at some moment and then becomes something else the next: it changes. But this book's rich discussion of diversity has caused me also to remember that change itself is a constant, a condition of all of life's experiences. And because all that we do is visited by change, it seems also true that questions of personal identity and association are not functions of condition, but of becoming. Who we are is not a snapshot, but a moving picture. Identity is not a conclusion, but a process of inquiry.

In my most recent reading of Lois Lowry's *The Giver,* I found myself thinking of this fine novel as a particularly provocative exploration of multicultural issues, in part because it explores change so insightfully. Jonas's community has become monocultural, a place where sameness abides and is honored. And what is it that enables this cultural sterility to continue? The key is not that community members have no differences, but that they are unable to perceive them. (Only Jonas and the Giver, for example, can detect Fiona's red hair.) And the reason they lack such perception is because they are without memory. Jonas is being trained as a "Receiver of Memory" in order that the community be relieved of knowing the past. And without a past, a people cannot know what is different (or remarkable) because they lack the ability to measure what has changed.

Read the selections in this volume, and you'll hear within them sometimes quiet, sometimes noisy calls for change. Some discuss how characters in young adult books change as they come to terms with matters of cultural difference. Some show how cultures or societies described in books become able to accept or even embrace the uniqueness of individuals within or outside them. Some YA authors confess here how they themselves have been changed by their works, and some acknowledge that their writing emerges from a need to influence the world (in other words, to change it). Finally, some teachers discuss how our classrooms might be changed as we orient literature study toward multicultural matters, or how our students might be changed by a heightened awareness and appreciation of both what we share and what makes us unique as different peoples.

This last thought—about the changes that our students might undertake—draws me back to my own recollections of the recent, local *Huckleberry Finn* debate. The one document that remains freshest in my memory from that particular controversy is a guest editorial written by an African American student who was ardent in her belief that Twain's novel had no place in American secondary schools today. I wholly disagreed with her position on the issue, but as I finished the piece, I found myself unable to simply put her view aside. "Good for you," I found myself whispering to this young writer. "You've not treated the issue simplistically, and you've not allowed me to conclude that it's simple. Thanks for rattling my thoughts. You've not changed my thinking at this point, but you have made me more disposed to change."

I should hope that our young students challenge thinking in that way as they read and respond to many of the fine young adult works discussed in these essays. Perhaps they themselves, or their classmates, will be challenged by the experience. Or perhaps it will be their parents, or us teachers, or the writers of young adult literature who benefit from our students' openness to change.

Enjoy and wrangle with this collection as your own personal invitation to explore identity and to embrace change.

Gary M. Salvner
Youngstown State University

References

Lowry, Lois. 1993. *The Giver.* New York: Bantam Doubleday Dell.

Rosenblatt, Louise. 1976. *Literature as Exploration,* Third Edition. New York: Noble and Noble.

Twain, Mark. 1948. *The Adventures of Huckleberry Finn.* New York: Holt, Rinehart, and Winston.

I Listening to Authors

We begin this volume with a series of chapters by authors who write for young adults. These authors have addressed the issue of diversity in their books and are sensitive to the rich fabric that varied cultures bring to our society. We believe that the selections in Part I, Listening to Authors, create for the readers a sense of immediacy with the authors' works as well as with the concept of diversity. In encouraging students to read multicultural young adult literature, teachers provide them with opportunities to experience places, cultures, and people beyond their own world, and to recognize a sense of shared humanity while recognizing and understanding differences. We believe that the readers of this book will be enriched by hearing authors talk about their work, their lives, and their philosophies. And, in turn, they will be able to help their students to make connections with multicultural young adult literature by sharing the authors' experiences and insights. For this reason, we have asked seven authors to discuss their experiences as writers who respond to the diversity in our culture.

The first chapter in this section is by Graham Salisbury. As he talks of his years growing up in the diverse culture of Hawaii, he directly addresses those critics who say that authors should write only of their own culture He makes the case that the sense of humanity common to all people supersedes cultural definition.

Nonfiction author Janet Bode draws from her experiences with teenagers around the world to present her discussion. In a series of vignettes, she focuses on areas of commonalities while urging us to recognize and honor cultural differences.

Joyce Hansen, building on her background as both an author and a former middle school teacher, provides readers with a dual perspective. She acknowledges the need for students to see themselves and their culture in the literature of the schools but also stresses their need to read beyond their own cultures to learn to appreciate others. She also provides specific suggestions and resources to help teachers introduce multicultural young adult literature in their classrooms.

Deb Vanasse, a first-time novelist, relates her experiences as a teacher in Alaska and demonstrates how those experiences led her to write her first novel, which is set in a Yup'ik village. She emphasizes sensitivity to other cultures and the importance of opening a dialogue among all people.

In an interview, Eve Bunting reflects on her life and her career. Expressing her concern about the self-imposed segregation of various ethnic groups, she stresses the need for people to come together. In particular, she speaks about her picture books that have examined significant social and cultural issues.

Joan Bauer expresses the need to dispel stereotypes in order to help students recognize the value in others. She sees humor and the ability to help students laugh together as unifying tools to bring about greater understanding.

Christopher Paul Curtis talks about his experiences as a youthful reader, looking for books to read about other African Americans, and about his attempts as an author to help fill the void he felt.

Works by each of these authors are included in the annotated bibliography at the end of this book.

1 Island Blood

Graham Salisbury

I was a mongrel. No question. As a boy in Hawaii I was more like somebody's wandering dog than somebody's kid.

I had burrs and fleas and goopy stuff in the corners of my eyes, just like all the other scraggly mutts I hung out with. We were a bunch of free-wheeling jokers who thought we owned the neighborhood, and maybe even did. I was a mixed-blooded WASP, but grew up part Anglo, part Hawaiian, part Japanese, part Chinese, part you-name-it, just because of where I lived. In the islands we all shared a few important things that bound us together: the most remote location in the world; a wild, strange-sounding dialect; a culturally kaleidoscopic society; and an unwavering love of personal freedom. Life was superb.

Today I'm a writer, just a regular white guy still running wild down the long ivory stretch of Kailua beach; hiking the muddy, mosquito-infested trails of Waipio valley; and ranging all over my several boyhood neighborhoods in Nu'uanu, Kaneohe, Kailua, Holualoa, Kailua-Kona, and Kamuela—only now it's all in fiction, of course, which to me is as alive and palpable as real life.

You see, I have this dinged-up chest of memories I can dig into if I need to, a tarnished box filled with dusty end-of-the-world adolescent dramas, old beat-up emotions, cuts, bruises, kisses, and a few billion ridiculously giddy memories of times telling gross jokes with the guys. These saved pieces of me are my springboard to fictional characters.

When I'm in the fictive world, I'm deep into my younger days, searching for the right voice, the perfect remembered detail, the true emotion. If I have to, I'll even step out of my race to get there. I'll write as a Japanese or Portuguese or Hawaiian or Chinese or, more likely, some mixture thereof. Sure, there are those who say this should not be done, that a white writer has no right to . . . blah, blah, blah. But you know, it doesn't really matter to me what anyone else says or thinks. It only matters that I remain true to what I know. And about the mixed cultures of Hawaii I know some little bit.

I hung out with white kids, Japanese kids, Hawaiian kids, Filipino, Chinese, Korean, whatever. On some mornings we started out as friends, and on others we didn't. But at the end of the day we were all as good as brothers, our many bloods looking pretty much like one: island blood.

As a writer, I don't feel the least bit awkward or guilty or deceitful if I step out of my race or culture or sex and enter the mind and heart of another. I don't because it's not the race or culture or sex that I explore. It's the human being. It's human emotion. It's survival, love, anger, sadness, fathers and sons, and the loyalty of friends. At the highest level, it's honor, integrity, and hope. Things common to everyone.

I am a result of my own personal suffering and soaring, just like any other person of any race and any culture. The emotion of my stories naturally flows from who I am. It is born of a time-lost world that even now shows scars of its turbulence.

At this moment I'm reaching into my memory chest to see what I come out with. Hmmm. Oh. Yes, I remember this. Yes, yes.

This one's from when my mom got married for the third time and my three younger sisters and I got yanked up and moved to another island. I was about twelve. My first stepfather, who was my sisters' real father, had recently died, and we were all still dizzy from that shock.

Anyway, this new guy—John was his name—was about twenty-five, ten years younger than my mother.

As stepfathers go he was not a breath of fresh air. And for a short while, neither was my mother. She seemed to have momentarily forgotten about us, mesmerized by her new love, this John guy, who sometimes looked at me as if I were somebody's spit-out gum.

Often—in the beginning, anyway—he and Mom would, on some late evenings, sit out on the beach in front of our newly bought used house on the Big Island and drink gin and laugh quietly at each other's jokes, and the sound of it would drift into my darkened bedroom window. I remember lying in bed listening, thinking about my lost buddies on Oahu, wishing I were still there, still one of them. But all that was gone now. Here, in my new village, I had no friends. Not at first. And being somebody's spit-out gum didn't make my life any better either.

The problem with John, I think, was that he'd gotten more than he'd bargained for. He wanted Mom, but had to take us four kids on as part of the package. Though he probably thought he knew what he was getting into, I think the sudden reality of stepfatherhood shook him. He had not one single clue what to do with us. None, zero, zilch. Forget it.

So mostly he ignored us.

He liked animals, though, which interested me.

He had a goose that roamed the yard and bit people, and a smelly, grunty pig he put in a pen in the weedy, mongoose-infested vacant lot just outside my bedroom window. Then the cats—Sticky Wicket, Lop Chong, Kung Hay Fat Choy, and Oreo—one of them screw-eyed and all of them part Siamese. John loved the cats. He teased them mercilessly, so much that they fought back with claws and teeth that drew blood. Then, in the evenings, he cuddled and stroked them on his lap while he read *Field and Stream* or *Saltwater Fisherman.*

I had no place in John's world, but I liked to watch him from the shadows. At first, I truly admired some of the things about him, and I studied him closely, mimicking his movements, his walk, his ways of speech, which were minimal, yet dripping with machismo.

From John, I also learned about hunting dogs, his real love. By watching, I learned how to keep them, feed them, train them. Mold and control them. Ruin them.

John built each dog its own flimsy iron-roofed cage, framed from old slabs of lumber he'd let me drag over from the vacant lot next door. At feeding time, I stood amazed as he'd toss them scraps of leftover people food, stuff you'd feed a pig, and each dog would devour his treasure in less than five seconds.

John liked the bat-eared, spotted and speckled, black, gray, and ugly brown, mostly pit bull mix-breeds. Dogs that couldn't stand still when there was another living creature anywhere in sight or smelling distance. Dogs that raised their lips and showed yellow teeth, or broken teeth. Dogs that would tear the head off any stranger who got too close, then tear into each other with their leftover energy.

Sometimes he staked them in the yard, just far enough apart so they wouldn't kill each other for something to do. You could pet them, if you wanted to. But anyone other than John had to approach them at a slug's pace, and maybe with something good to eat.

Mom hated these dogs and feared for our safety. But John liked them. Liked them a lot. And because John liked them, I liked them. He had several mad-insane types, and one gentle golden Lab.

John had names for all of them, but his favorites were Rastus, Melvin, and Scotty. Each resembled a particular bloodline, and because they did, they stood out.

Rastus was all black and could work himself into unspeakable frenzies. He was mostly pit bull and could tear the engine out of a jeep if he wanted to. Even his name sounded mean: *Rastus.*

Melvin was black and gray, mostly Australian Heeler, a rarity in Kona at that time. He was an excellent hunting dog, John said. The deceiving thing about him was that he always looked as if he had a smile on his face. And not only that, he had blue eyes, which was really weird.

But Scotty, the golden Lab, was John's favorite. The two of them were companions. At sunset, John took him down to the beach, which was only yards from our house. Sometimes they'd go swimming together. Then, back up on the sand, John would give the command and Scotty would do complete backflips, landing square on his feet. There was a nook in a date palm tree, and I curled up into it and watched it all from there. Once, I climbed down and went out on the sand and asked John if I could give Scotty the order to flip. John grunted that Scotty wouldn't do it for me, but he let me try it anyway. I gave the order, which was a circular hand movement. Scotty cocked his head, then lay down and looked at me.

Though I couldn't make him flip, Scotty was still a truly amazing dog. All of John's dogs were, actually. And, under different circumstances, they all could have been pretty decent people-dogs.

But that wasn't the reason John kept them.

He wanted hunting dogs, pig-dogs. Boar trackers. Blood smellers. Throat rippers. And to make them that way, he never exercised them, except when he took them hunting. They just hung around in their cages going crazy, or stood chained and staked-out in a six-foot radius of pummeled earth. So by the time John started up the hunting Jeep, they were as hair-triggered as nitroglycerin.

One morning, John took Scotty and Rastus and Melvin and another bolt-eyed dog named Willy and drove off in the Jeep before the sun came up. One of John's friends from Honolulu had flown over to go hunting with him. They took no guns, only knives, which was how they hunted.

The dogs did most of the work. It was up to them to race through the high-country jungle, track down the pig, and corner it. Then the human hunter would creep in and kill the boar with a knife. It had to be a knife and it had to be a boar, that's the way true men did it. John had the skill and the guts. He lived for this kind of stuff. Like I said, *dripping* with machismo.

After they drove off, I spent that morning in the weeds and bushes near our house, pretending to hunt like John, my silver-painted hard-rubber army knife in my teeth and four imaginary dogs fanning out in front of me. I hunted for an hour or more, bagging three huge pigs, then went home for lunch. In the afternoon I roamed the harbor, looking for something to do.

Just after sundown, John and his friend came home.

Thick globs of mud clung to the Jeep tires and spread in fan-shaped splatters around the wheel wells. Three dogs jumped out.

John's friend laughed at something John had said, then the two of them got out of the Jeep. The three dogs whisked around, sniffing, marking.

Wait a minute. *Three* dogs.

I looked in the Jeep.

Scotty and a huge black, sickle-tusked boar lay in the back. The pig was dead, and Scotty lay panting with blood caked all over his side. Gored. He could lift his head, but didn't much want to.

"What happened?" I asked.

When John didn't answer me, his friend said, "Got too close to the pig, I guess. He'll be okay in a couple of weeks. Dogs are pretty good healers."

John carried Scotty to the garage and settled him onto a bed of dirty towels. Then he and his friend carried the boar around to the ocean side of the house. There on the grass in the dusky light, they gutted it. Blood and white glistening, pulpy, smelly guts. John put the mess into a couple of buckets.

I stood just behind them with my arms crossed. Anne and Pat, two of my three sisters, came out to watch, too, their eyes pinched with curious disgust.

John noticed them and grinned. "Dump these guts in the ocean," he said, knowing it would appall them. He pointed his chin to the buckets. My sisters didn't question him. They simply did what he said. Each picked up a bucket and carried it down to the sand.

"Not there," John called. "Go out on the rocks so the eels can get it."

I followed them out, and together we tossed the guts into the foam that rolled in over the rocks and surrounded our feet. A rope of intestines washed back and wrapped around Anne's ankle. She shrieked and leaped back. Pat and I jumped back, too, then stood catching glimpses of bubbly gray pig guts bobbing around in the foam.

When we brought the buckets back, John said, "I hope you threw it way out. I don't want to see it stinking up the beach tomorrow morning."

They both nodded.

John grunted and turned his back on them.

I turned my back on them, too, believing I was one of John's men. A soldier in his army. John saw me do that, and snickered, right there in front of my sisters and his friend.

I left, mad as a wasp.

One muggy night a week or so later, I was lying in bed with the top sheet crumpled down by my feet. My room was off from the house, out behind the garage. Scotty, now able to limp around on his own again, lay just outside my door. He barked twice. A mongoose or something. He was healing, but he'd lost his energy. He slept a lot.

Faint music blew in through the window, and so did Mom's small laugh from out on the moonlit beach. Some guy on the radio in the house was singing, *"On a day like today we'll pass the time away. . . ."*

I heard Mom laugh again and got up and peeked outside. Nothing moved but the ghostly gray-white of the waves. I flopped back down on my bed and covered my head with my pillow. I threw it off a moment later.

Scotty heard me stirring. His tail thumped against the door.

I got out of bed and opened the door. Scotty struggled to stand. I kneeled down and stroked his head. "It's okay, boy. Lie down, lie down."

I sat next to him, and he licked my ear.

" . . . Writing love letters in the sand. . . ."

The two of us sat in the dark listening to the soft music, me squinting at the night shapes on the beach, and Scotty panting, his breath warm on my arm. Mom and John were out near the ocean. I could see them standing on the beach, the small silhouette of Mom and the dark shadow of John's powerful body. John skipped a stone out into the bay, both of them quiet now.

Scotty settled back down and lay his head in my lap.

"You like me, don't you Scotty?"

Scotty perked up and whined.

Does one have to be white to experience and write about the kind of adolescent loneliness I felt during that time in my life? No.

Does one have to be Hawaiian to know and love an island, an ocean, the jungles and valleys, the hearts and minds of dogs, the sun, the surf, the sand? Does one have to be Hawaiian to write about how rich all that natural life feels? No.

Does one have to be Japanese to know and write about how it feels to lose someone you love? To be mistrusted and mistreated? To be removed? No.

Well then what *does* one have to be?

Human. That's all. Just human.

2 Random Thoughts on the Passing Parade

Janet Bode

World of Difference?

I'm teaching ESL, English as a Second Language, to a room full of high school age *preparatoria* students in a private school in Guadalajara, Mexico. As the year goes by, some of them show me their journal entries, real-life stories of an angry stepsibling, a broken heart, concern about unknown futures.

I'm sipping thick, cardamom-flavored coffee with a Palestinian family in their home in Amman, Jordan. Fifteen-year-old Rula confides that her mom doesn't understand. They argue about her favorite rock-and-roll music, rules versus freedom, her choice of friends.

I'm skimming the daily paper in Nelson, New Zealand, a jewel of a seaside town surrounded by soccer fields, sheep, and in the distance, snow-capped mountains. Teen suicide rates are on the rise, reads an article. Ditto for eating disorders, according to another. A third reports that drug use among adolescents is up, too.

I'm meandering along the Li River in Guilin, China, when a bike rider of maybe eighteen brakes to a stop, comes over, and says in halting English, "How about those Chicago Bulls!" He wonders, can we walk and talk so he can practice his developing skills in my native language? "Sure," I tell him.

Worldwide, teenagers play their roles in the ongoing drama of being human. The problems and joys they share, the solutions and emotions they call forth feel to me oh, so familiar.

Mosaic of Their Souls

Closer to home I travel the nation talking with their U.S. peers wherever I'm invited—public and private schools, libraries, drug rehab programs, juvenile detention centers. When we meet in those structured settings, I try to leave time to have them jot down what's the best or the worst of their lives. These scraps of paper become my mosaic of their souls.

From Oregon, Florida, Iowa, Maryland, as well as my own greater New York City neighborhood come notes scrawled with heart and heat. As I unfold each one and read it, I'm no longer amazed by the complicated lives these young people lead. As you and I know, half of them are growing up in accordion families which expand and contract through adults' actions. You can find kids parenting their parents; kids working two jobs; kids wise and weary beyond their years. Still, in the same class are kids with involved, supportive families and communities, and futures ahead of them that almost seem to glow.

I remember a group of seventh graders from a Talented and Gifted (TAG) program with whom I meet in the auditorium of a public library. Afterwards I randomly study their messages. "What's best?" writes one student. "Two loving parents." I flip over the note and see the words "What's worst? My parents are divorced." A second student dashes off these words: "What's best is ice cream on a hot, hot day." A third pens letters so small it's hard to read them: "What's best is I realized that being sexually abused wasn't my fault." A fourth adds these thoughts to the pile: "I can't tell you best or worst. I haven't been paying attention to my life."

Other students write frantically, filling as much as a page in only five minutes. They are mini-autobiographies, and they always give me pause. I tack an ever-changing representative one to the bulletin board that leans against the wall opposite my computer. This passing parade of stories serves me as another reminder of the lives I'm allowed to enter.

The current posting is a numbered list of a single year's activity; it's handed to me by a graduating senior: (1) Homecoming queen. (2) Fall in love with a great guy. Homecoming is when we started dating. (3) Student Council president. (4) Had a great prom weekend, drinking, walking, singing. (5) Got pregnant on New Year's Eve, the *first* time I *ever* got drunk. (6) Started a part-time job at a bank, five hours a day. Will work full-time after graduation. (7) Had an abortion, very hard. (8) Moved in with my mother, haven't lived with her since I was eleven.

Tricky Business

In this brief sampling I know I only speak of sameness. I haven't focused on how separated these students are by culture and by color. This issue, however, has to be examined. Today it's not unusual to have students from a dizzying array of backgrounds sitting down together to untangle, say, the threads of the World Wide Web. But once they walk back out the door, more often than not, self-segregation shifts into place. The cafeteria at lunch time resembles the United Nations, each holding court at a separate table. "When we divide ourselves, we're just looking for a comfort level," reads a note I open over my meal.

I have countless pieces of paper, most of which I ponder, then file away in a bulging folder marked "race and culture." A Vietnamese student writes, "I love a beautiful American girl. But I don't know English good enough to speak to her."

An Afghan boy tells me he's opted out of that All-American teen pastime, romance and dating. He's Muslim. His marriage will be arranged, and that's the way he wants it. He asks to be interviewed for one of my books and I agree. His story is too rich to miss.

A Russian girl prints in her note: "My parents and me came here for a better life. As for me, my life never got better. It got worse. I went to school not knowing English. Kids teased me and called me names. They're not done teasing yet five years later. My parents got divorced, my grandparents died. They were in Russia so I couldn't say good-bye. I sometimes think back at what I left behind and feel so sad. Welcome to America Land of Opportunity. It makes me want to cry."

An anonymous fifteen-year-old immigrant turns in this reply: "The worst thing to me is trying to adjust to new surroundings and new cultural experiences. Life changes without letting you know."

Another student explains that until he was five, he spoke only Spanish, the language of his homeland. But he wasn't from a foreign country. He was born in Puerto Rico, a commonwealth of the United States. Still, day after day, he fights most of the battles that immigrants fight.

An African American passes me these few lines: "My behavior and thinking are positive. But people look at my skin and say, 'Another violent black male.'" He says I can quote him, but asks that I not let people know he's the one who said that. Here, too, I agree.

A teacher pulls me aside and says what helps in the multicultural classroom is an emphasis on respect, honesty, tolerance, and nonviolence. If you push shared values and individual achievement, academic success will follow. I think to myself: yes, of course. But then I think of my experiences in countries where a strong cultural lesson stresses cooperation. The family and community are more important than the individual. In fact, it's considered culturally inappropriate for the individual to shine.

This diversity stuff is tricky business. My hope and wish is that we at least keep talking.

Books by Janet Bode

1989a. *Different Worlds: Interracial and Cross-Cultural Dating*. Danbury, CT: Franklin Watts.

1989b. *New Kids on the Block: Oral Histories of Immigrant Teens*. Danbury, CT: Franklin Watts. Retitled *New Kids in Town: Oral Histories of Immigrant Teens*. 1991. New York: Scholastic.

1990. *The Voices of Rape*. Danbury, CT: Franklin Watts. Retitled *The Voices of Rape: Healing the Hurt*. 1992. New York: Dell.

1991a. *Beating the Odds: Stories of Unexpected Achievers*. Illus. Stan Mack. Danbury, CT: Franklin Watts.

1991b. *Truce: Ending the Sibling War*. Danbury, CT: Franklin Watts.

1992. *Kids Still Having Kids: People Talk about Teen Pregnancy*. Illus. Stan Mack. Danbury, CT: Franklin Watts.

1994. *Heartbreak and Roses: Real Life Stories of Troubled Love*. New York: Dell.

1995a. *Death is Hard To Live With: Teenagers Talk about How They Cope with Loss*. Illus. Stan Mack. New York: Dell.

1995b. *Trust and Betrayal: Real Life Stories of Friends and Enemies*. New York: Delacorte.

1996. *Hard Time: A Real Life Look at Juvenile Crime and Violence*. Coauthor Stan Mack. New York: Bantam Doubleday Dell.

1997. *Food Fight: A Guide to Eating Disorders for Preteens and Their Parents*. New York: Simon & Schuster Books for Young Readers.

3 Multicultural Literature: A Story of Your Own

Joyce Hansen

A multicultural education is an education for life in a free and democratic society. It helps students transcend their cultural boundaries and acquire the knowledge, attitudes, and skills needed to engage in public discourse with people who differ from themselves.

James Banks, *Multicultural Education*

As James Banks says, all of our students need to move beyond their cultural boundaries and widen their perceptions of the world. There is a dangerous parochialism in many sections of the nation, where the seeds of hatred and fear of other Americans are poisoning young fertile minds. Our schools and classrooms might be the last bulwark against the growing xenophobia that constricts our students' minds and ultimately their souls.

Our schools and classrooms should reflect those ideals of equality and democracy that our culture holds so dear, even if the ideal has yet to become a reality. Democratic principles are based upon concepts of tolerance and understanding. What better way to develop those concepts than to explore multicultural literature that exposes students to a wide range of human experience and helps them to realize that often our similarities outweigh our differences. In the end, we are one human family.

When I began writing *The Captive* I did not think of it as a multicultural story. I wanted, first, to write a story that youngsters would enjoy. Secondly, I wanted to try my hand at an adventure story—a genre I'd never attempted. Also, I wanted to create a heroic black boy—a character type not often found in contemporary stories in books and other media.

Kofi, my main character, would be kind, brave, intelligent, loyal, and proud. My readers would also be exposed to a little-known genre peculiar to American literature: the slave narrative. These autobiographical accounts, published in the eighteenth and nineteenth centuries, describe enslavement and subsequent escape from slavery. (One of the most famous of these is the *Narrative of the Life of Frederick Douglass, an American Slave, Written by Himself.*)

The Captive is based upon another slave narrative—*The Interesting Narrative of the Life of Olaudah Equiano, or Gustavus Vassa, the African; Written by Himself.* Vassa tells of being kidnapped as a boy in the West African Kingdom of Benin, his experiences on a slaver, and his adventures in the Caribbean, Virginia, London, and other places. The narrative also gives the reader an excellent portrait of everyday life in an African village—so different from the lurid and sensational accounts by European adventurers of savagery in the "dark continent."

I wanted to capture Vassa's voice with just a tinge of the intricate eighteenth-century prose that most of our twentieth-century youth would not have the patience to read. Besides the language, I took other liberties with the original narrative.

I set the story in the Ashanti Kingdom, part of present-day Ghana, instead of Benin. My character, Kofi, is taken to New England instead of Virginia. There he meets the real-life character Paul Curfee. However, my character's spirit, his bravery, honesty, curiosity, intelligence, and fears were all inspired by the original narrative.

I hope I have succeeded in creating an interesting adventure told in the style of a slave narrative. It seems I did, unwittingly, create a very "multicultural novel." Characters are African, European, Native American, and American. The story is set in Africa and New England. Yet it is an American story, which finally brings me to my point. When writers explore the full range of people and cultures that constitute the American republic, they bring a multitude of voices to their work; teachers should bring those same voices into their classrooms.

It is as critical for white students who live in all-white communities and attend all-white schools to be exposed to the rest of America (and the world) as it is for young people of color and other underrepresented groups (such as poor children of all races and urban children of all races) to see their lives reflected in the literature they read.

I am not saying that a class of African American students should be given only "Black" books to read, or that Hispanic students must read only Hispanic authors. I'm saying the lives and experiences of all underrepresented groups must be included in the broad range of literature we want to explore.

One of the purposes of literature is to help us understand our lives and the human condition. What message do youngsters receive when their image and world are absent from the literature they study? They learn that they are insignificant—and that books and literature have nothing to do with them.

Unfortunately, they never know the intellectual and spiritual sustenance that comes from an honest, well-told tale; a poem that touches your heart; or a play that miraculously explains your life.

When we need physical sustenance we are quite liberal and courageous about the food we eat. There seems to be no problem with multiculturalism when it comes to food. There are sections of the country where diverse cultures have blended to create something new and fascinating.

Take San Antonio, Texas, for example. You will find an interesting mix of Western and Mexican cultures, especially in food. When I ordered breakfast in the San Antonio airport, the bacon and eggs came wrapped in a taco shell.

In New York City, where people live in separate ethnic neighborhoods, the cultural boundaries of these communities often overlap when it comes to food. Every neighborhood has Italian pizza shops and small Chinese take-out restaurants that also offer fried chicken wings (an American influence on Chinese fare, I'm sure). And every native New Yorker knows that there are no roast beef sandwiches or dill pickles like those found in a Jewish deli (and, as my mother used to say, "the kosher frankfurters don't repeat on you").

We will often tolerate one another's food even when we think that we cannot tolerate each other. What do we think about when we eat a bowl of tasty wonton soup, a delicious plate of Spanish rice, a fresh bagel, or a tantalizing dish of candied yams? Do we dredge up our fears and stereotypes about Chinese, Hispanics, Jews, or Blacks? We think one thing—the food is good. We need to be as open about the literature.

Bringing Diverse Voices into the Classroom

Before we can even begin to include multicultural literature in our classrooms, we must do our homework. We need to be as knowledgeable as possible about the multicultural literature available to us and our students. We also need to understand the major issues in the evolution of the movement for multicultural education. And we need criteria to help us evaluate this literature. The following titles are excellent teacher resources:

Multicultural Education: Issues and Perspectives, James A. Banks and Cherry A. McGee Banks, eds. (1989)

Our Family, Our Friends, Our World: An Annotated Guide to Significant Multicultural Books for Children and Teenagers, Lyn Miller-Lachmann (1991)

Multicultural Voices in Contemporary Literature, Frances Ann Day (1994)

When evaluating any literature, literary quality is essential. How does the author develop the characters, plot, theme, and setting? Is the text appropriate for students? However, literary quality is not the only criterion we must use when evaluating multicultural titles. The annotated bibliography *Our Family, Our Friends, Our World* (Miller-Lachmann 1992) includes a helpful section on areas to assess when evaluating multicultural books. Topics such as accuracy, stereotypes, author's perspective, and other critical elements are discussed.

Most of all we want to bring those books and voices into our classrooms that engage our youngsters, so that they can identify with the characters and the story and come away from the text understanding more about the world and themselves. In order to do this, we must know the books and be able to empathize with our students. We have to be aware, as much as possible, of the issues that have an impact upon their young lives.

For example, I was reading with a small group of children in our school's bilingual program. I am not bilingual, so we had to read and talk in English. These were seventh graders who came from the Dominican Republic and had very limited knowledge of English. I wanted to find a text for them that did not insult their intelligence yet would not overwhelm them. I decided to try Allen Say's book *Grandfather's Journey,* about a Japanese American who describes his grandfather's journey from Japan to America and his love for both countries.

These teenagers responded positively to the book. It generated discussion about their own families—especially their grandparents, since many of them come from extended families where grandparents are held in high esteem. The students had experienced homesickness themselves and understood the desire to be in two places at once. They learned something about Japan besides karate and ninjas, and they all responded to the wonderful illustrations.

Ultimately, it is the quality of a work that allows it to engage, communicate, and draw youngsters into its world, even if that world is "foreign" at first. Maya Angelou's *I Know Why the Caged Bird Sings* is a powerful work that engages and communicates so that the reader sees and understands the life she shares with us. Every unfortunate teenager who has been abused and made to feel less than worthy knows Maya's mute pain.

And, because of an understanding teacher who exposed her to literature, Maya began to find her voice. You see, the teacher knew Maya. She knew that there was the heart of a poet locked inside this silent child. We also must know our students in order to help them find their voices, find themselves, find a story of their own. We have to listen to them as well, and not always impose our will on them.

Listen to Students

I have learned so much from young people during my years of teaching and writing. One of the most important things I have learned from students is that the author's and the reader's imaginations must connect before anything else happens. When I was a special education teacher, I had a student who was about fifteen years old and read around the fifth- or sixth-grade level. In his previous remedial reading class he'd been reading only out of workbooks. I kept a collection of young adult and middle grade literature in my classroom, believing that even students who had problems reading could benefit from quality literature.

I gave him the excellent book *Felita,* by Nicholasa Mohr. My student was Puerto Rican, like the family in the book. I knew that the characters and story would be familiar to him, and that it was a book he could read independently. Without introduction, I handed him the short novel, saying simply: "No more workbooks, Jose. Try this."

He began to read and after about ten minutes he called out, "Oh, Miss Hansen, this is a Puerto Rican family in this book. I never read a book with Puerto Ricans in it before." He was thrilled and so was I. He'd discovered himself in a book. He asked me for more books about family life. The fact that the family in *Felita* was Puerto Rican drew him into the story and aided in his understanding, but it was the theme of strong family values that captivated him. In his subsequent reading, he found other books about families. His successful reading experience with *Felita* gave him the confidence to pursue his interests to find stories of his own.

I had a group of African American girls who loved Mohr's *Going Home* (a sequel to *Felita*), which is set in Puerto Rico. I let them browse through the classroom library and they chose the book themselves. They really loved the book and some of them read it more than once. They related to Felita's feelings of being an outsider and not being able to "fit in" when she visited Puerto Rico. Many of our youngsters share those same feelings. In *Going Home,* they could learn about the Puerto Rican community and, at the same time, explore issues such as alienation, loneliness, and being different.

I have also learned much from the young people who write me letters. Whenever I receive a letter from a student, I am reminded of the great responsibility facing those of us who write for young people. We cannot afford to be careless with our pens. I also feel blessed whenever I get a letter from a young person indicating that I have written something that either brought them joy or helped them in some way to cope with their lives.

The letters inspire me. Some are from New York City, African American and Hispanic youngsters who are the audience I had in mind when I wrote my three Bronx novels, *The Gift-Giver, Home Boy,* and *Yellow Bird and Me.* Their letters often indicate that they enjoy reading about youngsters who are like them and about familiar settings. Other letters are from youngsters who are of racial and ethnic backgrounds different from the characters of my novels, but they too connect with the story and find the common humanity underneath the differences we make so much of.

Here is one of those letters:

> I came to United States from Russia one year ago. I just read your book, *The Captive,* and I think it's the best book that I have ever read. I am a little like Kofi. I also came from a foreign country not knowing the language and American customs. But as time passed, I became accustomed to America. Kofi did it too. Of course I am not a slave, but I still can understand him.

This letter is from a youngster in Virginia:

> I like to read books about black people and Africa. I also like to write stories about those things. . . . I look for your books all the time now because of one of them, *Which Way Freedom.* . . . That one book of yours got me the most interested in black people and Africa. . . . You gave me the inspiration to write the story about Shaza because I was thinking about *Which Way Freedom* and I thought to myself, that was a good book. I should try to write a good story like that.

The following letter is from a New York City youngster:

> Your books make me want to read because before I read your books I didn't want a reading book next to me. Do you know why kids like your book? It's because you write the truth. It's not a lie, kids like to hear the truth. I read two of your books. *The Gift Giver and Yellow Bird and Me.*

The last letter is from a youngster in Honolulu, Hawaii:

> I love the books called *Yellow Bird and Me* and *The Gift-Giver.* They kept my interest to the end. . . . I'll tell you a little bit of myself. Well, I was born in Cambodia and lived in an orphanage for ten years. I do not have any sisters or brothers—I did have someone who took care of me. I call her my sister. I got adopted by an American family. They are wonderful parents. . . . I have been living in America for 3 years now. I just had my birthday in July. So I'm now 13 years old. I'm going into 7th grade. I have other friends who are from Cambodia and live in America too. I have a friend who is just like Amir, but she's a girl. [We] have been friends since we were little. We've never been apart, until

> we came to America. Her parents had to go to Asia for her dad's business. Amir and [my friend] are a lot alike. They both face their problems, help other people, never get mad, and seem to see the best in other people.

As the writer Marshall Frady said, "We are all of us, finally, of one hope and one grief and one struggle." We cannot afford to ignore any of our children—each must have a story of his or her own.

References

Angelou, Maya. 1970, 1997. *I Know Why the Caged Bird Sings.* New York: Bantam.

Banks, James A., and Cherry A. McGee Banks, eds. 1989. *Multicultural Education: Issues and Perspectives.* Boston: Allyn & Bacon.

Day, Frances Ann. 1994. *Multicultural Voices in Contemporary Literature.* Portsmouth, NJ: Heinemann.

Douglass, Frederick. 1968. *Narrative of the Life of Frederick Douglass, an American Slave, Written by Himself.* New York: New American Library.

Equiano, Olaudah. 1969. "The Life of Olaudah Equiano or Gustavus Vassa, the African, Written by Himself." *Great Slave Narratives.* Ed. Arna Bontemps. Boston: Beacon Press.

Hansen, Joyce. 1982. *Home Boy.* New York: Clarion.

———. 1986. *Yellow Bird and Me.* New York: Clarion.

———. 1989.*The Gift-Giver.* New York: Clarion.

———. 1995. *The Captive.* New York: Scholastic.

Miller-Lachmann, Lyn. 1991. *Our Family, Our Friends, Our World: An Annotated Guide to Significant Multicultural Books for Children and Teenagers.* New Providence, NJ: R. R. Bowker.

Mohr, Nicholasa. 1979. *Felita.* New York: Dial.

———. 1986. *Going Home.* New York: Dial.

Say, Allen. 1993. *Grandfather's Journey.* Boston: Houghton Mifflin.

4 Cultural Sensitivity

Deb Vanasse

My first young adult novel, *A Distant Enemy,* deals with a culture to which I do not belong: the Yup'ik Eskimos of southwestern Alaska. Yet I believe the novel reflects a cultural sensitivity developed from years of living among the Yup'ik people.

The novel's protagonist, fourteen-year-old Joseph, resents the encroaching change brought to his village and his culture by the white people, the *kass'aqs.* His inner conflict is amplified by the fact that Joseph is himself half *kass'aq,* his white father having abandoned the family years before. The turmoil which results when Joseph tries to establish his identity between two cultures and the anger he feels when confronting cultural change are major themes in the novel.

Cultural conflict and change are realities of the world we live in, the global society of the 1990s. But these issues are particularly strong among the Yup'ik people. Elders in the fifty-two villages that span the deltas of the Yukon and Kuskokwim rivers can recall their first encounters with white people. Only in the last half of this century, when the Bureau of Indian Affairs (BIA) established grade schools in the region, did these nomadic people settle into the villages that now dot the map. Though these villages are still accessible only by boat, snowmobile, or small plane, over the last twenty years most have acquired electricity, phone systems, and satellite TV.

When I arrived in the village of Nunapitchuk in 1979 to begin my first teaching job in the recently opened village high school, I became quickly immersed in the Yup'ik culture. The village high schools were just being established, the result of a court settlement which mandated state-funded secondary education in all villages that expressed an interest. High school teachers had to find their own village housing, unlike the BIA teachers whose housing was part of the school complex, where they were an island unto themselves, complete with running water.

The term *immersion* conjures up images of dunking in water, and from my experience, cultural immersion is much like the blanching of vegetables. A teacher is forever changed by immersion in the village culture, but the teacher does not become part of the culture any more than the vegetables become water. Blanching involves quick immersion, an apt comparison for teachers who tend to stay only a few years in a village. Longer cooking may change the vegetables more profoundly, but they still never become water; so it is that the teacher who settles into a village for many years is much changed, but never Yup'ik.

I lived and taught in the Yukon-Kuskokwim area for eight years. Both of my children were born there; my son spoke Yup'ik before he spoke English. Those were wonderful, enriching, occasionally trying years, a vital part of my own coming of age. So it was only natural that when I wrote the short story that later grew into the novel *A Distant Enemy,* the Kuskokwim delta was the setting, and the characters were Yup'ik.

Two questions come to mind concerning my experience of writing about a culture not my own: What right do I have to describe the experiences of another people? And would this be a better novel, a truer novel, if written by a Yup'ik author?

The easy answer to the first question is, I suppose, that an author can write about whatever she chooses. But to write well, to write responsibly, the writer must always be sensitive, walking as it were in the shoes of others, seeing the world through different eyes. Cultural sensitivity is no less than this.

Living among the Yup'ik people did not make me Yup'ik, but it made me a different person than I had been, able to see differently than I had before. Eating frozen fish, subsisting on ptarmigan, and sewing a parka for my son did not make me an expert on the Yup'ik way of life, but these experiences contributed to a rich sense of setting for the novel.

But wouldn't *A Distant Enemy* have been a better book if it had been written by a Yup'ik author? Even my publisher said in the *Children's Writers and Illustrators Market Guide,* "Prefer books by authors of same ethnic background as subject, but not absolutely necessary." Nevertheless, I don't feel that *A Distant Enemy* would have been assuredly better if I were Yup'ik; it would only have been different.

If I have accomplished my task of listening and learning, of being culturally sensitive, then I can see the world through the eyes of a fourteen-year-old half-Yup'ik boy. Not a person on earth has lived through the exact set of experiences that Joseph has, so no one can say precisely how he sees. And as the author, I also see what Joseph cannot, adding a richness to the development of the story.

Although I must be on the lookout for "blind spots" in my view, a Yup'ik author would likewise contend with blind spots, albeit different ones. With Joseph's story told, a dialogue is opened. Fourteen-year-old Yup'ik boys can consider Joseph's strengths and flaws. They can discuss the credibility of his character. Isn't opening the dialogue what literature is all about?

In the end, every author's perspective is unique, and ultimately it is just that—a perspective. There are as many Yup'ik stories to be told as there are people to tell them, just as there are countless Chinese, Australian, Brazilian, and *kass'aq* stories. Immersion and sensitivity, not just birthright, give credence to their telling.

Reference

Vanasse, Deb. 1997. *A Distant Enemy.* New York: Dutton.

5 Reflections

Eve Bunting

Editors' note: In the spring of 1996, we had the opportunity to spend an afternoon talking with Eve Bunting about her work and her perspective on our diverse society: *"We are trying to reach out to all kids, to touch all kids, and to get into their lives,"* she said. As we replayed the tape of our conversation, we decided to let her speak without interruption from our questions.

I never start out saying I am going to write a multicultural book; but because we live in a multicultural society and I'm aware of this, it falls naturally into my way of writing. I think multicultural books are terribly important. It seems like in so many ways segregation is worse than it ever was. I live close to Pasadena City College and sometimes I walk around there—you see all Blacks at this table, all Asians at that table, all Mexican Americans at another, and all Whites at still another table. One way we can mix everybody and show that everybody is the same is in literature; and although I don't do it deliberately, intuitively I do. It's so wonderful what books can accomplish, even the simplest of books. Quite possibly the simpler they are, the more they get to the heart of things. Although I've written using many different genres, I'm happiest writing picture books. When I wrote *Terrible Things* (1980), an animal allegory about the Holocaust, it was a new kind of picture book. People liked it, but didn't know what to do with it. Now, of course, I know that it was ahead of its time, since today's picture books are dealing with more complex issues and are for older readers, too.

My head is like a beehive of ideas; unfortunately, most of them are worthless! For every ten ideas, only one or two is workable. Most of my ideas tend to come to me full blown, at least the nucleus of them, because they tend to come from something that amuses me totally or because something is so sad or thought-provoking or unfair. Most of my ideas come from the newspaper or perhaps something someone tells me—something that touches me emotionally. When I get a very poignant idea, I can usually condense and say what I want to say rather simply and in a few short words. If an idea is rather shallow or rather slight, it doesn't appeal to me. The story has to really say something to me before I become completely interested in doing it. I want to say something that will give some take-home value to the story, that is not just a fun story. The ones that give me the most satisfaction are the ones where I feel I am saying something important.

I wrote *Smoky Night* (1994) after the Los Angeles riot because I was thinking about how it would be for a child in central Los Angeles or any large city when there is rioting. I was very careful not to get into ethnic differences. The only name used is Mrs. Kim, probably Korean. I was very careful not to blame anyone for anything, because in my own personal opinion, there is enough blame to go around for everyone. There was no one group who was the bad guy—we were all guilty for that happening. There were Blacks, Whites, Mexicans, and Asians among the rioters. They were all there and I didn't single out anyone; I think we all should equally share the blame. I wasn't being critical—I wanted to know why the riot happened. I was trying to understand. Did this happen because we are grouped like we are and we don't know each other and we don't try to know each other? Perhaps if we did try to know one another, then we could avoid this sort of thing happening again.

This is not the message some people got from the book. I'm not really sure what message they got, other than children should not know about riots. But I don't believe the truth is going to hurt kids. They know what is happening, but they need help to ask questions and get true answers, not just what is being said on the streets. *Smoky Night* has become controversial, but it wasn't until it received the Caldecott Medal Award for David Diaz's illustrations. The controversy made me feel hurt and angry, probably more hurt than angry, because I had done my best to be fair. Having lived in Northern Ireland and having seen my share of unfairness, that is something I can't stand.

I've been writing for over twenty-five years and have published more than 150 books, but the one book I get the most reaction from is *The Wall* (1990). When I autograph books, people will hold my hand and talk about a grandfather or father who died in Vietnam. I receive more letters from readers of *The Wall* than any other. One letter had newspaper clippings about a class that was so touched when their teacher cried while reading *The Wall* to them, revealing that her husband had died during Vietnam, that they held a car wash to raise money to send her to Washington, D.C. Their teacher went and for the first time saw her husband's name engraved on the Vietnam Memorial Wall.

I've been asked if there is anything special I would like to tell teachers. I guess it is to allow their students to express their feelings about books. I hope that my readers will understand what I'm trying to say, and sometimes I think they do more at an intuitive level than at a level they can verbalize. I just hope they will read them and enjoy them and gain some new knowledge of themselves.

Picture Books by Eve Bunting

1980. *The Empty Window.* New York: Warner.

1989a. *Terrible Things: An Allegory of the Holocaust.* Philadelphia: Jewish Publication Society.

1989b. *The Wednesday Surprise.* Boston: Houghton Mifflin.

1990. *The Wall.* Boston: Houghton Mifflin.

1991. *Fly Away Home.* Boston: Houghton Mifflin.

1994a. *A Day's Work.* Boston: Houghton Mifflin.

1994b. *Smoky Night.* San Diego: Harcourt Brace.

1994c. *Sunshine Home.* Boston: Houghton Mifflin.

1995. *Cheyenne Again.* Boston: Houghton Mifflin.

1996a. *The Blue and the Gray.* New York: Scholastic.

1996b. *Going Home.* New York: HarperCollins.

1996c. *Secret Place.* Boston: Hougton Mifflin.

1996d. *Train to Somewhere.* Boston: Houghton Mifflin.

Novels by Eve Bunting

1983. *Karen Kepplewhite Is the World's Best Kisser.* Boston: Houghton Mifflin.

1984. *Someone Is Hiding on Alcatraz Island.* Boston: Houghton Mifflin.

1985. *Face at the Edge of the World.* Boston: Houghton Mifflin.

1988. *A Sudden Silence.* San Diego: Harcourt Brace.

1990. *Such Nice Kids.* Boston: Houghton Mifflin.

1991a. *The Hideout.* San Diego: Harcourt Brace.

1991b. *Jumping the Nail.* San Diego: Harcourt Brace.
1991c. *Sharing Susan.* New York: HarperCollins.
1995. *Spying on Miss Muller.* Boston: Houghton Mifflin.
1996. *S.O.S. Titanic.* San Diego: Harcourt Brace.

6 Helping to Improve Multicultural Understanding through Humor

Joan Bauer

I have a six-inch-long rock in my office that my husband gave me for Christmas. No, he is not a boor or a cheapskate; he is a wise, instinctive man. For carved into the rock is a word: LAUGH. And the laugh rock, as it has come to be called, sits on my desk as a reminder of a truth about life that, for me, is carved in stone: Laughter is imminently, undeniably crucial.

E. B. White said, "A life without humor is like a life without legs." But why? What is it about humor and laughter that provides such support?

I believe, firstly, that humor intersects life and our humanness. There has yet to be a culture discovered where humor is not evident. Babies laugh the world over. Funny stories are shared in all countries and religions. The clown who fails miserably at some task and the adolescent storming off after a row with her impossible mother are reminders to us all that we are imperfect, fallible human beings. We learn about life through laughter. It is one of the great gifts we've been given as thinking souls. Humor puts life in perspective. It builds bridges between people, brings connections, and can take us from pain to redemption. But it does not stand separate from serious issues. Laughter and tears are connected. How many of us have laughed so hard that we've cried or, depending on our physiologies, wet ourselves?

The sheer magic of humor is present all around us. In a classroom setting it can provide an uproarious "welcome to the club." Humor, by its very nature, is uniting and multicultural. The task for educators, then, is to uncover the humor in multicultural settings that is already there.

As a children's and young adult novelist, I am constantly looking for passageways between life's difficulties and humor. When I speak at schools, I encourage students to "perform" stories. I find this can often best illustrate where conflict, character development, and resolutions intersect. On one occasion, in a seventh-grade classroom, I tried an experiment. I asked two male students to come forward, one white, one black, and told them to talk about how they felt about school, but that they must exchange races when they did it.

"You be the white kid," I instructed the young black man who grimaced. "You be the black," I said to the white student.

They and the class looked at me like I'd just grown a third eye. This is not for the faint-hearted. After some resistance, they agreed to try.

We went through several false starts when the black student finally said, "I don't know how to act white."

The white student shifted nervously in agreement and smoothed back his hair. The black student watched him, then grinned broadly, and did the same thing.

The white student flopped deeper in the folding chair. The black student copied him perfectly.

The white student, catching on, crossed his legs and raised his hands to the ceiling as the two began a back-and-forth mimic of great complexity and good-natured laughter. Finally, the black student, in the ultimate tour de force, jumped up and spun around in a spectacular twirl; the white student attempted to follow, but knocked over a chair, ending the exercise. They returned to their seats to riotous applause—distinct, yet together.

"I'll teach you the spin," the black student said to the white student. And he did, at recess.

Sometimes multicultural influences can be mighty plot thickeners and the key to fostering understanding.

At another school I visited, the class and I were brainstorming about a story that I hoped would illustrate the role of conflict and motivation in fiction writing. The class (mostly boys) had come up with an idea about a middle school boy who wanted more than anything to play football.

"What's keeping him from doing it?" I asked.

Viable answers came. He's got a broken leg. His mother doesn't want him to get hurt. He can't afford the equipment.

But I saw the light go on in the eyes of a Japanese student who raised his hand and announced, laughingly, "Because he lives in Japan."

"So what?" asked several students, less than charitably.

"Because," the Japanese student replied, "in Japan there is no football."

"Now *that's* story conflict," I shouted.

And we proceeded to roar into a wonderfully comic, twisting plot about a boy living in Japan who dreamed of becoming a professional football player, and all the crazy things he did to get his parents to move to the United States so he could play the game. There was great laughter and discovery shared that day, and the students learned two lessons about humor writing:

1. Conflict breeds laughter.
2. Always push the envelope as far as it will creatively go.

Also, happily, throughout the exercise, the Japanese student starred—patiently, proudly instructing his American classmates about life and sports in his country.

Finding the Voices

As a novelist, I'm intrigued by how a simple exchange between characters can be layered to have deeper meaning. In my third novel, *Sticks,* which is the story of a ten-year-old boy and his math genius sidekick who learn about life, determination, math, and science in a pool hall, I've attempted to describe a multicultural setting in the first-person narrative of Mickey Vernon, age ten, without him ever describing another character as black, white, or Hispanic. In fact, I wanted Mickey to be color-blind in that sense—to distinguish and celebrate people for their accomplishments while respecting their cultural milieus. Here, Mickey is sitting in art class trying to gain courage about facing his thirteen-year-old nemesis, Buck Pender, in the local pool tournament:

> I'm working on my African warrior mask, painting the papier-mâché cheeks bright gold and purple. I stick feathers at the top and make the mouth look angry and I picture this huge warrior with a spear doing a death dance around Buck Pender. T. R. Dobbs is working on his mask next to me. He's descended from African Zulu warriors and he says a Zulu never retreats in the face of the enemy. I'm descended mostly from potato farmers, which isn't a lot to hold on to when you need to be tough. I lift the mask to my face and shout the Zulu war cry T. R. taught me.
>
> "Zuuuuluuuu Zuuuuluuuu!"
>
> Mr. Pez, the art teacher, looks up. I look down and keep painting. Nobody turns me in.
>
> It's easy to be brave when the enemy isn't around.

Blasting stereotypes gives me soul satisfaction. And blasting them in a classroom setting bridges the way to common ground as students are brought into a larger place of acceptance of others.

Certainly the joy of finding universal experiences draws people together wonderfully. I spoke during an assembly at a New Jersey high school and announced to the assembled masses: "I promise you this will be the easiest test any of you have taken all year. True or false: Teenagers repeatedly have conflicts with their parents."

A pulsating, thundering "True!" rang out.

I continued: "True or false: These conflicts can be a royal pain, particularly when the parents are being thick-headed and unfair, particularly when they're not paying attention to anything the poor kid says."

The "True!" was a hundred times louder.

Of course, I knew how they would respond, and they knew that I knew. But their affirmation was the connection—black, white, Asian, Hispanic, old, young, rich, poor—united by adolescent angst.

"Anybody ever been in love with somebody who didn't know you were alive?" I asked.

Knowing nods.

So I read to them from *Thwonk,* my second YA novel, about a seventeen-year-old lovelorn photographer who learns about love, self-esteem, and forgiving her father from the hands of an exasperated cupid. Here, pre-cupid, she explains her lot.

> The whole thing with Peter Terris started five months ago, and I'd like to say from the outset that I wasn't looking for trouble. I was walking through the Student Center, speed-reading *Beowulf,* when I tripped over Peter's flawless foot and crashed at his feet like a complete spaz. I would have written the whole thing off to consummately bleak timing had I not gazed into his ice-green eyes, observed that they were positively riveting, and frozen in time.

Humor at Our Very Roots

The power of humor to lift, heal, and define in all facets of life and culture is well documented, from author Norman Cousins's bold remission from cancer that he chronicled in *Anatomy of an Illness* to every joke told by every comic down through the ages trying to make sense of their cultural heritage. Here's one of my favorites, written by Milt Josefsberg for Jack Benny:

> A rabbi receives a phone call from an IRS investigator. "Rabbi, do you know a man named Hyman Shapiro?"
>
> "I do."
>
> "Does he belong to your congregation?"
>
> "He does."

"Did he make a $10,000 donation to your temple?"
"He will."

Why do we laugh at that joke? Because in some ways, we've all been there. Because with a few short lines it tells us all we need to know about the rabbi and Hyman Shapiro. Does that make it a universal teaching tool?

Yes!

Humor is appreciating the ludicrous and comic absurdity of life. Humor works when it allows us to laugh *with,* not *at,* another person or different culture. Humor teaches when it springs from life's experiences, especially if those experiences are painful, because laughter can help put painful experiences and feelings in perspective and allow us to move toward healing.

Children, however, will not all laugh at the same thing. But neither will they cry, be moved, or respond to anything uniformly. I believe, though, that they must be taught the difference between humor that uplifts and regenerates and humor that is thoughtless and cruel. In that, humor can be a bridge to the wider world view we seek for ourselves and our future.

As literature removes boundaries and explores universal themes, as the heart of cultures are examined and differences celebrated, we make another step toward unity and understanding. I believe that the simple, profound gift of shared laughter can help to show us the way. Garrison Keillor said it all: "Humor isn't tricks, it isn't jokes. Humor is like grace and falls on everyone."

References

Bauer, Joan. 1995. *Thwonk.* New York: Delacorte.

———. 1996. *Sticks.* New York: Delacorte.

Cousins, Norman. 1983. *Anatomy of an Illness as Perceived by the Patient.* New York: Bantam.

Josefsberg, Milt. 1987. *Comedy Writing for Television and Hollywood.* New York: Harper & Row.

7 Michael and Me (and Other Voices from Flint)

Christopher Paul Curtis

Anyone who has any sympathy must wince every time my hometown, Flint, Michigan, is mentioned. In recent decades, Flint has gone from being known as the automobile capital of America to the nation's unemployment capital to its murder capital. Finally, the city's reputation has lighted on being known as the subject of a disparaging documentary. Whenever I tell a non-Michigander I'm from Flint, I inevitably watch as a glimmer of recognition lights their face while they search their memories before they finally come up with some variation of, "Flint? Flint . . . oh yeah, isn't that the city that that guy made that movie about? Wasn't his name Roger Moore? And what was that movie? Wasn't it called, 'Rodney and Me' or something?"

Actually, it was Michael Moore and the movie was *Roger and Me,* and this unfortunately seems to be Flint's legacy. Recently I was in Minneapolis at a booksellers' convention and saw that Michael Moore was one of the featured speakers. I was only able to hear the end of his speech but was especially struck by his summation. Michael thanked the audience and said something to the effect of, "and particularly let me thank you for giving me, somebody from Flint, Michigan, and others like me a chance to be heard. It is so rare that our voices are noticed."

After my knee-jerk reaction passed (Wait a minute, Mike, you're not actually from Flint; you grew up in the suburbs), I liked that thought. I liked the idea that he was recognizing that there are voices out there that are largely either silenced or ignored. However, I don't think Mike and I have the same voices in mind.

The year that my young adult novel *The Watsons Go to Birmingham—1963* has been published has been a tremendous learning experience for me. I have learned a great deal about the publishing process and book promotions. I've learned much about speaking to students and have, for the first time in my life, done a great deal of traveling, all of which have given me a new perspective on what voices are and are not being heard. One of the strongest lessons I've come away with is the blunt honesty of young people's questions. I have become aware that there is no such thing as an easy or predictable appearance.

Students seem to come up with the most thought-provoking, embarrassing questions. (And I don't mean the big two either: "If you're a writer you must be making pretty good cash; if that's true how come you're wearing shoes like that?" or "How old are you? My dad is fifty and you've gotta be a lot older than him.") Rather, the question that caused me the most problems was when a girl asked me, "What books really touched you when you were a kid?" I paused when she asked, thought, and realized there weren't any.

For the longest time I felt really bad about this. I mean here I was an author of books for young people; it seemed as though I should have been able to recite a litany of books that had deeply moved or affected me as I was growing up, but nothing was coming to mind. It wasn't that I hadn't been exposed to books; books were readily available in the Curtis household. Both of my parents were avid readers who had made a tremendous financial sacrifice to buy us a set of *Childcraft* and *World Book* encyclopedias one Christmas. Also, my oldest sister, Lindsey, used to regularly read to me. Neither was my inability to name a memorable book caused by my having difficulties reading: I could read at levels much higher than my age group. Nor was it that I didn't enjoy reading; I loved looking through *Childcraft* and reading magazines and comic books. After much thought I decided that the problem wasn't as much with me as it was with the books that were available.

Of course, I remember being made to read many different books but none of them really stuck with me, none of them really spoke to me as a young person in the same way that so many books do now. In hindsight, I think there were far too few books that reached out to me in a voice I could relate to, and even fewer books that used "my" voice. I could enjoy only so many *Johnny Tremaine*s or *Oliver Twist*s or *1984*s or *Bridge*s *at Toko Ri*s or *Huckleberry Finn*s before I became starved for quality books that were about me. I say *starved* because that's precisely what I felt. I remember being so hungry to read about me that the word "Negro" (as we were called once upon a time) would jump off the page two paragraphs ahead of what I was reading. I would skip forward and see what brothers or sisters this book was talking about and what kind of character this "Negro" was going to be. Ninety-nine times out of a hundred I would be badly disappointed. Or embarrassed. Or, most often, angry.

As far as I knew there simply weren't any books that were told by me, about me, or for me. I'm certain that this isn't the muted voice that Michael Moore was referring to, but it is a voice I'm sure he'd agree is needed now as desperately as it has ever been.

I think young adult literature is at the same point that television was many decades ago. There was a time, and most African Americans who are at least in their thirties can remember this, when black faces were so rare on television that their appearance was an event. I can remember rushing to the living room after hearing one of my parents scream, "Hurry up, there's a Negro on channel 12!" We'd all stare at the TV, smiling mouths agape, amazed that black faces could actually ride the air waves. In young adult literature we're just about at the same point. There are so few African American voices filtering through that there is a palpable stir when a new voice "rides the air waves."

There are many reasons we are in this sorry state, but to end it, everyone involved in the process of teaching young people the love of reading has to redouble his or her efforts. This has to start with publishers and editors, who must develop a more sensitive ear when it comes to recognizing and encouraging new talent from underrepresented groups. Unfortunately, my experiences at Delacorte Publishing with *The Watsons Go to Birmingham—1963* are far from the norm. There, my editor Wendy Lamb plucked my manuscript from a pile of four hundred others that she'd read for their annual Young Adult Writer's Contest, took a chance, and helped give Kenny Watson's voice life.

I coped with the lack of books for and about "me" by reading comics, magazines, and newspapers. In so doing I learned to love reading. Unfortunately, many other minority students will cope as many in my generation did—by giving up on books. They will never learn the joy of reading for pleasure's sake; they will be turned off before they have a chance to see the beauty and power of literature. They will be robbed of the single most precious enduring gift education can give them. Of course, a lack of voice is not the only factor that comes into the equation of why children won't read, but it is an extremely important part.

What more can we do? As an author I can only try to produce the types of books that weren't around when I was a child; I am unqualified to suggest what you as teachers can do. In my visits to schools I have seen many of you work and I am in awe. All I can do is paraphrase my homeboy, Michael Moore: I, too, want to give my sincerest thanks to the many librarians and teachers who have embraced me and my book. I am so grateful that you have provided an opportunity for a long-ignored, long-muted voice from the choir of voices in Flint to be heard.

References

Curtis, Christopher Paul. 1997. *The Watsons Go to Birmingham—1963*. New York: Bantam Doubleday Dell.

II Connecting with Students

In Part II, Connecting with Students, we hear the voices of teachers, from upper elementary grades, middle school, high school, and teacher education, telling their stories and sharing their insights on how they make connections between multicultural young adult literature and their students. Teachers use literature as they strive to help young people become literate individuals who understand themselves and the world. They help students to be able and willing to make personal connections with the curriculum. Perhaps there is no other area in the curriculum that has the potential to elicit such significant responses from students as literature. To this end, we believe that it is essential to expand the traditional offerings of the school curriculum to reflect both the emergence of excellent works written for the young adult audience and the emergence of powerful books and stories about women, people of color, people from distant lands, and people of different perspectives and religions.

Deborah Forster-Sulzer describes how she used multicultural young adult literature to help the young women in her high school class find appropriate role models. Ellen Shull presents the work she did to help middle school students understand commonalities among people by reading and writing poetry. Jean Brown and Elaine Stephens describe a literature involvement strategy to help readers gain in-depth understanding of characters from other cultures. Betsy Noll, Charlotte Valencia Lindahl, and Debra Salazar describe a variety of strategies to help readers respond to multicultural literature. In each of their chapters Denise Emery, Diane Hoffbauer, and Mitzi Witkin describe various strategies they have used in their classes to help students understand their own cultures and heritage as well as those of others. Jeff Kaplan presents books and strategies for heightening students' understanding of Jewish culture and history. Louise Garcia Harrison illustrates the impact that Cisneros and Soto have on helping her students to write personal narratives.

The young adult books cited in each of these chapters are included in the annotated bibliography at the end of this book.

8 We Are All Phenomenal Women: Finding Female Role Models through Multicultural Poetry and Literature

Deborah Forster-Sulzer
Orange County Schools

Pretty women wonder where my secret lies.
I'm not cute or built to suit a fashion model's size. . . .
Maya Angelou, *Phenomenal Woman*

My first-period sophomore English class buzzes quietly as the students flip through piles of magazines searching for the perfect symbolic pictures to describe their identity. At 7:30 on a rainy Monday morning, they are actually impressive in their persistent pursuits of creative collage material.

After taking attendance and setting the envelope outside, I pick up some magazines and a pair of scissors and join Liza's group, wanting to model and participate in the learning activity that I have assigned at this inhumanly trying hour. Christina leafs through the latest editions of *Glamour* and *Cosmopolitan,* frowning and sighing with distaste.

"I will never have a chest like that, a waist like that, or thighs like that," she whines with frustration. "It's no wonder that Chris doesn't even know that I exist."

"You know, if I am not constantly on a diet then I don't feel good about myself, and then when I cheat and eat pizza, I feel like throwing it up," replies Michelle, who can't actually be larger than a size three.

Liza mumbles without conviction, "I just wish that I could look in the mirror and like what I see, inside and out." She tries unsuccessfully to avoid the well-knowing glances from Christina and Michelle. These teenagers, like a majority of my female students, lack the self-esteem necessary to see and understand the phenomenal traits that lie within each one of them.

I resist my dark places, and try to hide them
from other people, but mostly myself.
Sark, *Succulent, Wild Woman*

I honestly look at myself, and I have to wonder if I am truly phenomenal. Can I look at my students and practice what I preach?

"You've got to believe in the individual power that each of you has." I can hear my own words ringing in my head. Do I believe in my own power? I have to listen to the questioning of Christina, Liza, and Michelle and wonder how such extraordinary girls can doubt themselves and the brilliance of their abilities. But then, why do I doubt my own abilities? What must it be like to be able to gaze into the objective mirror and totally love the woman that stares back at you? I would like to think of myself as a strong, independent woman who could handle anything that is thrown at her, but would I describe myself as phenomenal? Unfortunately, my English teachers never really offered me any types of literature that suggested that women truly are phenomenal. No one ever introduced me to the passion of Maya Angelou or the wit of Angela Shelf Medearis. I admit this readily, simply because of the alarming fact that not only are many women desperately trying to define themselves as adults, but many of the female students who stare at me each day for guidance and inspiration are similarly struggling to define themselves during the trying teenage years. And, teachers have the perfect self-worth–building tools to help build a young female's sense of purpose: multicultural poetry and adolescent literature.

Let's face it—women truly want to be phenomenal. We want to use the inspirational words of Maya Angelou and "rise up" to be all the things that women before us never had the opportunity to be. We want to have it all: peace, love, education, family, career, a meaning in life, a drive to be a part of the big picture of existence. When I look into the eyes of my first-period class, I see twenty-two females and five males staring expectantly back at me. It seems like my male students can often look to the world for role models. They can argue about the political campaign of Bill Clinton and Bob Dole. They look to the television to hear the commentary of Peter Jennings and gaze to the corporate world to idolize the Microsoft giant, Bill Gates. Even down our west hallway, the males can go to the front office to talk shop with our high school principal, Mr. Brinker, who has been a pillar in our school community for decades.

I look into the eyes of my teenage female students, and I know that I have to help them to find their defining role models just as healthily as their male peers. I want to be the teacher who recognizes that there is a need to help all girls believe that they are indeed phenomenal, and that they will look into the mirrors of life and love every part of their existence. I missed out on having a teacher who saw this as a priority. I think we spent most of English class diagramming sentences and constructing five-paragraph essays.

Mandy worries me because she is afraid to talk during class discussions for fear of being ridiculed by the boys. Shannon feels that there will never be a woman president, and thus she will not waste her time pursuing politics. Melissa believes that the only thing that will make her happy in life is to find the perfect man to marry, because her father does not feel that girls should go to college. The majority of my teenage female students, when asked to describe themselves, use words such a *lonely, plain, shy, afraid,* or *reserved* to explain their inner personalities. Not one of my female English students used a positive adjective to describe her personal identity. Why do negative self-images haunt these girls? How do these negative self-images begin? Is society to blame? Is television to blame? Regardless of the blame, negative self-images can be changed with the help of literature that portrays strong, female protagonists, literature that can be used as a means of celebrating the phenomenal abilities of woman. Through the inspirational words of Maya Angelou, Angela Shelf Medearis, Sandra Cisneros, and Sara Holbrook, my sophomore English students not only discovered valuable multicultural and female role models, but also learned about their own inner identities and their phenomenal possibilities for the world.

Early in the school year, I decided that my students would grow from an integration of multicultural, female literature into the traditional male canon of our high school's literature program based upon the diverse personal needs of my students. As sophomores, my students were expected to read, analyze, and know a great deal about William Shakespeare, Homer, and John Steinbeck, but they were never required to experience multicultural literature or any type of literature with a strong, female perspective. Because all students are looking, in some way, for a definition of who they are and what they believe in, I began our school year with an Identity Quest to create a Personality Portfolio. This quest started out as a not-so-simple task: discover who you are, define who you are, and distinguish what personal role models and individual authors and literature brought you to this understanding. My students were asked to read a multitude of poetry, short stories, adolescent literature, novels, music lyrics, and so forth, in hopes of discovering some unique language to personally and positively describe themselves as individuals. The students were introduced to such books as *Phenomenal Woman, Life Doesn't Frighten Me,* and *I Shall Not Be Moved* by Maya Angelou; *The House on Mango Street* by Sandra Cisneros; *Skin Deep* by Angela Shelf Medearis; and *Chicks Up Front* by Sara Holbrook. Through the use of Personality Portfolios, the students began a collection of artifacts that would ultimately describe who they were as individuals. These artifacts included self-written poetry and short stories, copies of meaningful, relevant literature, art pieces, magazine clippings, song lyrics, and so on—anything that could help define their actual "status of being."

> I would like to baptize myself under a new name. . . .
>
> Sandra Cisneros, "My Name . . ."

Sandra Cisneros's *House on Mango Street* is dedicated "a las mujeres—to the women," and offers a variety of engaging writing prompts that can help male and female teens think about their own personal stories and how these combine to define the unique person that each one of them is. One of Cisneros's vignettes, "My Name," describes the frustrations that many young adults feel in looking at their names as a rock-solid defining factor of their personality.

Even as an adult, I can easily look back at my high school years and remember wishing that I were a Samantha or a Whitney, anything but a Debi. Debi was so plain sounding, and it reminded me of the type of person who would spend a lot of time saying "like wow, man." "My Name" looks at a teenager's frustration with her own name, regardless of why it was chosen by her mother or what it might symbolize. My students thought it was extremely relevant to write about their own names, their likes and dislikes, and what they would rename themselves if they had the chance to. Many of the girls grew to like the honesty of Cisneros's writing, and Kelly pointed out that Cisneros "talked about the details of life that mattered to me—she made me feel that I'm not alone or crazy or anything."

The beauty of the Personality Portfolios was that, like a writer's scrapbook, these portfolios were authentic, working documents that students continually added to all year long. As we explored themes of study such as "through freedom and bondage we come to know who we are," students automatically jotted down phrases from survival stories, poetry, films, and music that helped them to define their thoughts, beliefs, and attitudes. For example, as I read Maya Angelou's picture book *Life Doesn't Frighten Me* to my first-period class, Sandra immediately grabbed the book from my hands because this poem symbolized her, and she had to copy it down immediately into her portfolio. The portfolios became extensions of the students' personalities as they discovered the powerful words of multicultural authors to help them with the often tough job of figuring out how to define their own individuality.

> I just can't seem to find
> a language. . . .
>
> Angela Shelf Medearis, "As Soon As I Find Out Who I Am You'll Be the First to Know"

I believe that we are all searching for words and voice to define ourselves, to express our beliefs, our values, and our sense of home. *Skin Deep and Other Teenage Reflections,* by Angela Shelf Medearis, is a fantastic collection of teenage poetry that offers great examples of personal voices for young writers to model and experiment with as they search for their own. "As Soon As I Find Out . . ." is a poem that many teenage readers, male or female, can easily relate to because of the pressure endured in trying to provide answers about feelings that they often don't have solidified.

"I've just started high school, and my parents already want to know exactly where I am going to go to college, how I am going to pay for it, and what I want to do for a living. How am I supposed to tell them that I want to be an actress?" explained Candace during a discussion that we conducted after our daily journal writing in our Reflective Log. I had posed the question, "Do you always trust your gut feelings?" Students immediately dived into writing an answer to this question because they could use written expression in favor of or against relying on true emotions for decision-making purposes. Our discussion, following the quick write, included those students who believed in the power of their emotions and those who trusted only reason, and the debate continued with great passion and energy. As an extension activity, students read "As Soon As I Find Out . . ." and applied the emotions of the speaker to their own lives and then to the lives of the characters from *House on Mango Street.* A significant majority of my female students believed that they could relate to Medearis's speaker because they, too, had a difficult time articulating their true feelings about personal issues to friends, parents, and teachers.

To practice finding personal voice, my students created a Travel Diary, as a reader-response technique, for responding to the reading that they were doing. Students attempted to assume the persona of the speaker or any other character that emerged in the poetry and literature that they were reading. After assuming the identity and point of view of a character within the piece, the students created diary entries of their "travel" through the literature, commenting on inner feelings of the character not stated in the actual writing. These responses occurred nightly, varied in length, provided a multitude of discussion ideas, and always allowed the individual student to bring personal meaning to a text. For some of my girls, this personal meaning making and articulation was one of the first times that they had ever been encouraged to trust their personal interpretation of a piece of relevant literature.

I am looking
for that place
beyond resign and cope. . . .
Sara Holbrook, from "Still Looking"

I think, in reality, we are all "still looking" for positive methods of celebrating our phenomenal, individual personalities, whether we are male or female. Our challenge as teachers is to provide meaningful tools for all students to build on their individual sense of self-worth, especially during the trying times of adolescence. Through the powerful words of Maya Angelou, Sark, Sandra Cisneros, Angela Shelf Medearis, and Sara Holbrook, adolescent females can find strength and power in the pages of multicultural poetry and adolescent literature.

References

Angelou, Maya. 1993. *Life Doesn't Frighten Me.* New York: Stewart, Tabori & Chang.

———. 1995. *Phenomenal Woman: Four Poems Celebrating Women.* New York: Random House.

Cisneros, Sandra. 1994. *The House on Mango Street.* New York: Random House.

Holbrook, Sara. 1996. *Chicks Up Front.* Ohio: Milkweed Press.

Medearis, Angela S. 1995. *Skin Deep, and Other Teenage Reflections.* New York: Simon & Schuster.

Sark. 1997. *Succulent Wild Women.* New York: Fireside.

9 Creating a Talisman: Reflecting a Culture

Jean E. Brown
Saginaw Valley State University

Elaine C. Stephens
Saginaw Valley State University

As teacher educators we use multicultural young adult literature with our students, both preservice and practicing classroom teachers, in all of our teacher education courses. We do this because we believe that muliticultural young adult literature is a vital addition to the school curriculum that "has the potential to integrate and to unify learning in all content areas by celebrating the uniqueness of different cultures and their people while reaffirming the universal traits that define our humanity" (Brown and Stephens 1995, pp. 4–5). We want our teacher education students to experience the power of literature to transport readers into new and different environments and heighten their awareness of other peoples and other cultures.

We believe that today's youth benefit from involvement with the increasing amount of high-quality young adult literature that reflects the diverse cultures in our society and in the world.

> When cultural differences remain hidden or misunderstood, fear and suspicion frequently overcome rational understanding. Learning about the customs, beliefs, and traditions of others helps students become more open to differences. This openness, when nurtured and developed, fosters tolerance. (Brown and Stephens 1996, p. 3)

As we use multicultural young adult literature with preservice and inservice teachers and they, in turn, use it with their own students, we discover that it is essential for readers to connect with the characters. This connection must occur if readers are to develop more than a superficial understanding of the characters, their life circumstances, their families, their cultures, and their environment. When readers read about characters who are similar to them, this connection is fairly easy to foster, but when the characters are dissimilar in significant ways, readers frequently struggle to find a satisfying way to make a connection.

Although we have explored a number of literature involvement activities to help readers make this connection, we have found that the

"Create a Talisman" activity is particularly effective when students read about characters from diverse cultures, other ethnic groups, or unfamiliar life situations. A talisman is an object or charm thought to avert evil and bring about good fortune. When engaged in the "Create a Talisman" activity, the reader selects a specific character for intensive study, culminating in identifying, creating, or designing a talisman for that character. In order to select an appropriate talisman, the reader must have a well-developed understanding of the character. This understanding should also reflect an awareness of the character's heritage and the objects and symbols of that character's culture that represent positive images. Therefore, this activity necessitates that readers have a sensitivity to and understanding of the cultural perspective from which the character comes. The talisman does not need to be an object that is part of the character's background; however, it should reflect an awareness of it. Ultimately, a goal of this strategy is to enhance the multicultural understanding of all readers. For readers, this perspective helps them to recognize the context and circumstances from which the character evolves.

Some books feature objects that function as talismans, and these serve as good models for helping students to understand the concept. An effective example is in Will Hobbs's *Bearstone.* The protagonist, Cloyd, discovers a cave with relics of the Ancient Ones. Amidst the pottery and blankets he finds a small, turquoise bear, polished smooth from years of handling. Cloyd knows from his grandmother that, in his Ute heritage, bears play a significant role.

> The most important of all animals to the Utes, she'd said—friend and relative of man, bringer of strength and luck. If you could make a bear your personal guardian, you would be a strong man and lucky. (p. 15)

Bears are talismans to the Utes, representing an ongoing cultural belief. But a talisman may be more abstract and more personal. For example, in *The Catcher in the Rye,* Holden carries his brother Allie's baseball glove in his suitcase with him. The glove is decorated with poems written in green ink so Allie could have something to read when he was in the field and waiting for a batter to come to the plate. Holden grieves for Allie, who is dead, and the baseball glove helps him to feel connected to his younger brother.

As we work with our teacher education students to use the literature involvement activity, "Create a Talisman," we ask them to go beyond the text to create a meaningful talisman that is reflective of the character. The three-phase process for the talisman development begins with readers doing an intensive character study (phase 1), followed by an examination of the culture and traditions that the character comes from (phase 2). The character study and culture examination then serve as the springboard for the talisman creation (phase 3). The process for each of these phases is as follows.

Phase 1. Select any character from one of the books you have read for this class. It may be either a major or minor character. Pick a character that intrigues you and whom you wish to examine more fully. Use the following to assist you:

> What is the character like?
>
> What motivates him or her?
>
> How is the character viewed by other characters?
>
> Identify key words that give insights into the character.
>
> What objects remind you of the character? Why?
>
> Are there objects that you think represent aspects of the character? What and why?
>
> Close your eyes and visualize the character. Jot down characteristics that you think the character has. If you were to visualize an object that reminds you of the character, what might it be?

Phase 2. Identify the cultural heritage of the character. What customs, traditions, rituals, or symbols of the culture have played a role in the character's life? What is their impact on the character? How does this heritage influence his or her actions and behavior?

Phase 3. Given the insights you have gained about the characters and culture from which they come, design a talisman for the character. The talisman may be either a concrete object or an abstract one. Select an object that the character does not own in the book. Pick something that will give special insight into the nature of the character, the circumstances of the character's life, and an awareness of the culture. Remember that by its nature a talisman is largely symbolic. Don't immediately settle on the obvious.

Examples

The following are examples of talismans created for three different characters, Kofi from *The Captive,* Tomi from *Under the Blood Red Sun,* and Ellie from *Squashed.*

> Kofi, from Joyce Hansen's *The Captive,* is kidnapped from his home in Africa and sold into slavery in Massachusetts, even though there are laws against slavery there. When he was taken

from his family, all he was able to keep was the flute that his father had given him. A number of times people try to take the flute, but Kofi always gets it back one way or another.

The talisman I would give to him would be a bag for him to carry the flute in. When he was brought to New England, Kofi was dismayed about the plain, scratchy clothes that he was force to wear. So I would make the bag from a soft cloth of bright colors like the African robes that he wore before he was captured. The bag would have a narrow rope around the top to close it and also to hang around his neck. The rope, as it circles his neck, represents his capture, then being set free in New England, returning to Africa on a trading ship, and then returning to his new family in America.

In *Under the Blood Red Sun,* by Graham Salisbury, the main character has a rough time when the Japanese bomb Pearl Harbor because his family is Japanese and lots of people blame them. It's really hard on him because he was born in Hawaii and felt like he was American, not Japanese. The talisman I would give him is a medallion with an American flag on one side and a Japanese flag, like the one his grandfather had, on the other side. Although Tomi thinks of himself as totally American, his Japanese heritage also has a big influence on him. Once his father and grandfather are sent away, his cultural heritage becomes more obvious to him as he must be the head of the family. The two sides of the medallion represent the two cultures that Tomi lives in.

The talisman that I would choose for Ellie from *Squashed* by Joan Bauer is a Petosky stone. Like any other rock, Petosky stones are really hard and I think Ellie was hard or tough, but in a good way. She had to be to keep to her dream and to win in the pumpkin growing contest. Petosky stones are also rare—you can only find them on the northern shores of Lake Michigan. I think that Ellie is also kind of rare or unusual. Not many teenaged girls are going to put all that energy into growing a giant pumpkin. But the biggest reason that I would give Ellie a Petosky stone as a talisman is because when you find one, they seem to be just gray stones. They are really plain until they are either wet or polished. Then they reveal a complex pattern and are quite interesting and pretty. Ellie never thinks that she is pretty, but she really is under the surface. That's why I think it's a good talisman for Ellie.

In each of these examples, readers envisioned an object that connects with the character according to their reading of the novel. The conceptualization of the character and the creation of the talisman provide readers with opportunities to have authentic connections with their reading. We also believe that the heightened understanding that readers gain about the character and the culture she or he is from will help them to be more sensitive and tolerant of differences.

References

Bauer, Joan. 1994. *Squashed.* New York: Bantam Doubleday Dell.

Brown, Jean E., and Elaine C. Stephens. 1995. *TeachingYoung Adult Literature: Sharing the Connections.* Belmont, CA: Wadsworth.

Brown, Jean E., and Elaine C. Stephens. 1996. *Exploring Diversity: Literature, Themes, and Activities for Grades 4–8.* Englewood, CO: Teacher Ideas Press.

Hansen, Joyce. 1995. *The Captive.* New York: Scholastic.

Hobbs, Will. 1989. *Bearstone.* New York: Macmillan.

Salinger, J. D. 1945, 1984. *The Catcher in the Rye.* New York: Bantam.

Salisbury, Graham. 1994. *Under the Blood Red Sun.* New York: Delacorte.

10 Painting Pictures with the World: Reading and Writing Multicultural Poetry in the Middle School

Ellen Shull
Palo Alto College
San Antonio, Texas

After the exciting parade of Thanksgiving, Christmas, Hanukkah, and New Year's, with the accompanying music, gifts, rich food, and the requisite parties, mid-January can be a letdown. I found a way to revive it a few years ago. Now I start the new school year by bringing poetry to students in the middle school grades at a nearby elementary school. It's good for me, for their teachers (who get a break), and for the students who hesitate at first but end up with creative juices flowing and pens scribbling poems even on the back of math homework and the side of a grocery bag. This is also an opportunity to introduce poetry and poets not to be found in textbooks, poets from cultures and lands not their own. It has been a great success, this multicultural, midwinter poetry.

We take time for reading from poetry books I bring in to connect reading poetry with writing poetry, but time is set aside also for hearing their poems and the poems of their classmates. I stop by the school and pick up freshly written student poems every few days so I can read and comment on them and keep our connection strong over the few weeks we work together. By the third and final session, a special day, the students have written at least four complete poems and have collected a portfolio with numerous in-progress writings. They also have prepared one poem to present for The Reading, a celebration of poets and their poetry. It is invigorating.

Meeting One

I begin every year the same way: "I am going to give you something, but I am also going to take something away." What I give them is sense imagery, similes, metaphors, and other poetic devices. I take away rhyme. The first time, a howl went up: "We can't write poems without rhyme. What kind of a poem would that be anyway?"

"It would be a poem rich in images and detail, one you will be proud of. Trust me," I said the first year and held my breath. Since then, resistance has been minimal.

Now the seventh and eighth graders who have been through the drill the year before smile when rhyme is discussed. The new students in the three grades plus the entire sixth-grade class blanch. What kind of poems are these with no rhyme? They soon find out.

Reading lots of poems in the first meeting creates the poetic atmosphere. We begin by talking about what makes poetry different from stories. I read poems to them, making the reading as dynamic and dramatic as I can. Poems about friends, school, sports, the lion at the zoo, a rainy day. Poems coming from Argentina, Kenya, Indonesia, Vietnam, Denmark, Israel. Then we read poems together. The idea is to have fun and to make poetry familiar and comfortable.

I pass my books around so the students can handle real books, full books devoted to poetry. When Ashley Bryan, the Maine artist and writer, visited San Antonio a few years ago, I acted as his chauffeur and so was privileged to attend the readings he presented for groups as diverse as English teachers, girls in a Catholic high school, and kids off the streets at an inner-city center. I noticed he always held the book in his hands even though he appeared to be too familiar with the poems to need it. I asked him why and he told me, "Children have got to see the books, handle the books, value the books. We are becoming a nation without books." I like to speak to students about beginning or maintaining their own personal libraries, but now I have taken his admonition to heart and do so with the book in hand.

At that first session, once we have read aloud a variety of poems, we begin a warming-up exercise. We might write group poems or use a model so everyone can produce something poetic for the initial piece in what will become their portfolio of poems. Previously, I have used William Carlos Williams's "This Is Just to Say" and "The Red Wheelbarrow" as poems to emulate because they center our attention on the image. Students write their own transformations, coming up with some great ideas. Instead of plums I have met a student who was sorry to have burned the 400-page book someone was writing, but thought it allowable because "you were going to rewrite it anyway." And as far as red wheelbarrows, today's student has no sense of them. Much more depends upon a red Porsche or a computer hooked up to the Internet. I talk to them about poetic language and the notion of the narrator as a creation of the poet. I tell them, "You don't have to tell the truth in poems! You can make it up just like you do for stories." Their homework assignment is to write a poem suggested by one of those we read.

Now, however, I begin with the multicultural poems even for the initial exercises. This year I am using *The Tree Is Older Than You Are,* a collection of poems and stories from Mexico, printed in Spanish and in translation. It includes Manuel Ulacia's "The Word," an intriguing short poem which compares the use of language to a magician's tricks or an astronaut's hanging by a thread—tenuous perhaps, but what an example of the creative imagination at work. It is useful as well for showing students effective similes. Another poem, this one by José Juan Tablada, compares a turtle and his shell to someone carrying a load of household furniture, an apt simile here, too. The piñata which falls out of the tree in Jennifer Clement's poem "Piñata" makes a comparison between ripe fruit falling from a tree and piñatas, which also might fall and spill their candy. But then there's Alberto Forcada's "Waking," which presents a mother with a "harpoon voice" getting her child up for school by scaling, cooking, garnishing him with books, and then casting him out the door into the "numbered teeth of Mathematics." Chilling. The students understand this situation—especially those weak in mathematics—though the poem comes from Mexico. They make a number of connections: that poems can be short but must show with images rather than explanations to make them good poems, that my mother getting me ready for school can be compared to a deep sea fisherman sometimes, and that children in Mexico might have a school problem similar to mine. "I guess we're in the same boat," said one seventh grader. Then he laughed when he realized his metaphor matched.

Next we look closely at a single poem of greater length. "Little Girl with Chocolates" by Mexican poet Hugo García González has a two-part construction. The first two stanzas look closely at a young girl who must sell chocolates on the city streets to help her family survive. We are invited to look closely at her hair, clothing ("a green dress / with seven flowers"), shoes, and the candy. The second two stanzas look at her situation ("she must sell her chocolates / and care for her brothers and sisters") and also imagine her hopes and dreams.

Students can approximate this poem for themselves by starting with a picture cut from a magazine or newspaper, preferably of someone they do not know. By first painting with details so particular as to even number the flowers on a dress, they transfer the picture to the paper. Only then may they infer the rest. A successful exercise, this helps students create good poems.

Meeting Two

For the second session I select two or three poems to study closely. We begin by having volunteers read the poems so we can hear them in many different voices. Students point out all the sense imagery and look at poetic devices, especially simile, metaphor, and personification. We look up any unfamiliar words. We talk about who the narrator might be and look also at the scene and action of the poem. Only then do we discuss what the poem means. By this time everyone has an opinion.

Two years ago we used our second meeting to work with poems from *This Same Sky: A Collection of Poems from Around the World.* Even the book's endpapers are multicultural, a collage of envelopes the poems came in with stamps and postmarks from around the world. Tarapada Ray's poem "My Great Grand Uncle" brings us to his homeland of India and introduces an eccentric uncle who collected feathers. On the day he died ("How did he know it would be that day?" asked three or four students in unison) he let all the feathers fly from the roof of his house, and even to this day ("Could that possibly be true, Mrs. Shull?") some of them are still floating in the air. What great possibilities that poem presented. "Let's write a poem like this," I said. "Most of you have relatives or know someone who does something that you think is slightly odd, don't you?" The imaginations exploded. "And maybe you could leave some element floating at the end like Ray does," I added. During the next week I read poems about a grandmother who collected angels so that she would be used to them when she got to heaven, a grandfather who collected neckties but never ever wore one, a great aunt who collected string ("enough to tie up the world"), and a cousin who had so many old cars that he had to move to the country to have a place to keep them. An odd, quirky poem, yes. But it speaks of things understood in south Texas, too.

A poem from Pakistani Sameeneh Shirazie reminded us to give attention to elderly relatives while they are still with us. Surely, that too is a universal maxim, one which knows no boundaries. "Grandmother" is a poem of sudden understanding. The narrator-granddaughter enumerates the many household tasks accomplished by her grandmother throughout the day and realizes how difficult they can be for her now that she's older. Suddenly, she is ashamed that she was merely going to say hi and run, instead of give time and attention to her grandmother, and actively appreciate what this old woman has suffered to make their house a home. This poem elicited sensitive response. One student wrote about his grandmother, who constantly tried to stop him to tell about the times she lived through, but he always escaped with one excuse or another, only recently realizing that her history was his history too. Another poem was about a grandmother who wanted to talk about death, but no one would listen. And then she died, the poem said, "but I'll never know if she was afraid of death or saw it as another adventure."

Last year all our poems came from Naomi Shihab Nye, an Arab American who lives in our city. She had just published a collection of her works called *Words under the Words,* so we had a brand new book with her Arab grandmother's picture on the cover. We found out that Nye traveled all over the world but especially to Palestine, the native home of her father, where she collected many ideas for poems. We read about Arabic coffee, the man in the village who makes brooms, the gypsies of the desert, and "The Garden of Abu Mahmoud." Nye, who frequently works as a poet in the schools to help young people write poetry and understand the brotherhood of man, will often "give" her students a first line of a poem to get them started on their own poem. So I felt no hesitation in presenting these students with the beginnings from two Nye poems to be found in *Red Suitcase.* "Voices" was our grandmother poem last year. With understanding, poignancy, and resolute love, the speaker sees now—probably as an adult—what sadness her grandmother carried, the sadness of a woman whose "voice / had been pushed down hard inside you / like a plug." The first stanza reads like this:

> I will never taste cantaloupe
> without tasting the summers
> you peeled for me and placed
> face-up on my china breakfast plate.

I gave the students "I will never taste (fill in the blank) / without tasting the (fill in the blank)" and they soared. One student wrote about summer and picking strawberries with her grandfather. When their hands got red, they used stalks of rhubarb magically to take the red out, a memory that stays though he is gone. Another wrote that he would never smell the ocean without remembering his father going to the Gulf War. Still another wrote that roses would always remind her of losing her sister—to marriage.

Nye's "Valentine for Ernest Mann" is taken from a true experience, according to the poet. A man wrote and asked her to write a poem for him. She was so startled that she did write a poem in spite of herself, beginning "You can't order a poem like you order a taco." I gave that line to the student writers, extracting *poem* and *taco* in favor of their own ides. What a great opener. They wrote about ordering good grades, love, a baby sister, a friend, and a winning basketball season. But one wrote about the kind of understanding that can't be ordered, only worked on until people and nations get together in peace: "You can't order peace like you order a valentine."

Meeting Three

After two meetings for reading, discussing, and creating poems, plus the tidelike movement of poem packages from them to me over the six-week period, these poets sit proudly on our reading day with their own portfolio or mini-chapbook. One after another they go to the front of the room, read their poem, and then tell the source of inspiration, mostly the poems we have been reading. As I sit in the back of the room, smiling and applauding their efforts, I hear the connections with Turkey, Latvia, Japan, Sri Lanka, Chile—countries these youngsters had only a vague notion about until they found the poem and realized someone in that country experienced life and talked about it in poetry as they did in this country. What a small thing a poem is, I think once again. But how powerful.

References

Nye, Naomi Shihab, ed. 1992. *This Same Sky: A Collection of Poems from Around the World.* Portland, OR: Four Winds Press.

———. 1994. *Red Suitcase.* Brockport, NY: BOA Editions.

———. 1995a. *The Tree Is Older Than You Are.* New York: Simon & Schuster.

———. 1995b. *Words under the Words: Selected Poems.* Portland, OR: Eighth Mountain Press.

11 Who Am I? What Is My Heritage?

Christa Goldsmith
Maire Elementary School
Grosse Pointe, Michigan

I teach in a midwestern suburban school system adjoining a major urban city. The predominately white community ranges economically from middle and upper middle class to affluent. Many families have lived in this community for several generations and share with newcomers the desire for a family-oriented area with a strong educational system. Generally conservative, the community can all too often become a world unto itself and the children can grow up with a limited understanding of other people and their cultures.

My team-teaching partner and I wanted to help our students develop a broader perspective of other people and cultures beyond the familiar life in our own community. Sitting before us each year is a group of approximately fifty fifth-grade students whose ancestors traveled from more than twenty countries bringing cultures and customs that have withstood the test of time. These children haven't begun to learn, let alone comprehend, how such diversity has enriched and enhanced life in America in general and specifically, life for each one of them. Thus, we created a year-long theme, "Who Am I? What Is My Heritage?"

This theme offers numerous opportunities for students to become familiar with a wealth of wonderful literature that enriches their understanding of their own heritage as well as that of others. Student comments such as the following testify to its effectiveness:

> Just reading the social studies text isn't enough. There is so much more about history in literature. It is definitely more interesting to learn about other cultures this way.

> I never understood what immigration was about before now. I really liked *Journey of the Sparrows* and *Night Journey.* Now I want to read more, especially books about specific people and their adventures and hardships. The ideas I had before have changed completely.

> I didn't know much at all, but reading *Lyddie* helped me realize how difficult life was and much more sad than I could imagine. I want to read more now.
>
> After reading *The Keeping Quilt,* I told my mother I wanted to make my own keeping quilt so we went to the library for some books on quilt making.
>
> Reading about my own culture has attracted me to learning more about other cultures. I learned a lot about Turkey reading *Against the Storm.*

Because I believe it is important for teachers to take time to read aloud to their students, I read many books to them throughout this unit. Two riveting ones that are particularly successful are *Letters from Rifka* by Karen Hesse and *Friedrich* by Hans Peter Richter. *Immigrant Kids* by Russell Freedman is excellent and has the added benefit of serving as a useful tool when teaching note taking to the class. Students also enjoy *The Star Fisher* by Laurence Yep.

As the school year unfolds, the students select one country of their ancestors and begin their search for knowledge and understanding of their lifestyle, customs, traditions, hardships, and what it meant to come to America. They use an Information Chart to focus on specific topics. They begin by gathering basic facts from the encyclopedia, then move onto additional resources such as nonfiction, historical fiction, interviews, periodicals, and travelogues. The Information Chart helps students to organize this information and is referred to often as they work on various activities and projects.

We encourage students to work together as they gather information. In each classroom students who are researching the same country become a team. They sit together and assist one another by sharing resources and ideas. A student working alone on a country may also form a team with someone researching a country with close proximity. For example, students researching Wales and England may work together, and those working on Greece and Italy may also share ideas. Each day, after thirty to forty minutes of silent reading, dialogue journals are used to communicate personal feelings and thoughts with a member of their team. Later, they have a dialogue with someone from another team. Sometimes both students will be reading the same book. Frequently, a specific assignment is given for discussion in their journals. For example, if they are reading historical fiction, they may be asked to name two life skills that one of the main characters possesses and describe how they are manifested. If they are reading nonfiction, they may be asked to name and explain two life skills that would be most important for a person to possess. Our team-teaching situation allows us to maintain a flexible schedule so that one day per week is Open Classroom Day. This enables teams studying the same country from our two classrooms to unite, share, and begin to prepare for their presentation at the culmination of this unit.

I display a time line in the classroom so the students are aware of all deadlines. We allocate two weeks for the research, but many students finish ahead of time, since they are eager to begin the activities based on their research. They all know that when the basic research is completed, their time to be creative begins. Posted near the time line is a list of activities designed to develop higher-level thinking skills. I also encourage the students to add new ideas to this list, and some eagerly rise to the challenge. Some of the suggested activities are as follows.

Individually

Design, write, and "send" a postcard to a classmate who is researching a different country. Explain at least one holiday and state a minimum of six additional facts about your country.

Become a pen pal with someone in another country (i.e., a classmate who is researching a different country). Write as if you are actually living in the country you are researching. Describe your life and include some pictures. Write at least three letters to each other.

Design a banner with a personal motto that describes some inner thought or feeling that kept your family going on your journey to America or helped you hold onto some hope once you settled in America.

Select two famous people from your country and compare and contrast them. Include at least one hardship and one important achievement for each person. List at least five words to describe each one and explain why the words are appropriate.

Individually or with a Partner

Create an easy-to-read book about your country with photos and/or illustrations. It must contain at least twenty interesting facts and a full explanation of at least one holiday. Share this with primary grade children.

Create your own folktale and put it in booklet form or write it as a script to be performed with other students.

Small Group (2–4)

Create a song or parody containing a minimum of fifteen facts about your country. Teach it to the class.

Learn a dance or song from your country and teach it to a group. Present it and teach it to the class.

Join one or two students from another team and compare and contrast one famous person from each of your countries. Provide the same information as stipulated in the above activity.

Team

By a specified date (noted on the time line), be prepared to share the following with the class: What art, music, literature, food, inventions, and vocabulary would be missing from America if your country never existed? (Visual aids are encouraged.)

Two or three of the activities are mandatory for everyone. Then, depending on the individual, we set a minimum number of activities of the student's choice. Because of their appeal, nearly everyone completes more than is required. Any activity labeled "Individually" indicates that the student is solely responsible for the work but may confer with the team for suggestions and additional information. Each day I move from team to team answering questions, providing assistance, and evaluating and assessing completed assignments. At the end of the week, each student shares with the class something he or she has written or created. We also take a few minutes during this time to discuss any concerns, problems, or suggestions relating to this unit.

All of the activities created during this unit; the Information Chart; and any additional materials including notes, photos, projects, and illustrations are placed into a student-made, stitched and bound book. The front flap of the book contains a brief summary and the back flap displays a photo of the student author and a short biographical sketch. The back of the book jacket has excerpts from reviews of the book by the "critics." These books become personal treasures to most students and their families.

I also establish specific Learning Centers with teacher-directed activities related to the theme. Students are also required to complete at least one activity from two of four of the following centers:

The Creative Writing Center has multiple activities, ranging from various forms of poetry and journal writing to creating board games or a trivia game.

The Folktale Center displays the elements of a folktale, a world map, and folktales from around the world. Examples of activities for students are as follows: Explain how to make a sociogram analyzing relationships between characters. Keep an ongoing list of character qualities that other students may add to. Lead a discussion with other students about the similarities and differences in the folktales of three or four different countries.

The Classroom Calendar Center encourages students to mark special holidays pertaining to their country and to celebrate them throughout the year.

The Bulletin Board Center sets aside space to share words from various countries. Example: Say "Hello" in any language. Students write the name of their country on a card along with the way that word would be spoken in their language and post it on the board. Periodically, change the word.

Two additional activities, Celebrating Foods from Around the World and the Class Multicultural Cookbook, directly involve the parents. Information and dates are clearly stated in a parent newsletter at the onset of this unit, with follow-up reminders as necessary and thank you notes afterwards. To celebrate foods from around the world, students bring a special dish from their country on a specified date. They are encouraged to relate a unique family story or custom associated with the food. To create a Class Multicultural Cookbook, we collect one favorite family recipe from each student representative of their ancestral country. We encourage parents to add any anecdotes or family stories to accompany the recipe. The books are duplicated and sent home with each student.

In addition to learning about one particular country, I ask students to give their minds an opportunity to expand in more than one direction. They must also read any nonfiction or historical fiction book about a country other than the one they researched and be prepared to discuss some changes in their thinking and knowledge they gained about the people of this country. Also, they are asked to relate any interesting information they learned that was not mentioned during the final presentation. One student commented to me as follows: "I was interested in another country from my past, so I am reading beyond the country I am researching for the team work and presentation. I am discovering my ancestors are from many different countries."

Finally, after six to eight weeks of hard but invigorating work, each team is ready for the culminating activity on our time line: Presentation Day. This is their moment of glory. Each team is assigned a specific presentation date. They design and distribute invitations to parents, friends, and relatives. Together, each team is responsible for teaching all of us about their country. They arrange the room so they can hang posters, maps, and other large pictures. Artifacts from their country are displayed on tables. Also, each student is expected to bring a simple, inexpensive, and sometimes imaginative food representative of their country for the class to taste.

All students receive "passports" with countries listed and dates of travel (presentation dates). As tourists in each country, they are expected to take notes during the presentations. After all the countries have been visited, students create a booklet, poster, game, or song highlighting things they learned during their travels through this wide world of cultures. This is added to their bound book along with their passport and a photo of their team on Presentation Day. At the end of their presentation, a one-page, team-designed test is distributed to the tourists. Later, it is collected and graded by the team.

Notes may be used while giving the presentation, but students are expected to speak "from the heart" rather than read to the class. They may also use the overhead projector, slides, and videotape. Presentation time is limited to thirty to forty minutes. Students must be well organized and prepared to share as much information as they can in an interesting manner. Music or dance demonstrations are encouraged as well as teaching the class a simple game or craft. All artifacts and food are also explained. Additionally, each team must create a souvenir to present to each "tourist" (class members). For example, some choose to make a variety of bookmarks with sayings or facts on them, which are duplicated for everyone.

Visits from grandparents, relatives, and family friends sharing stories and experiences from the "Old Country" or from their trip to America make history truly come alive. The parents frequently admit that this unit generates lively discussion at home, and some traditions are often revived or a custom learned from another culture is adopted.

This unit ignites an enthusiasm and appreciation for other cultures and the innumerable contributions and talents these people brought to America. The manner in which the students share the knowledge gleaned from literature only heightens their desire to understand more about other cultures. The most frequent comment made by the students is how similar we are in our hopes, dreams, and desires. This is always a discovery they reach on their own.

Every year, former students return to visit and they always say, "Remember the fun we had when we learned about other countries and their customs? Do you still do that?" They tell me they still have their book or their family still observes the special customs or, best of all, they comment on how special it was to learn about and better understand one another. I smile and my heart does a little flip and I know why I love being a teacher.

Suggested Readings

Brown, Tricia. 1991. *Lee-Ann: The Story of a Vietnamese-American Girl.* New York: Putnam.

Buss, Fran Leeper, with Daisy Cubias. 1993. *Journey of the Sparrows.* New York: Dell.

Fisher, Leonard Everett. 1986. *Ellis Island: Gateway to the New World.* New York: Holiday House.

Freedman, Russell. 1994. *Kids at Work: Lewis Hine and the Crusade against Child Labor.* Boston: Houghton Mifflin.

———. 1995. *Immigration Kids.* New York: Puffin.

Gilson, Jamie. 1985. *Hello, My Name Is Scrambled Eggs.* New York: Luthrop.

Harvey, Brett. 1987. *Immigrant Girl: Becky of Eldridge Street.* New York: Holiday House.

Hesse, Karen. 1992. *Letters from Rifka.* New York: Holt.

Hicyilmaz, Gaye. 1993. *Against the Storm.* New York: Dell.

Lasky, Kathryn. 1986. *Night Journey.* New York: Puffin.

Leighton, Maxinne. 1992. *An Ellis Island Christmas.* New York: Viking Children's Books.

Levitin, Sonia. 1993. *Journey to America.* New York: Atheneum.

Lord, Bette Bas. 1984. *In the Year of the Bear and Jackie Robinson.* New York: HarperCollins.

Maestro, Betsy. 1996. *Coming to America: The Story of Immigration.* New York: Scholastic.

Muggamin, Howard. 1995. *The Jewish Americans.* Broomall, PA: Chelsea House.

Murphy, Jim. 1993. *Across America on an Emigrant Train.* Boston: Houghton Mifflin.

Nixon, Joan Lowery. 1993. *Land of Hope.* New York: Dell.

———. 1994. *Land of Promise.* New York: Dell.

———. 1995. *Land of Dreams.* New York: Dell.

Oberman, Sheldon. 1993. *The Always Prayer Shawl.* New York: Viking Penguin.

Palacco, Patricia. 1988. *The Keeping Quilt.* New York: Simon & Schuster.

Paterson, Katherine. 1996. *Lyddie.* New York: Dutton.

Richter, Hans Peter. 1987. *Friedrich.* New York: Puffin.

Rutledge, Paul. 1987. *The Vietnamese in America.* Minneapolis: Lerner.

Yep, Lawrence. 1975. *Dragonwings.* New York: HarperCollins.

———. 1992. *Star Fisher.* New York: Puffin.

12 Seeking *Cuentos*, Developing Narrative Voices

Louise Garcia Harrison
Heritage High School
Saginaw, Michigan

In the mid-1980s I returned to teaching after a twelve-year absence raising my family. I spent the next few years in an urban school system, dividing my teaching day between a middle school and a center for academically talented students, grades 8 through 12. As urban schools go, this system reflected the typical challenges as well as the advantages of having students of varied backgrounds, beliefs, and cultures. In fact, the city, with its diverse population, has a reputation for being racially divided. There is a long history of distrust and uneasiness between the urban and suburban areas. After eight years I transferred to a high school in a nearby suburban system where students are predominately white and middle class. As I came to know my students, I learned that many of them were uneasy or actually fearful about going into "the city." They too often based their opinions on the sensational accounts from our local paper or on ethnic stereotypes.

I began my second year of teaching in this suburban system knowing that I wanted to try to effect a change in their views. I felt that their perspectives needed to be broadened and their sensitivity to other cultures and traditions enhanced, while also giving them opportunities to be more reflective about themselves and their lives. The initial unit for the year in my ninth-grade class was designed to introduce examples of multicultural young adult literature to my students and to have them use their reading as models for their own work with narrative writing. I felt that the choice of multicultural young adult literature would address both the need to provide my students with strong narrative voices as well as provide opportunities to expand my students' perspectives. I selected initial readings from the work of Maya Angelou and Graham Salisbury and then moved on to a more in-depth study of works by Gary Soto and Sandra Cisneros. These authors often presented worlds and images that were totally new to my students, thus helping them to gain insights and perceptions that many of them had not previously had.

I used my own experiences of growing up in the inner-city community of Gary, Indiana (where my parents settled after they emigrated from Spain), as a bridge to help my students look reflectively both at themselves and at the literature that we were reading. My world on 11th Avenue in Gary was a rich one filled with my extended family. Aunts, uncles, and cousins—three families—lived in one building. Our lives were enriched growing up around family with a shared heritage and the traditions, language, and customs brought by my parents and their generation from Spain. In the multiethnic setting where I grew up, there were people who had come from all over the world. We shared our customs and traditions. Our community reflected the rich tapestry of this country with families from Eastern Europe, Great Britain, Mexico, South America, and Africa via southern states. I used *cuentos,* my growing-up stories, to help my students understand the stories of Soto, Cisneros, Salisbury, and Angelou. Our experiences were significantly different from those of my students.

I began the year with a unit combining readings from multicultural young adult literature with assignments in narrative writing. We began the unit with some short excerpts from Maya Angelou's *I Know Why the Caged Bird Sings* and Graham Salisbury's *Blue Skin of the Sea* and then moved into more intensive reading and discussion of selections from Gary Soto's *Living Up the Street* and Sandra Cisneros's *The House on Mango Street* and *Women Hollering Creek.* The selections were presented both as models and as springboards for students to practice "finding their voices" as they began the process of telling their own stories. I found that using strong narrative voices (such as those found in the writings of Cisneros, Soto, Salisbury, and Angelou) provides students with appropriate models for their own writing as well as a heightened awareness of the significance of narration. The selections by these authors also present an authentic sense of place and a sensitive portrayal of the community and the culture in which each of the authors grew up.

We began the unit by reading aloud sections of the first three chapters of *I Know Why the Caged Bird Sings.* I wanted my students to hear the language and see the images that Angelou weaves. We focused on the ways in which she creates a sense of place in these chapters. We talked about the role of the store as a center for the community. Students were asked to write their first narrative, a paragraph beginning with the words "In my neighborhood . . ." The students were beginning to find their narrative voices by telling their own *cuentos* (stories). Next, the students read "The Year of the Black Widows" from *Blue Skin of the Sea* by Graham Salisbury. In this chapter, Sonny and his cousin Keo are unduly influenced by Jack, a new boy in school. As a response to this reading, students were asked to recount either an experience about what it was like when they were new to a school or to relate what it is like to be part of a group and the pressures that it places on its members. I urged them to recall specific places and people—in fact, to try to recreate the memory. This assignment served as a bridge to Gary Soto's "Being Mean." After reading this story aloud in class and discussing it, students' told their *cuentos* from the perspective of being a bully. Among the other stories that students read during this unit were "Baseball in April" by Soto and "Barbie-Q" by Sandra Cisneros. Students then related stories about games that they played and told who they played with. Cisneros's "Salvador Late or Early" served as a model for having students write about a classmate.

These and other daily reading and writing assignments were preparatory to the unit project, a scrapbook of "snapshots" from their lives. All students were to use the format of *The House on Mango Street* as a model for creating seven short narrative pieces. Each of these writings was to be about 250 words and serve as a "snapshot" of their personal lives. The students were directed to include events from their own neighborhoods, focusing on family and friends and providing a clear sense of place. Students were to include three things that related personally to the selections that they had read. They could also illustrate the *cuentos* of their growing up with sketches, photos, maps, or souvenirs.

Young children are natural storytellers. They have what my mother called "a thousand *cuentos*," but as they get older it is more difficult to harness their abilities and willingness to share the stories that reveal who they are and what their lives are and have been. These factors contribute to the challenge involved in helping my ninth-grade students to establish their own narrative voices, which this project began to address. Although many of these students are storytellers, they frequently resist or are unwilling to tell their own stories. "My life is boring—nothing ever happens to me" or "I don't have any stories" are common comments that they make. Life may seem dull for students who are inundated with MTV, video games, and the Internet, so my initial challenge is to help my students see that *cuentos* can be found even in the simplest events.

References

Angelou, Maya. 1970, 1997. *I Know Why the Caged Bird Sings.* New York: Bantam.

Cisneros, Sandra. 1994. *The House on Mango Street.* New York: Random House.

———. 1991. *Woman Hollering Creek & Other Stories.* New York: Random House.

Salisbury, Graham. 1997. *Blue Skin of the Sea.* New York: Bantam Doubleday Dell.

Soto, Gary. 1992. *Living Up the Street: Narrative Recollections.* New York: Dell.

13 Beyond the Holocaust: Exploring Jewish Themes through Contemporary Young Adult Literature

Jeffrey S. Kaplan
University of Central Florida

The world of young adult literature is filled with many wonderful books about distinct cultures and religions. Young people can visit the homes and neighborhoods of people and families of all walks of life, comparing and contrasting how their cultures are similar to or different from their own. These fascinating journeys of self-discovery are made possible by writers who combine their love for fun and adventure with a well-developed understanding of time and place. I remember reading Charles Dickens's *Great Expectations* and Arthur Miller's *The Crucible* as a high-school student and thinking "Who are these strange people?" Who are these characters who inhabit Dickens's world of nineteenth-century England and Miller's colonial America? What are their beliefs? Their fears? Their hopes? Their dreams? And can we compare them to people who are living today?

Clearly, members of every generation bring to the table their own experiences and desires. Americans today are different from Americans who lived during the Revolutionary War, the Civil War, or, for that matter, the Vietnam War. To be sure, basic human emotions do not change—as individuals, we still feel love, hatred, and shame—but our surrounding circumstances differ greatly. Our prosperity, our schooling, and our technological advances have transformed us.

One thing, however, remains constant: we are a country of great diversity, and this heterogeneity includes many schemas, religious and otherwise, of conceptualizing the world (and the cosmos) and one's place in it. Each of these belief systems, whether religious or secular, offers a unique perspective on the human condition. Daily, we face each other at work and at play, and, more than likely, we ask the same questions. What makes one belief system differ from another? What customs do others practice? What rituals do they observe? What prayers, if any, do they recite? What ethical codes of conduct do they live by?

School, I believe, is an appropriate place for such questions to be addressed, and one surefire way for teachers to begin discussions about such issues is to motivate their students to read young adult novels which talk openly and candidly about questions such as "What it is like to be a member of a certain belief community?" Whatever their beliefs, all children bring their own understandings and can enlighten others about their specific practices.

As a Jew, I am particularly sensitive to this issue. In America the Jewish people constitute a very small segment of the population—about 3 percent. And outside of large metropolitan communities—New York, Miami, Chicago, Los Angeles—the Jewish communities are often small in number. Thus the opportunity for young people to meet and associate with other Jews becomes increasingly difficult. So it becomes vitally important that teachers introduce their youngsters to the abundance of young adult literature which addresses Jewish concerns—and not just stories about the Holocaust. Although some of the best literature written is about the Holocaust, teachers must remember that now there are third- and fourth-generation American Jews who experience life in a multidimensional and progressive world—far removed from Hitler's unspeakable atrocities.

There are many excellent young adult novels about contemporary Jewish issues and concerns. They address a population that is often overlooked in today's media and speak with an urgency that can be appreciated by diverse readers, including Jews as well as members of other belief communities. So I encourage educators to read these novels, share them with their students, and teach them in imaginative and informative styles.

On Being Jewish

In Sandy Asher's *Summer Begins,* Summer Smith, an eighth-grader, learns what it means to be a media celebrity. For her school paper, she writes an editorial pondering what it must be like for a non-Christian to act and sing in the yearly school Christmas pageant. Suddenly, her world erupts. Everyone from close friends to the town's mayor becomes upset at Summer's words, leaving her baffled and stunned by what she thought was an honest question. Eventually, Summer resolves her dilemma by reaching out to friend and foe alike, learning considerably about religious feelings and influences. As a Christian, Summer gains a firsthand understanding of what it is like to be Jewish in a non-Jewish world.

For anyone, especially young people, moving to a new home can be a traumatic experience. Leaving family, friends, and familiar surroundings can be most trying, especially for twelve-year-old Hannah Brand in Naomie Karp's *The Turning Point.* With her family, Hannah must leave her crowded and noisy life in the Bronx for a quiet and idyllic place in the suburbs. On the surface this sounds wonderful, but to Hannah, leaving means giving up her Jewish roots for a home in a predominantly Protestant community. Quickly, she realizes that she "does not fit in"; her demonstrative behavior and outspoken demeanor get her in trouble. Ostracized for her "Jewish ways," Hannah must adjust to her new life by learning consideration and tolerance for others.

Another realistic tale—though not contemporary in setting—is Barbara Barrie's *Lone Star.* The time is 1944, and the place is Corpus Christi, Texas. The Miller family has just moved there from hustling, bustling Chicago, hoping to find a more secure and safer place to raise their children. And like Hannah Brand in *The Turning Point,* young Jane Miller must adjust to life in a town where Judaism is considered a strange and foreign custom. Rural Texas is not the home to a thriving Jewish population, so Jane must learn to reconcile her "ways" with those of her new neighbors. All this occurs as news of Hitler's Europe reverberates in the background. *Lone Star* is a poignant tale of a young girl's coming of age in a lonely and often terrifying universe.

Moving from the city to rural areas is a theme that appears in many young adult books about contemporary Judaism. Another two are Miriam Chaikin's *I Should Worry, I Should Care* and Mary Anderson's *The Rise and Fall of a Teen-Age Wacko.* Although neither book is overtly Jewish in context, each describes what it is like for young Jewish children to move from predominantly Jewish to non-Jewish areas. Both display a funny and smart sensibility, with *I Should Worry, I Should Care* suitable for younger children, and Anderson's *Teenage Wacko* suitable for older children.

Speaking of older children, Kathryn Lasky's *Pageant* would be appropriate for young adults wanting to read about life in a private boarding school. Teenager Sarah Benjamin finds herself at an exclusive Catholic girls school in Indianapolis, where she buckles under the intense pressure to conform. As the lone Jew, she encounters one disaster after another—from participation in the annual Christmas play to terrible first dates. Seeking refuge from the school's conservative atmosphere, Sarah runs to her sister in New York City, where she finally comes to terms with herself, her family, and her Jewishness.

The anxiety of feeling different and apart from the mainstream greets the central character in Wendy Lichtman's *Telling Secrets,* the emotional wrenching tale of the pain one young woman feels because her father is in prison for embezzling. Praying in Hebrew and vowing to keep the family's shame a secret, this religious young woman must wrestle with her conscience about whether to tell her college roommate the truth. For older students this is a painful account about what it is like to be both religious and the child of a man who has sinned.

On Jewish Religious Practices

To understand specific Jewish practices, students can choose from a number of easy-to-read works. Eth Clifford's *The Remembering Box* is a touching tale of a young boy's learning about his Jewish heritage and rituals from a box that contains his grandmother's memorabilia and religious objects. *Miriam,* by Iris Rosofsky, tells the story of one young girl's questioning of her faith when her brother dies at thirteen. As we read, we learn about Jewish rituals and customs, and of Miriam's agony to preserve her Jewish identity in the face of a devastating tragedy.

Two other good books about Jewish customs for young readers can be found in E. L. Konigsburg's *About the B'nai Bagels* and Charlotte Herman's *What Happened to Heather Hopkowitz?* Both books are amusing, insightful tales about Jewish rituals and practices in contemporary America. In *B'nai Bagels,* Konigsburg takes the time to explain Jewish customs, and in *Heather Hopkowitz,* a young Jewish girl finds herself staying with very religious Orthodox Jews when her parents take a vacation. The family's strict dietary and spiritual practices leave her in a quandary, but she learns to adjust, and so do we.

When Jewish children reach the age of thirteen, they are allowed to be formally introduced into the Jewish religion as a participating adult. This rite is known as *bar mitzvah* (for boys) or *bat mitzvah* (for girls). In Sandy Asher's *Daughters of the Law,* Ruthie Morgenthauis, who is approaching thirteen, must decide whether to observe this ancient ritual. She is torn because her aunt wants her to participate, but her father, now dead, hated organized religion. She wants to honor her religion but, at the same time, not discredit her father's memory. Through her dilemma, we learn about becoming a formally recognized Jewish adult. On a somewhat lighter note, Myron Saltz in Stephen

Kaufman's *Does Anyone Here Know the Way to Thirteen?* wants to skip his dreaded bar mitzvah and instead become a little league superstar. And in Barbara Girion's *Like Everybody Else,* a seventh-grader lives through the ordeal of planning a bat mitzvah as the daughter of a famous mother. Not wanting a "big deal," this young woman learns what it really means to be a grown-up Jewish person in the face of her mother's elaborate preparations.

On Interdating and Intermarriage

For young Jewish people, especially those living in non-Jewish areas, the question of "who to date" becomes a central theme of their teenage lives. Being torn between their love for another and their allegiance to their religion can be a tricky and problematic concern. Judy Blume drives this home in her seminal work *Are You There, God? It's Me, Margaret,* the story of a twelve-year-old girl's struggle to understand who she is—since her parents are of different religions. Young Margaret struggles with the typical pains of adolescence—puberty, menstruation, falling in love, and loneliness. Moreover, she questions openly and honestly which God to believe in.

One of the more famous young adult novels which deals with falling in love outside of ones' religion is Bette Greene's *Summer of My German Soldier.* This novel packs a double whammy—dealing with the problems of both interdating and anti-Semitism—for the lead character falls in love with a Nazi prisoner of war. In rural Arkansas during World War II, young Patty Bergen falls for a German prisoner of war who has escaped from a nearby prison barrack. The ensuing love affair and the eventual discovering of her secretive liaisons leads to an explosive and emotional climax. This is a must-read for all.

Three other good novels deal with dating across religious faiths: Cynthia Blair's *Crazy in Love,* Mort Grossman's *The Summer Ends Too Soon,* and Joan Merrill Gerber's *Handsome as Anything.* What happens when a young Jewish girl realizes that someone who has been sending her love notes is Puerto Rican? And that her best friend loves the same guy? With wit, insight, and compassion, *Crazy in Love* tells the story of an intriguing love triangle. *The Summer Ends Too Soon* tells the story of a Jewish boy and Protestant girl who fall in love at an all-Jewish summer camp. Will their love last the summer? Will their parents approve? And can they ever resolve their religious differences? And finally, in *Handsome as Anything,* "Who should I marry?" is the central question. Young Rachel, a high-school senior, is weighing possible spouses. A serious rabbinical student? A Zen Buddhist? A reserved homebody? In her search for Mr. Right, Rachel learns who she is and what she believes.

On Anti-Semitism

Few fictional books confront the problem of anti-Semitism as well as Fran Arrick's *Chernowitz!* This is a strong narrative, complete with snappy dialogue and strong characters. Timid and hesitant, Bobby Cherno faces a school where he is the religious outsider, and where he is tormented because he is Jewish. Forced to defend himself, Bobby plans a plot for revenge that teaches us all a lesson in the problems of confronting religious bigotry. It's a great book for middle-school readers and a perfect discussion starter.

Felice Holman's *The Murderer* tells the story of a young Jewish boy, Hershy, who lives in Ashlymine, Pennsylvania, during the Depression. Although not contemporary in tone, this book is a gripping tale of how a young boy is tormented just because he is Jewish. Ridiculed mercilessly, Hershy is eventually accused by the neighborhood children of a murder that he did not commit. Confused and lost, Hershy struggles to defend himself as he wonders why a merciful God would allow him to be tortured.

Set in a faraway time and place, Leonard Everett Fisher's *A Russian Farewell* is another narrative which describes the horror of religious persecution. In the Ukraine of the early 1900s, a Jewish family sets across their native land in search of a better life in America, free of the threat of continual harassment and torture.

Or students can enjoy Gloria Goldreich's *Lori,* the touching story of a young girl's move from New York to Israel and her eventual friendship with a young Palestinian. Lori learns firsthand about religious intolerance when she becomes very close to a young Arab girl and a young Israeli soldier.

On the Holocaust

Books about the Holocaust, naturally, are plentiful. Fictional and nonfictional accounts abound, and any teacher can select from many well-known titles. Elie Wiesel's *Night, The Diary of Anne Frank* (both book and play), and Lois Lowry's *Number the Stars* are a few examples of fine literary accounts of this horrific event. Similarly, Chana Byers Abell's *The Children We Remember* is a powerful retelling of what happened to Jewish children during the Holocaust. Told in simple, declarative sentences and vivid, black-and-white photographs, this work is a terrific resource for learning more about this tragedy.

Surprisingly though, there are fewer works which dramatize the feelings of young Americans about the Holocaust. And most existing fictional works speak in a voice that seems strange or outdated to young readers. Few bring a contemporary perspective.

Two books told in a contemporary voice, however, are Mel Glenn's *Squeeze Play,* and M. E. Kerr's *Gentlehands.* In *Squeeze Play,* a sixth-grader must wear a patch over his eye because he has been hit in the head by a baseball. Teased mercifully by his teammates, he seeks solace in his school teacher, who he learns is a Holocaust survivor. Together, they learn something about each other—the young boy about the teacher's horrid past, and the teacher about the boy's feelings of inadequacy as a young ball player and his torment at the hands of his so-called friends.

Finally, one of the most realistic novels about contemporary youth and their feelings about the Holocaust is M. E. Kerr's haunting young adult novel *Gentlehands.* In a spine-chilling tale, one seventeen-year-old boy comes to learn that his beloved grandfather is actually an escaped Nazi war criminal. And to complicate his life even more, he learns that his girlfriend harbors anti-Semitic feelings. Kerr's powerful and penetrating tale forces young adults to come to terms with questions about social responsibility, family loyalty, and unbridled love.

On Teaching

Good teaching about literature begins with sharp questions: What happened? Why did it happen? And what does it all mean?

Thus, to teach these novels, I would begin by asking students the same questions: What do they know about Judaism? What did they learn by reading these novels? Did they ever know someone who was Jewish? Did they ever have concerns similar to those of the characters in their readings? And more importantly, what did they learn through reading about other belief systems?

Productive, informed, and guided discussions should be the hallmark of all instruction, particularly about a topic as sensitive and unique as belief systems. Students need time to share aloud and in comfortable settings their thoughts and opinions about religious faiths and, naturally, to learn more about the multitude of spiritual and ethical beliefs practiced in American society and in the world as a whole. By encouraging such discussion in public schools, we promote diversity in a unified setting.

Smart discussions can be followed by creative and critical writing assignments, allowing students to voice their concerns in quiet and contemplative thought. Students can write about their own beliefs, their understanding of other belief systems, and the unique role that religious and other value systems play in society. And to sharpen their critical-thinking skills, young people can begin to compare how life in a given belief community differs from generation to generation. To be sure, American Jews today live differently than their grandparents and great-grandparents did. My grandparents lived in Poland and Russia and managed to come to America before the rise of Hitler. But many of their relatives stayed, and died at the hands of the Nazis or Russian Cossacks. My father knew the sting of religious persecution when he served in World War II, aiding in the defeat of the German army, yet I grew up in a comfortable suburban community, surrounded by tolerance and goodness. Three generations, three different perspectives.

One final word for teachers: these novels need not be read from cover to cover for students to fully appreciate them. Passages can be selected which best exemplify the author's intent or creative imagery. Or better yet, students can read these selections and then imagine their own possible scenarios. They can script their own debates or confrontations, pen poems about beliefs and persecutions, or create artistic renderings of spiritual or other insights and awakenings. In any event, these books about contemporary Judaism should inspire educators everywhere to discuss openly and honestly what it means to be who you are and to openly practice your beliefs.

Reading can inspire a generation of caring and tolerant citizens. Through good books, we can explore cultures and customs and foster mutual understandings.

References

Anderson, Mary. 1981. *The Rise and Fall of a Teen-age Wacko.* New York: Atheneum.

Arrick, Fran. 1983. *Chernowitz!* New York: Signet.

Asher, Sandy. 1983. *Daughters of the Law.* New York: Dell.

———. 1982. *Summer Begins.* New York: Bantam.

Barrie, Barbara. 1990. *Lone Star.* New York: Delacorte.

Blair, Cynthia. 1988. *Crazy in Love.* New York: Fawcett Junior Books.

Blume, Judy. 1970. *Are You There, God? It's Me, Margaret.* New York: Bradbury Press.

Brooks, Jerome. 1986. *Make Me a Hero.* New York: Dell.

Chaikin, Miriam. 1979. *I Should Worry, I Should Care.* Illus. Richard Egielski. New York: Yearling Books.

Clifford, Eth. 1985. *The Remembering Box.* Illus. Donna Diamond. NewYork: Houghton Mifflin.

Fisher, Leonard Everett. 1980. *A Russian Farewell.* Portland, OR: Four Winds Press.

Gerber, Joan Merrill. 1990. *Handsome as Anything.* New York: Scholastic.

Girion, Barbara. 1980. *Like Everybody Else.* New York: Scribner.

Glenn, Mel. 1989. *Squeeze Play: A Baseball Story.* New York: Clarion.

Goldreich, Gloria. 1979. *Lori.* New York: Holt, Rinehart, and Winston.

Greene, Bette. 1993. *Summer of My German Soldier.* New York: Dell.

Grossman, Mort. 1975. *The Summer Ends Too Soon.* Philadelphia: Westminster.

Herman, Charlotte. 1981. *What Happened to Heather Hopkowitz*? New York: Dutton.

Holman, Felice. 1978. *The Murderer.* New York: Scribner.

Karp, Naomie J. 1976. *The Turning Point.* New York: Harcourt Brace Jovanovich.

Kaufman, Stephen. 1985. *Does Anyone Here Know the Way to Thirteen?* New York: Houghton Mifflin.

Kerr, M. E. 1978. *Gentlehands.* New York: HarperCollins.

Konigsburg, E. L. 1971. *About the B'nai Bagels.* New York: Atheneum.

Lasky, Kathryn. 1986. *Pageant.* Portland, OR: Four Winds Press.

Lichtman, Wendy. 1986. *Telling Secrets.* New York: Harper & Row.

Lowry, Lois. 1989. *Number the Stars.* New York: Houghton Mifflin.

Rosofsky, Iris. 1988. *Miriam.* New York: Harper & Row.

Wiesel, Elie. 1982. *Night.* New York: Bantam.

Suggested Readings about Judaism

Abells, Chana Byers. 1986. *The Children We Remember.* New York: Greenwillow.

Arnold, Catherine, and Herma Silverstein. 1985. *Anti-Semitism: A Modern Perspective.* New York: Julian Messer.

Bial, Morrison D. 1978. *Your Jewish Child.* New York: Union of American Hebrew Congregations.

Chaikin, Miriam. 1986. *Sound the Shofar: The Story and Meaning of Rosh Hashannah and Yom Kippur.* Illus. Erika Weihs. Boston: Houghton Mifflin.

Fiedler, Jean. 1981. *The Year The World Was out of Step with Jancy Fried.* New York: Harcourt Brace Jovanovich.

Frank, Anne. 1989a. *Anne Frank's Tales from the Secret Annex.* Trans. Ralph Mannheim and Michael Mok. New York: Doubleday.

Frank, Anne. 1989b. *The Diary of Anne Frank: The Critical Edition.* Trans. Arnold J. Pomerans. New York: Doubleday.

Goodrich, Frances, and Albert Hacket. 1956. *The Diary of Anne Frank,* Drama. New York: Random House.

Gubby, Lucien, and Abraham Levy. 1990. *Jewish Book of Why and What: Custom, Practices, and Beliefs.* New York: Sure Sellers.

Herman, Charlotte. 1989. *Our Snowman Had Olive Eyes.* New York: Puffin.

Hirsh, Marilyn. 1988. *I Love Passover,* Illus. Marilyn Hirsh. New York: Holiday House.

Kerr, Judith. 1987. *When Hitler Stole Pink Rabbit.* New York: Putnam.

Kripke, David. 1981. *Let's Talk about Being Jewish.* Ktav Publishing House.

Lasky, Kathryn. 1986. *The Night Journey.* New York: Puffin.

Levoy, Myron. 1987. *Alan and Naomi.* New York: HarperCollins.

Reuben, Stephen Carr. 1991. *Raising Jewish Children in a Contemporary World: The Modern Parent's Guide to Creating a Jewish Home.* Rocklin, CA: Prima.

Rose, Anne. 1977. *Refugee.* New York: Dial.

Sussman, Susan. 1988. *Hanukkah: Eight Lights around the World.* Illus. Judith Friedman. New York: Albert Whitman.

14 The Web of Life

Diane Hoffbauer
Alaska Pacific University

In the story *Two Old Women,* Ch'idzigyaak and Sa' discover that isolation and power are interwoven as they strive to understand themselves and the people they love, who have abandoned them. As the two women begrudgingly take control of their lives and their survival, "We will die trying" becomes their rallying cry. *Two Old Women* is a story about dignity and human integrity, as the two old women learn that betrayal, friendship, community, and forgiveness mold their vision of life. These themes can be explored in a number of books for adolescents, and they are themes that can help adolescent readers reflect on the meanings of their own lives.

At Alaska Pacific University in Anchorage, Alaska, the Education Department is responsible for preparing teachers to work in urban centers, rural communities, and isolated Alaska Native villages. Because a diverse range of cultural and ethnic groups live in Alaska, teacher education programs must pay particular attention to helping preservice teachers understand the importance of thoughtfully selecting curriculum materials. Choosing and using adolescent literature is an especially critical process for teachers in Alaska because of the state's isolation, the variety of Alaskan lifestyles, and the importance of providing students with culturally accurate educational materials. Studying the human condition through carefully chosen adolescent literature such as *Two Old Women* provides Alaskan students with an opportunity to appreciate their own local culture while expanding their understandings of cultures less familiar.

A culturally diverse group of students in an undergraduate teacher education literature class at Alaska Pacific University reviewed four young adult books to identify concepts and themes that demonstrated similarities between seemingly different stories, lifestyles, and characters. These preservice teachers then explored activities and teaching strategies that could be used with upper elementary and middle school Alaskan students. The purpose of this chapter is to describe this literature and the strategies and activities that were developed.

Hatchet (Gary Paulsen), *Two Old Women* (Velma Wallis), *Sadako* (Eleanor Coerr), and *Morning Girl* (Michael Dorris) were chosen for this project. Each of the four books has as its theme a historical event or concept that has affected Alaska. At the same time, each book provides an in-depth look at a culture while raising issues familiar to all people. Although illustrations are included in two of the books, the strongest images of all four books are created by the authors' abilities to write powerful stories that contain conflict, capable characters, a well-developed story line, and resolution (although not always happy) of a problem. A brief summary of each story's highlights follows.

- Based on an Alaskan Athabascan Indian legend, *Two Old Women* was selected because its main characters are two old Gwich'in women abandoned by their tribe during a brutal winter famine. As the women rediscover strength and skills to survive, their views of their roles and value to their community change. When after many months the women are accidentally reunited with The People, they share their food and furs to save starving and freezing adults and children. As the women tell their survival stories and extend forgiveness to the tribe, the chief appoints them to honorary positions within the band.
- *Hatchet* was selected because it is an adventure story of an adolescent boy who survives in the wilderness after a small plane crash. As the months pass by before he is rescued, the boy takes control of his life, his survival, and his outlook on his family's problems.
- *Sadako* tells the story of a young heroine who dies of leukemia as a result of radiation from the atom bomb dropped during World War II in Japan. This book also is a true recounting of the creation of the Hiroshima Peace Park, a monument signifying peace. *Sadako* lends itself to many discussions of topics relevant to Alaskan children. The only World War II battles on North American soil were fought in Alaska's Aleutian Islands, which were bombed and invaded by the Japanese. Alaskan Aleuts, the native inhabitants of the Aleutians, were caught at home unprepared for the battles. Aleut villagers on Attu Island were captured by the Japanese and sent to prison camp in Japan. Most all the other Aleuts were removed from the islands by the U.S. government and shipped to faraway internment camps, similar to the way the government resettled Japanese Americans throughout the nation in internment camps during the war. More recently, health concerns similar to those described in *Sadako* have been raised among Alaska Natives since the discovery of secret atomic testing sites and waste burial sites in northwestern Alaska.
- *Morning Girl* shares with the reader the life of a young Taino girl in 1492 who sees Columbus's party of explorers as they land in the New World; this book raises the issue of encoun-

> ters between cultures. Alaska Natives experienced many of the same concerns, problems, issues, and conflicts as explorers and fortune seekers from Russia, Scandinavia, the United States, and other nations pressed into and had an impact on Alaska's native cultures.

A variety of strategies, such as the use of perspective taking and graphic organizers, worked well for analyzing the ideas presented in the four books just described. Perspective taking is a way readers respond to literature. Without the ability to take various perspectives, readers have difficulty making the links between the characters' lives and their own lives. The development of a sense of perspective taking was critical for the discussions of similarities and differences in people and events, and the class began by exploring the use of perspective in each individual book. It was important for students to understand their own viewpoints and remember those as they switched perspectives and looked at the characters' situations.

After reading *Morning Girl,* class members completed a "porthole" assignment. Students were required to simply create two things: one that would exemplify what the girl saw and one that would exemplify what the explorers saw during the encounter scene at the closing of the book. The issue of differing perspectives was clearly presented as students shared the variety of art projects they had developed representing their visions of the encounter. Whereas some students creatively displayed a sense of fear, violation, or curiosity, other students shared projects that focused on opportunity, trust, and excitement. Further discussion helped students understand how the characters of *Two Old Women* and *Hatchet* survived only because they changed their perspectives: they quit seeing themselves as helpless victims and started seeing themselves as powerful and decisive individuals. In *Sadako* the young girl dramatically touched the world because of her strong and positive perspective about her health and the need for peace. The class could most easily relate to *Hatchet.* By understanding the survival skills and problem solving of that character, they then could look at those same issues through the perspective of an old Athabascan woman or a young Japanese child.

After reading *Two Old Women,* students were then assigned the task of developing a book cover that visually highlighted the key events or ideas presented in the story. Because the story describes people and land familiar to students in Alaska, they were able to link their own prior knowledge with additional pictures created by the words of the story. The "book cover" activity provided students an opportunity to bring their own perspectives to the understanding of the story and its characters. After discussing their various perspectives, students looked at concepts presented in each book, applying additional strategies that would visually represent their knowledge and thoughts.

Conceptual webbing proved effective for helping students see the connections between concepts and isolated pieces of information in *Morning Girl.* Students were assigned the task of individually identifying the key concepts or points and supporting details of the story. After students shared their own webs, the class created another web together. This web illustrates the key points (family, community, daily rituals, self-confidence, and survival) the students pulled from the story.

Students took their key points from the book cover activity and transferred them into class webs for both *Two Old Women* and *Hatchet.* Although the ideas of survival, tools, and food appeared first in both webs, the class members quickly realized many more things in common between the two books. Students began to compare and contrast the people who supported or abandoned the characters in both books. They also identified emotions felt by the characters in both stories, such as fear, dependency, helplessness, hope, and confusion. Other similarities were identified, including the creation of shelter in both situations, the value of food and the necessity of accumulating it, the meaning of survival, and the fate of the characters in both books after they were reunited with their communities. Students quickly saw that examining two stories from two different cultures led to rich exploration of the human condition.

The last book the students read was *Sadako.* Rather than creating a web from this story, students explored the book by creating a comparison/contrast diagram (see Figure 1) for *Sadako* and *Hatchet.* The diagram provided the class with a structured way to look at similarities, differences, and overlapping concepts in the stories. Students began the discussion by deciding what points were unique to each individual story. They quickly realized that most of what was said about one story could be said about the other and that the stories and characters had many things in common. The students explored hope and death, and they realized that loneliness could exist whether or not a person has many people around him or her. Friendship, the meaning of abandonment and betrayal, and the meaning of survival were debated. The class added *Two Old Women* to the diagram and began to explore the ideas of self-preservation, problem solving, and decision making. Lastly, *Morning Girl* was added to the diagram. The students swiftly filled the diagram with connections between *Morning Girl* and the other three stories, thoroughly exploring additional ideas such as courage and anticipation.

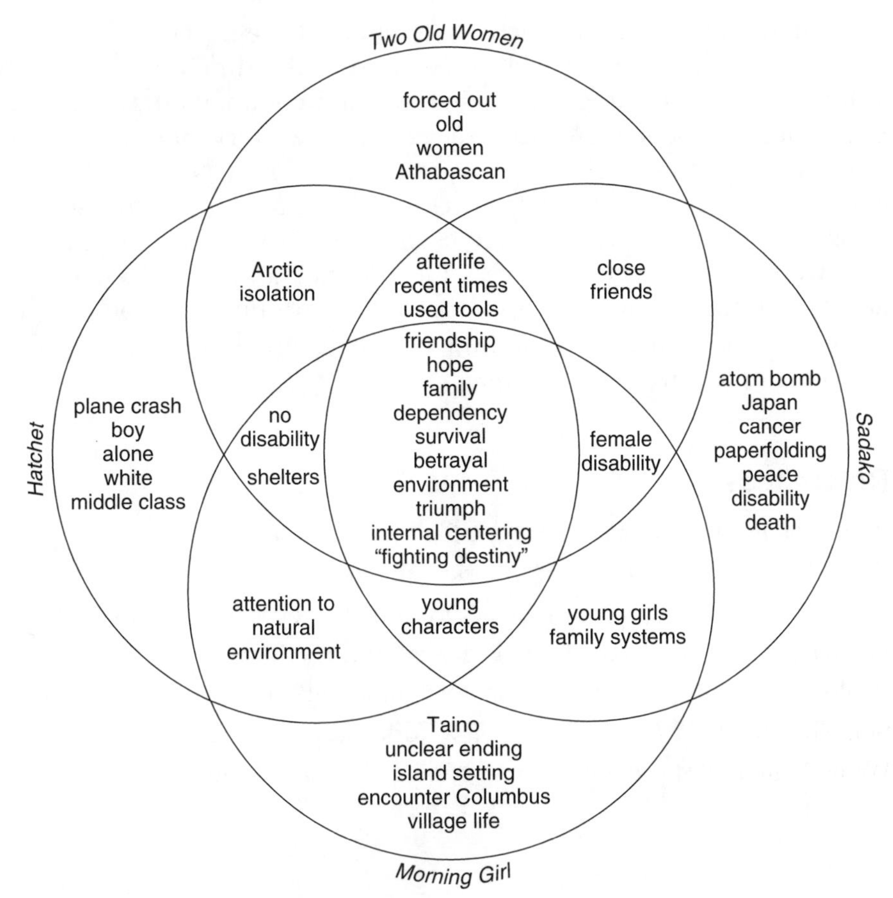

Figure 1. Comparison/contrast diagram.

A final piece to this study of human characteristics and conditions was a brainstorming session to determine other books that would work well in continuing the discussions of similarities and differences. Students suggested that adding *Chive, Maniac Magee,* or *Secret City, USA* could provide additional depth by introducing changing definitions of family and homelessness. New approaches for analyzing the books were discussed as well: a graphic organizer could be used to analyze cause and effect, and a sequential organizer could be used to put each story's events in order while at the same time providing an opportunity to discuss what might happen to the books' characters in the future. Creating alternative endings to each book would encourage students to conduct research and to solve any new problems highlighted by research.

In this class, four distinctly different books representing four cultures and events worked well for exploring the differences between cultures while accenting the similarities and commonalities. Alaskan preservice teachers were able to see how a story about two old Athabascan women related to experiences of non–Native Alaskans and people who represent cultures outside the state. Although the books and related activities were used with Alaskan college students, they were all chosen because of their connection and appeal to Alaskan adolescent readers and are appropriate for any upper elementary or middle school class, whether the students are located in Alaska, Hawaii, or the Lower 48.

References

Barre, Shelley. 1993. *Chive.* New York: Simon & Schuster.

Coerr, Eleanor. 1993. *Sadako.* New York: Putnam.

Dorris, Michael. 1992. *Morning Girl.* New York: Hyperion Books for Children.

Holman, Felice. 1990. *Secret City, USA.* New York: Scribner.

Paulsen, Gary. 1995. *Hatchet.* Boston: Houghton Mifflin.

Spinelli, Jerry. 1996. *Maniac Magee.* New York: HarperCollins.

Wallis, Velma. 1994. *Two Old Women.* New York: HarperCollins.

15 Using Literature to Combat Stereotypes

Denise R. Emery
Midland Public Schools
Midland, Michigan

Give me knowledge, so I may have kindness for all.
Plains Indian proverb (Zora 1994, p. 16)

The ones that matter most are the children.
They are the true human beings.
Lakota Indian proverb (Zora 1994, p. 49)

In August of 1995 I left Michigan, along with seven other helpers and teachers, to lead a vacation bible school for the Cree Indian tribe in Norway House, Manitoba. In preparation for our trip, it was suggested that each of us make ourselves familiar with the customs, literature, and beliefs of the Cree tribe. As I began to read and explore the North American Indian culture, I was impressed with the inclusive nature of these people.

A basic North American Indian belief is that all things are connected. The symbol of a circle is often used in their literature, storytelling, and art; the circle is the visual representation that one being, event, or object affects others. The Sioux Indian tribe has a proverb that reflects this belief: "With all things and in all things, we are relatives" (Zora 1994, p. 13).

As I was in Norway House teaching, I began to see examples of the collectiveness of this culture. The entire community saw that each child's safety was their responsibility; therefore, the children had much more freedom than the children in the United States. The adults tended to let children explore and learn on their own, believing that the lessons one learns alone are more important than those taught by another.

When I returned to Michigan I began to think of the students that I teach and how they are similar to the Cree children of Norway House. An overwhelming commonality is that most children seem to crave knowledge, time, the freedom to explore, and a chance to be heard. Therefore, my approach to multicultural literature and writing in my classroom has been molded to allow for these needs.

In the past, a few multicultural books in a classroom library or an essay devoted to Black History Month seemed to satisfy the need for diversity demanded by the educational system and minority groups. In the last twenty years, however, there has been a move to celebrate the commonalities of the human race through its differences. No longer is the subject of diversity simply a cry from a state department or a minority group; rather, it is a desire and a need of many teachers.

It is my goal as an English teacher to have all of the literature I use be multicultural. This may sound impossible, but it isn't. My idea of multicultural literature is not only literature that focuses on racial and ethnic groups; my choices expand to literature that explores the differences in people in relation to religion, age, gender, and physical abilities.

It is important for students to have authentic experiences with multicultural literature. The goal for my eighth-grade students is to have them appreciate themselves while having the ability to see commonalities and differences with others. Rochman (as cited in Schwartz, 1995) stated in the spring 1995 edition of *The ALAN Review:*

> The stories you read can transform you because you imagine beyond yourself. If you read only what mirrors your view of yourself, you get locked in. It's as if you're in a stupor or under a spell. Buried.

The last thing that I want for my students is for them to be buried or to explore those things that will not change or affect them. When selecting books for free-reading time, most of my students choose books that reflect themselves; therefore, it is very important that I select multicultural books for in-class reading that reflect different traits.

My teaching partner, Deanna Knox, and I have developed an eighth-grade program that focuses on the themes of prejudice, struggle, and stereotypes. We have found that by using general themes we are able to find influential and enriching literature, and we are able to make connections among reading, writing, and various units throughout the year. In the 1996–97 school year my eighth-grade English program will be team-taught with eighth-grade American history. The history connection will allow for even more development and exploration of prejudice, struggle, and stereotypes, since these readings pertain to historical events.

The year starts with a look at self-image and adolescence. This is a time for students to reflect upon themselves and their heritage. In this beginning unit, students do reflective writing responses, and they also create an ideal family. This ideal family is fictional, but they may have traits that the students admire in real individuals. The ideal family is developed in a journal, based on what each student determines "ideal" to mean. Throughout the year, the ideal family members will be put up against the prejudices and struggles experienced by the characters we read about. This project allows for lessons in fictional character development, but it also allows for the student to become personally involved with what the characters are going through in each piece of literature we explore.

The first unit that has a strong literature base is our unit on Anne Frank and World War II. We read the dramatic form of *The Diary of a Young Girl,* and then we watch the film *The Attic: The Hiding of Anne Frank,* which is told from Miep Gies's point of view. We ask our students to either put a member of their "ideal family" in the place of Anne or Miep and to discuss the character's thoughts and feeling in their journal. As a class, we then share the entries, and we find the contrast in the points of view an interesting source of discussion.

In the past I have discovered that most students do not have much knowledge of the Holocaust, so this is a vivid and meaningful unit for them. We also discuss the individuals and the groups of people that risked their own lives to help hide and shelter the persecuted people.

During this unit I read aloud Elie Wiesel's *Night.* It is an autobiographical look at Wiesel's experience in a concentration camp when he was a young boy. Upon completion of this unit, students write a choice piece that is reflective of the Holocaust. Many students in the past have written about how studying the Holocaust affected their lives, contrary to their initial impressions.

Young Adult Novels That Are Effective with a World War II Study

Adler, David. 1995. *We Remember the Holocaust.* New York: Holt.

Erman, John. 1988. *The Attic: The Hiding of Anne Frank,* Marietta, GA: Cabin Fever Entertainment.

Filipovic, Zlata. 1995. *Zlata's Diary: A Child's Life in Sarajevo.* New York: Viking Penguin.

Finkelstein, Norman H. 1993. *Remember Not to Forget: A Memory of the Holocaust.* Illus. Lois and Lars Hokanson. New York: Morrow/Mulberry.

Greene, Bette. 1993. *Summer of My German Soldier.* New York: Dell.

Hahn, Mary Downing. 1991. *Stepping on the Cracks.* New York: Clarion Books.

Lowry, Lois. 1989. *Number the Stars.* Boston: Houghton Mifflin.
Matas, Carol. 1987. *Lisa's War.* New York: Scribner.
———. 1992. *Kris's War.* New York: Scholastic.
———. 1993. *Daniel's Story.* New York: Scholastic.
Pettit, Jayne. 1993. *A Place to Hide: True Stories of Holocaust Rescues.* New York: Scholastic.
Strasser, Todd. 1981. *The Wave.* New York: Laurel Leaf.
Van Der Rol, Ruud, and Rian Verhoeven. 1995. *Anne Frank: Beyond the Diary: A Photographic Rememberance.* New York: Puffin.
Volavkova, Hana. 1994. *Never Saw Another Butterfly.* New York: Schocker.
Vos, Ida. 1993. *Anna Is Still Here.* Boston: Houghton Mifflin.
Wiesel, Elie. 1996. *Night, Dawn, Day.* Northvale, NJ: Aronson.

We start the next unit, which is called our Struggles Unit, by brainstorming about different types of people or groups of people that are underrepresented in books, movies, television, and other media. After creating a list of examples we then focus on the struggles that these people had and continue to have in order to live life as they desire.

During this unit we focus on famous "strugglers" (e.g., Rosa Parks, Cesar Chavez, Native Americans and the Trail of Tears, Malcolm X, Dr. Martin Luther King Jr., South Africa's struggle with apartheid, etc.). Our students write about some of their personal struggles, and they are asked to choose a novel that is about a person or a group of people who went through some sort of struggle that they would like to learn more about. While the students are reading their books they also keep a reader-response journal, where they answer questions (e.g., What does the character learn from his struggle? How would you have handled the situations that your character came across? Who in history could your main character be compared to and why? What do you admire most about your character?) or they react with thoughts, feelings, and ideas. *Long Journey Home* by Julius Lester and *Nightjohn* by Gary Paulsen are two books that we read aloud to our classes, either in part or in their entirety. Both of these novels portray a realistic picture of life as a slave.

Young Adult Titles That Uplift and Broaden One's View on Struggles

Armstrong, Jennifer. 1992. *Steal Away.* New York: Orchard.
Berry, James. 1992. *Ajeemah and His Son.* New York: HarperCollins.
Borland, Hal. 1984. *When Legends Die.* New York: Bantam.
Cohlene, Terri. 1996. *Turquoise Bay: A Navajo Legend.* Mahwah, NJ: Troll Communications.

Collier, James L., and Christopher Collier. 1985a. *The Blood Country.* New York: Scholastic.
———. 1985b. *The Winter Hero.* New York: Scholastic.
Cooper, James Fenimore. 1982. *The Last of the Mohicans.* New York: Bantam.
De Jenkins, Lyll B. 1989. *The Honorable Prison.* New York: Puffin.
De Paola, Tomie, ed. 1991. *The Legend of the Indian Paintbrush.* New York: Putnam.
Douglass, Frederick. 1960. *Narrative of the Life of Frederick Douglass: Written by Himself.* Cambridge, MA: Belknap Press.
Ekoomiak, Normee. 1990. *Arctic Memories.* New York: Holt.
Esbensen, Barbara J. 1988 . *Star Maiden: An Ojibway Tale.* Illus. Helen K. Davie. Boston: Little, Brown, and Co.
Feldmann, Susan, ed. 1991. *The Storytelling Stone: Traditional Native American Myths and Tales.* New York: Dell.
Ferris, Jeri. 1991. *Native American Doctor: The Story of Susan LaFlesche Picotte.* Minneapolis: Lerner.
Gordon, Sheila. 1989. *Waiting for the Rai.* New York: Bantam.
Hansen, Joyce. 1992. *Which Way Freedom?* New York: Avon Camelot.
Hicyilmaz, Gaye. 1993. *Against the Storm.* New York: Dell.
Highwater, Jamake. 1993. *Anpa: An American Indian Odessey.* New York: HarperCollins.
Hirschfelder, Arlene, ed. *Rising Voices: Writings of Young Native Americans.* New York: Simon & Schuster.
Hudson, Jan. 1991. *Sweetgrass.* New York: Scholastic.
Hunt, Irene. 1986. *Across Five Aprils.* New York: Berkley Books.
Hurston, Zora Neale. 1990. *Their Eyes Were Watching God.* New York: HarperCollins.
Jahoda, Gloria. 1995. *The Trail of Tears.* New York: Random House.
Kazimiroff, Theodore L. 1982. *The Last Algonquin.* New York: Walker.
Kroeber, Theodora. 1964. *Ishi: Last of His Tribe.* New York: Houghton Mifflin.
Lasky, Kathryn. 1986. *The Night Journey.* New York: Puffin.
Lester, Julius. 1985. *Long Journey Home: Stories From Black History.* New York: Penguin.
Lester, Julius. 1985. *This Strange New Feeling.* New York: Scholastic.
Levinson, Riki. 1985. *Watch the Stars Come Out.* New York: Dutton.
Levitin, Sonia. 1987. *The Return.* New York: Atheneum.
Marshall, James Vance. 1992. *Walkabout.* Portsmouth, NH: Heinemann.
Martas, Carol, 1994. *Sworn Enemies.* New York: Dell.
McGraw, Eloise Jarvis. 1986. *Moccasin Trail.* New York: Puffin.
Meyer, Carolyn. 1993. *White Lilacs.* San Diego: Harcourt Brace.

Meyers, Walter Dean. 1992. *Somewhere in the Darkness.* New York: Scholastic.
———. 1993. *Malcolm X: By Any Means Necessary.* New York: Scholastic.
O'Neal, Zibby. 1990. *Language of Goldfish.* New York: Puffin.
Paterson, Katherine. 1989. *Of Nightingales That Weep.* New York: HarperCollins.
Paulsen, Gary. 1995. *Nightjohn.* New York: Dell.
Porter, A. P. 1992. *Jump at de Sun: The Story of Zora Neale Hurston.* Minneapolis: Lerner.
Price, Susan. 1989. *The Ghost Drum.* New York: Farrar, Straus & Giroux.
Rochman, Hazel, ed. 1988. *Somehow Tenderness Survives: Stories of South Africa.* New York: HarperCollins.
Rosen, Michael, ed. 1995. *South and North, East and West: The Oxfam Book of Children's Stories.* Atlantic Highlands, NJ: Humanities Press.
Salisbury, Graham. 1994. *Under the Blood Red Sun.* New York: Delacorte.
Staples, Donna. 1993. *Arena Beach.* Boston: Houghton Mifflin.
Whelan, Gloria. 1992. *Goodbye, Vietnam.* New York: Knopf.
Yep, Laurence. 1975. *Dragonwings.* New York: HarperCollins.

The next unit in our program focuses on stereotypes—the stereotypes of the past and those prevalent today. Ironically, good examples of stereotypes from the past can be found in outdated textbooks. The roles of women, children, the elderly, African Americans, Native Americans, the homeless, and the poor were often stereotyped. *The Keeper of the Isis Light* by Monica Hughes is used as a whole-class novel during this unit. This book focuses on a young girl, Olwen, who is physically adapted to survive on the planet Isis, but later Olwen is faced with great prejudice and stereotyping because of her appearance. As we read *Isis,* students are asked to think about their definition of beauty and happiness, and the stereotypes that they have made or that have been made of them.

The unit is beneficial for our students because many of them experience stereotyping because of their age, gender, physical appearance, and physical abilities. The students are asked to take their ideal characters through situations in which he or she faces stereotypes. We also look at employment skills and ask our students to fictitiously apply for an occupation that stereotypically wouldn't fit their persona. It is through this application that students find themselves discovering the differences and similarities that they have with others, specifically those who, on the surface, seem different from themselves.

An addition to this unit for the 1996–97 school year was to ask my students to face some of the concerns and stereotypes that they may have about the elderly. My history team-teaching partner, John Lupanoff, has developed a club called Adopt-A-Grandparent, and throughout the school year he takes young people to a local nursing home to play bingo, bowl, or share in birthday celebrations with the residents. It is the goal of our team-teaching efforts to get our students to interview and write a living history of one or more elderly individuals. We are hoping that, through this immersion, students will break some stereotypes. Walter Dean Myers's *Won't Know Till I Get There* presents a great connection between a group of youths and a group living in a center for the elderly.

The following are three story books that I use to introduce the Living History Unit: *The Two of Them* by Aliki; *Just Listen* by Winifred Morris; and *Annie and the Old One* by Miska Miles.

Young Adult Novels and Story Books That Deal with Stereotypes

Adoff, Arnold, ed. 1995. *My Black Me: A Beginning Book of Black Poetry.* New York: Puffin.

Aliki. 1987. *The Two of Them.* New York: Mulberry Books.

Angelou, Maya. 1970, 1997. *I Know Why the Caged Bird Sings.* New York: Bantam.

Ash, Maureen. 1989. *The Story of the Women's Movement.* Danbury, CT: Children's Press.

Baker, Rachel. 1987. *The First Woman Doctor.* New York: Scholastic.

Bauer, Marion Dane, ed. 1995. *Am I Blue? Coming Out from the Silence.* New York: HarperCollins.

Craven, Margaret. 1980. *I Heard the Owl Call My Name.* New York: Dell.

Fox, Mary Virginia. 1991. *The Story of Women Who Shaped the West.* Danbury, CT: Children's Press.

Hughes, Monica. 1981. *The Keeper of the Isis Light.* New York: Atheneum.

Johnston, Norma. 1995. *Remember the Ladies: The First Women's Rights Convention.* New York: Scholastic.

Miles, Miska. 1990. *Annie and the Old One.* New York: Trumpet Club.

Morris, Winifred. 1990. *Just Listen.* New York: Atheneum.

Myers, Walter Dean. 1988. *Won't Know Till I Get There.* New York: Puffin.

Pitts, Paul. 1992. *The Shadowman's Way.* New York: Avon.

Soto, Gary. 1993. *Local News.* San Diego: Harcourt Brace.

Stavsky, Lois, and I. E. Mozeson. 1992. *The Place I Call Home: Faces and Voices of Homeless Teens.* New York: Sure Seller.

Sullivan, Georgie. 1994. *The Day the Women Got the Vote: A Photo History of the Women's Rights Movement.* New York: Scholastic.

Taylor, Theodore. 1987. *The Cay.* New York: Doubleday.

———. 1995. *Timothy of the Cay.* New York: Avon.

We have found that after the Stereotype Unit is completed many students will point out, want to discuss, or write about the stereotypes that they see in today's art, media, and literature. This involvement is a good measure of success because it suggests that it does make a difference for students to study those different from themselves; it is then that they begin to appreciate the differences. The passion that my students begin to feel carries over to the last unit, which centers on the reading of *Flowers for Algernon* by Daniel Keyes. This novel focuses on a mentally retarded man who is given an experimental operation that temporarily makes him a genius, and it explores the different treatment that he receives at different stages of his development. Along with *Flowers* we read aloud *The Acorn People* by Ron Jones and/or *Tunes for Bears to Dance To* by Robert Cormier.

The reading of these pieces is accompanied by reader-response entries, ideal-person applications, and most importantly a debate-style discussion. We debate the treatment of the characters and the implications of assumptions and stereotyping.

Our year ends with a culminating activity. Every year this final project changes its shape and form based on the discussions, explorations, and directions that the students have found interesting. The writing of list poems, the scouring of current media for examples of prejudice and struggles, and community volunteer activities are all possibilities.

We hope that through our students' exposure to stereotyped and repressed groups they grow in knowledge and become more open minded, they tend to open up in their writing, and most retain the hunger to learn more about those who are different from themselves. We ask that they continue to remind themselves of the Hopi Indian proverb:

> What should it matter that one bowl is dark and the other pale, if each is of good design and serves its purpose well? (Zora 1994, 76).

It is our job as teachers to introduce the similarities and differences, encourage humanizing choices, and nurture the most important human beings. It is our hope that each of them will do the same for another human being . . . someday.

References

Cormier, Robert. 1994. *Tunes for Bears to Dance To.* New York: Dell.

Jones, Ron. 1996. *The Acorn People.* New York: Dell.

Schwartz, Gretchen. 1995. "Growing Up, Reaching Out: Multiculturalism through Young Adult Literature and Films." *The ALAN Review,* Assembly on Literature for Adolescents of NCTE. http://scholar.lib.vt.edu/ejournals/ALAN/spring95/toc.html

Keyes, Daniel. 1996. *Flowers for Algernon.* San Diego: Harcourt Brace.

Zora, Gary A. 1994. *The Soul Would Have No Rainbow If the Eyes Had No Tears: And Other Native American Proverbs.* New York: Simon & Schuster.

16 Parallel Lives: Anne Frank and Today's Immigrant Students

Mitzi Witkin
North Middle School
Great Neck, New York

As an eighth-grade English teacher who serves all students ready for entry into regular school classes, I often reflect on the practical ways I might integrate my immigrant students into my heterogeneous, mainstreamed classes. Teachers affect the social ambiance of the classroom when they successfully include ESOL students (English speakers of other languages) in collaborative activities requiring students to interact in small groups. But when teachers draw out the students' past so that the youngsters can connect it to the present, teachers penetrate the innermost recesses of their students' minds and hearts. This inner awakening was my mission recently with a class assignment on memoir writing sparked by the reading of *The Diary of a Young Girl*, by Anne Frank.

Three ESOL students with a rudimentary knowledge of English were assigned to my English classes recently. Originating from Taiwan, Japan, and Iran, they sat mute for the most part, reluctant to call attention to their faltering English in classrooms that were overwhelmingly populated by students whose birthplace and upbringing in the United States endowed them with facility in their native tongue. Though confident in English expression, many of these young people, born in the United States, were undergoing their own adolescent anxiety about their ability to fit in, and ESOL students brought out their xenophobia. The symptoms were as subtle as changing a seat or as obvious as a fight, but either way, the distancing was palpable.

What countermeasures could I, an English teacher, use to diminish criticism, distrust, and fear in a classroom already electrified by the cliques that thirteen-year-olds form out of their need to develop their own identity? How could I discourage the adverse treatment of ESOL students when their faltering, fractured English labeled them outsiders? Above all, how could ESOL students contact their past and connect it to their present in psychological wholeness?

The answer for me was to carry on the regular English program but to find ways for the culture and past life of ESOL students to work to their advantage. My assignment in memoir writing became an occasion for ESOL students to present themselves as reporters, stand-up comics, and heroes in a classroom where they had been sitting cautiously, uncertain of their reception. The experience of remembering their past and sharing it with their classmates elevated them to celebrities, who had lived an adventure marked by danger and survived to tell the tale. Young people haunted by events that they had witnessed in their past had an opportunity to relate them to an interested audience and to integrate them in a new setting.

I introduced memoir writing after the class had completed reading and discussing *The Diary of a Young Girl* by Anne Frank. This book proved especially appropriate, for Anne's experience as a German-Jewish teenager seeking refuge in Holland during World War II resembles the dislocation of some of those ESOL students who had more recently escaped as refugees from the zones of turmoil. Of course, these students surmounted perilous obstacles, whereas Anne Frank was destroyed by them.

My immigrant students tackled Anne Frank's *Diary* with the help of their ESOL teacher, who supplied an abridged edition and devoted some of her class time to elaborate on the content. In my English classes, *The Diary of a Young Girl* was used as the centerpiece of a unit of study on the Holocaust. I focused on "the inner and outer worlds of Anne Frank." Materials from the Anne Frank Center USA, the United States Holocaust Museum, and library research provided the historical background for Anne's experiences. In addition, students examined the writing in the *Diary* for its literary merit. For example, Anne's tendency to act as a reporter, frequently quoting her co-residents of the Secret Annexe, was validated in her stated goal in life—to become a journalist. Her candid examination of the physical and emotional changes she was undergoing and her introspective analyses of her vicissitudinary relationships with her parents; her sister Margot; Mrs. Van Daan; Dussell; and especially Peter, her romantic attachment, were all sources of compelling interest to students who were also experiencing the roller coaster ride of adolescence. All of these elements—the personal, the historical, and the literary—may have paved the way for my ESOL students' responses in their memoirs, written after their experience of living vicariously with Anne Frank confined to the Secret Annexe.

Connections between Anne Frank and my immigrant students were delineated several ways in the writing of their memoirs. First, early in her diary Anne writes about her reputation in school as Miss Chatterbox. Anne's teacher punishes her for talking too much, and she has to write compositions as penalties for her misdemeanors. This she does by turning them into witty stories that eventually win over her teacher. The old-fashioned discipline wreaked on Anne by her stern teacher reminded Lin in my class of her own harsh education in Taiwan. Her classmates listened intently as Lin reported the severe treatment she received in her school there:

> The terrible life began when I was going to elementary school. I couldn't sleep until 11 o'clock because I had to study for homework and test. If I got bad grades on the test, the teacher would hit me with a stick. And we had a lot of homework and tests. We had to go to school six days a week. Only on Sunday I can rest and do whatever I what. [*sic*]

Lin's description of her rigorous school life in Taiwan contrasted painfully with students' freer life here. As Lin concluded, "But now I am happy to live here because now I have some free time and I can do whatever I what [*sic*]." Lin's remembrance, her feelings of strain and relief, contributed to her classmates' understanding of her past and her personality. But even more welcome was her willingness to reveal herself, a component of her desire to participate in the class as an equal partner. As she disclosed something about her past, she won status among her classmates. Her errors in pronunciation and grammar paled in the light of her candor and courage.

Anne Frank's *Diary* also proved valuable for Hideo's memoir. Inspired by Anne's humorous description of dentist Dussell's examination of Mrs. Van Daan's teeth, Hideo recalled and wrote about the time he gave himself a haircut and his mother reacted to it. When he was five years old, unwilling to face the barber, Hideo decided to trim his own hair:

> I started to cut my hair by myself looking at the mirror, watching my face in the mirror. After finishing my hair cut I thought I've done it well, so I ran into my mom's room and woke her up. She woked up slowly and angrily. I told my mom that I went to a barber shop. Then she looked at my face and suddenly she screamed. (I was little so I didn't know what my mom was saying.)

Hideo concluded his dramatically conceived comic scene with a playful metaphor worthy of a haiku. "After that, she hid my head so no one can see my hair, then took me to the barber shop. So after that my hair became so weird so she said my hair is like a acorn." The sincere laughter of his classmates showed Hideo that he had triumphantly rendered his recollection of himself as a mischievous child, a Japanese "Dennis the Menace."

Mehran's memoir spoke to the heart of Anne Frank's *Diary* since his was an eyewitness account of the start of the Iran-Iraq war written from the point of view of an eleven-year-old worried about a test in school.

> Two years ago when I was in Iran, I went to my friend's house in the afternoon at 3 P.M. We had a very big test in math the next morning. We were studying together for the test. Then, it was 6 P.M. and it was in the winter. The sky was dark and cold. I had to walk home alone by myself. When I got outside to go back to my house I felt scared and I started to run. When I stepped up to my house and rang the bell, I heard a very very loud sound like a bomb and my whole house shook very hard. I didn't know what it was. Then I heard some more and then when I turned on the TV, the announcer said that Iran was going to start a war with Iraq and the sound like a bomb was a missile from Iraq to Iran. After that Iraq sent many missiles and my family and my other relatives and I went to some other city and I didn't take the test and I didn't go to school for two months.

This memoir solidified Mehran's standing in the class. He had evoked an unexpected, harrowing event experienced as a child—first feeling frightened and helpless; then discovering the circumstances and finding safety; and finally living through an extraordinary, disruptive period when he could not attend school. Mehran earned recognition as hero of the class that day and for some time after.

This assignment in memoir writing allowed my students to dig into their past, examine a portion of it, and share that memory and its meaning with their classmates. The incidents selected, after much discussion, varied considerably—from a family vacation to the death of a pet. But the contributions of the ESOL students took center stage. Because their memoirs contained harsh references (corporal punishment, the Iran-Iraq war) or exotic echoes (hair compared to an acorn), they infused a vigor and novelty absent from the writing of the American students. Moreover, as immigrants they were disconnected from their past in ways the children born in the United States were not. Writing their memoirs gave them the opportunity to bridge the gulf between the past that had been lost and the present that is found in a classroom in the United States. Longing for a reconnection, these children used the resources of language and recollection to win over their classmates, thus achieving a place in the society that is the American classroom. Yes, the past the ESOL students recalled was different from that of the American students in some ways, and that is what made their contributions interesting.

Furthermore, the element that aided the immigrant student's acceptance by their classmates was the ghost of Anne Frank herself. Written after the students read Anne Frank's *Diary,* these memoirs echoed her revelation of intimate details and anguished longing for freedom from the confines of the Secret Annexe. Because of Anne's immediacy, her ghostly presence lingered in the classroom as the immigrant students related parallel experiences from their own lives. Expressed in faltering English, their memoirs breathed new life and affirmed Anne's life at the same time.

17 Supporting Active and Reflective Response to Multicultural Literature

Elizabeth Noll
University of New Mexico

Charlotte Valencia Lindahl
University of New Mexico

Debra Salazar
University of New Mexico

Last fall, the three of us met in an education course called Literature for Adolescents, which I (Noll) taught at the University of New Mexico. Composed of undergraduate and graduate education and English majors, our class met weekly to read and discuss a wide range of young adult literature and to explore methods and issues surrounding the teaching of literature in middle school and high school. Throughout the semester, we read a variety of literature reflective of both mainstream and culturally diverse groups that included fiction, nonfiction, poetry, and other genres. Among our choices were writers such as Rudolfo Anaya, Lawrence Yep, Maya Angelou, and Langston Hughes, and books such as *The House on Mango Street, The Color Purple,* and *Rio Grande Stories.* Our discussions ranged from the selection of literature for the classroom to the influence of popular media on adolescents' experiences with literacy to the portrayal of cultural and ethnic stereotypes in young adult literature.

One of the activities in this course was small-group collaboration and presentation on different topics of interest. We (Lindahl and Salazar) chose to examine the teaching of multicultural literature through the use of picture books. Thus, for our presentation to the class we decided to use a book not actually intended for adolescents; a picture book. We chose *Chato's Kitchen,* written by Gary Soto and illustrated by Susan Guevara, as a book which would work well in demonstrating to the class the interplay between print text and visual imagery. Following our reading and dramatic interpretation of the book, we planned to lead a discussion on Soto's satirical humor, his use of code switching in the text, and the potential appeal of this book to secondary school students. Our classmates had other ideas. They were more interested in examining Soto's portrayal of Latinos, Guevara's use of animals to represent humans, and the intended message of the book. Thus, our simple invitation following the reading—"Tell us what you thought of this story"—resulted in a discussion far different (and far livelier) than what we had envisioned. As the discussion gained momentum and headed in unexpected directions, we set aside our well-laid plans and followed the class's lead in exploring issues of interest and concern.

Even though the resulting discussion involved nearly the entire class in active exchange of ideas, we were left feeling rather confused about the unexpected turn of events. When the three of us met later to discuss the presentation, we addressed the class's diverse interpretations of *Chato's Kitchen,* then moved on to the topic of discussion facilitation. We agreed that this experience of having a discussion take on a life of its own—though initially somewhat disconcerting—actually offered valuable insights into the use of multicultural literature with middle and high school students. We recognized, for example, the importance of a responsive stance and varied strategies in encouraging lively class involvement and expression of multiple perspectives. In this chapter we discuss specific strategies characteristic of this stance designed to actively and reflectively engage middle school and high school students in a variety of multicultural literature.

Expanding Understandings with Multicultural Picture Books

Although picture books are generally considered to be the domain of young children, they can be used very effectively with older students as well. Of benefit to all students, and in particular to those learning English as a second language, picture books offer two media—print and visual imagery—through which in-depth personal understandings of literature can be developed. Unfortunately, the value of such intertextuality of written language and illustrations goes largely unrecognized in the upper grades. The illustrations in picture books evoke immediate response, and the language is rich and clear. The vivid images and strong themes offer middle and high school students valuable means for examining cultural representations, unfamiliar dialects, and historical information. *The Lily Cupboard: A Story of the Holocaust,* for example, informs students about the Nazi occupation of Holland through the story of a Jewish Dutch girl who is protected by a kind farmer and his family, and *Dreamplace* describes the lifestyle of the Anasazi eight hundred years ago.

Pairing picture books with novels, short stories, and poems by the same author offers students opportunities to explore cultural images, author's voice, and literary conventions across levels. For example, Alice Walker's picture book *To Hell with Dying* might be paired with *The Color Purple* to explore the roles of African American females in each. Similarly, text sets composed of picture books and young adult literature by multiple authors provide a means of examining certain cultural topics, issues, and themes. I (Noll) have developed text sets of multicultural literature for use with middle school students that focus on themes such as survival, family, and journey. The literature selections in these text sets portray the themes in contrasting and unexpected ways. For example, the titles in the text set on the journey include the following: *Journey of the Sparrows,* about a family who is forced to leave war-torn El Salvador; *Fly Away Home,* about a homeless boy and his father who live in an airport; *Dogsong,* about a Native Alaskan boy's journey to manhood; *Journey to Topaz,* about the evacuation of Japanese Americans during World War II; *Grandfather's Journey,* about the immigration of Say's grandfather to the United States and his later return to Japan; *Homecoming,* about four siblings who are abandoned and set out to find a home for themselves; *Encounter,* about a Taino boy's memories of Columbus's arrival in San Salvador; and *Over the Green Hills,* about a South African mother and child who travel miles by foot to visit the grandmother.

Such text sets lend themselves well to small-group discussion, in which four or five students gather to read the assorted texts and to share their observations, questions, and personal understandings. Using the text set just described, for example, students might examine the multiple ways in which the concept of journey is portrayed in each of the selections and discuss what their findings tell them about the cultures portrayed in the literature. Students who are uncomfortable expressing their thoughts in a large group will often participate more readily in the "safer" environment of small discussion groups.

Supporting Multiple Interpretations through Dramatization

Dramatization of multicultural literature is another effective strategy for actively engaging students and encouraging them to explore multiple interpretations of texts. Just as illustrations in picture books enhance the meanings that students construct, so too does movement—the walk, gesture, facial expression—in dramatization. In the presentation of *Chato's Kitchen,* dramatization of the text as it was being read aloud gained the immediate attention of students in the class. In fact, it was our dramatic interpretation of the characters that launched the class into such spirited discussion. Students questioned our representation of Soto's and Guevara's intended meanings, and they wanted to compare it with the written text and illustrations.

Likewise, role playing in the secondary school classroom can be performed before an entire class followed by small group discussion. In small groups, students have opportunities to move back and forth between the text and their own dramatic interpretations as a means of negotiating and developing varied understandings of topics such as author's purpose or characters' attitudes and actions. They might try reading aloud or "ad-libbing" selected scenes in a book or experiment with various personas of characters as a way of understanding different cultural perspectives. A few examples of texts that lend themselves especially well to interpretation through dramatization are Langston Hughes's poetry; the short stories in Sandra Cisneros's *Woman Hollering Creek* (1994); and Walter Dean Myers's books, with their rapid dialogue.

Both picture books and dramatization encourage active collaboration among students. Unlike these strategies for engaging students in multicultural literature, reflective writing provides an independent forum for students to express their thoughts and ideas. In reflective writing, students periodically pause and reflect on, or "take stock," of all they have been reading, thinking, and discussing.

This writing can be done in a number of ways, two of which are described here. First, teachers might ask students to take a few minutes at the end of class to write informally about issues addressed that day. Rather than being a response to assigned topics, this writing is intended to be open ended and exploratory. Students may pose questions, express ideas and opinions, or make connections to personal experiences, other pieces of literature, or broader issues. Although teachers may choose to read and/or respond to this writing periodically, its primary purpose is simply to provide students—and teachers—an opportunity to free-write about topics raised in class. Using a notebook or journal keeps the writing in one place and provides chronological ordering of the entries.

I (Noll) have found that students are likely to write most spontaneously following heated class discussions. For students who are hesitant to voice opinions aloud in class, reflective writing offers a welcome means of expressing themselves. One of my former middle school students commented as follows in her journal:

> I have so many ideas in my head during discussions but, by the time I get up the courage to say them out loud, the talk has moved on. I'm kind of like Dicey [in *Dicey's Song*, Voigt, 1982] when she wants to be able to talk to her grandmother but holds back. She sorts out her thoughts working on her boat. I sort out mine here in my journal.

Finally, reflective writing in journals helps students make connections from one day or week to the next, and it provides a valuable record—for both students and teachers—of their thinking and growth.

Alternatively or in addition to the informal reflective writing in journals, teachers might periodically assign short (one- to two-page) reflective essays on pertinent issues. For example, students might be asked to express their views on the importance (or lack thereof) of authors belonging to cultures about which they choose to write. Or students might make connections between the culture of a particular character and their own culture. Such essays are more formal than the journal entries and, in fact, ideally grow out of those informal writings. Both, however, are exploratory in nature and encourage students to connect in personal ways with the cultures about which they are reading.

Conclusion

The three strategies described in this chapter are designed to engage students in active and reflective response to multicultural literature. Picture books, dramatization, and reflective writing encourage students to explore multiple understandings of the cultures depicted in literature. Critical to the success of these strategies, however, is the role of the teacher. As the class discussion of *Chato's Kitchen* demonstrated to us, having a responsive stance and a willingness to listen openly encourages expression of diverse—and sometimes unexpected—interpretations of literature. Such a stance provides an important model for middle and high school students as they encounter a wide range of perspectives, not only in multicultural literature, but also in their daily interactions with others in and out of school.

References

Bunting, Eve. 1993. *Fly Away Home*. Boston: Houghton Miffin.

Buss, Fran Leeper, with Daisy Cubias. 1993. *Journey of the Sparrows*. New York: Dell.

Cisneros, Sandra. 1991. *Woman Hollering Creek & Other Stories.* New York: Random House.

———. 1994. *The House on Mango Street.* New York: Random House.

Isadora, R. 1992. *Over the Green Hills.* New York: Greenwillow.

Lyon, G. E. 1993. *Dreamplace.* Illus. P. Catalanotto. New York: Orchard.

Meyer, Carolyn, ed. 1994. *Rio Grande Stories.* San Diego: Harcourt Brace.

Oppenheim, S. L. 1995. *The Lily Cupboard: A Story of the Holocaust.* Illus. R. Himler. New York: HarperCollins.

Paulsen, Gary. 1985. *Dogsong.* New York: Simon & Schuster.

Say, Allen. 1993. *Grandfather's Journey.* Boston: Houghton Mifflin.

Soto, Gary. 1991. *Baseball in April and Other Stories.* San Diego: Harcourt Brace.

———. 1995. *Chato's Kitchen.* Illus. S. Guevara. New York: Putnam.

Uchida, Yoshiko. 1971. *Journey to Topaz.* New York: Scribner.

Voigt, Cynthia. 1982. *Dicey's Song.* New York: Atheneum.

———. 1993. *Homecoming.* New York: Atheneum.

Walker, Alice. 1982. *The Color Purple.* New York: Harcourt Brace Jovanovich.

———. 1993. *To Hell with Dying.* Illus. C. Deeter. San Diego: Harcourt Brace.

Yolen, Jane. 1992. *Encounter.* Illus. D. Shannon. San Diego: Harcourt Brace.

III Expanding the Curriculum

Fundamentally, we believe that literature forges authentic connections between the reader and the work. Additionally, literature is an effective way to connect ideas. For example in this section, the authors have presented ways to infuse literature into other academic areas. In recent years we have seen the artificial boundaries of the subject matter curriculum erode, especially in elementary and middle schools where thematic units and team teaching often focus on the complementary aspects of content. Literature, with its life lessons, provides a natural connection to other content areas. In Part III, Expanding the Curriculum, six authors suggest ways in which multicultural young adult literature bridges to other areas of study. Kelly Chandler connects Paulsen's historical novel *Nightjohn* with Frederick Douglass's account of his early life, with implications for American history as well as English classes. Alyce Hunter provides an interdisciplinary perspective of the varied aspects of Chinese culture. In his chapter, Jeff Wilhelm describes means of involving students in drama activities using young adult literature. David Pugalee demonstrates that math is more conceptual than numerical as he provides ways to use literature in the math classroom. Amy Hackett provides a data bank of young adult novels that can be illustrative of scientific concerns and realities. The young adult books cited in each of these chapters are included in the annotated bibliography at the end of this book.

18 Considering the Power of the Past: Pairing *Nightjohn* and *Narrative of the Life of Frederick Douglass*

Kelly Chandler
University of Maine

I've known and taught a lot of high school students who complain about having to learn history. Many fail to see the relevance of past events in their own lives, and some show an unfortunate lack of empathy for members of cultural groups other than their own. Given the bland, tedious, and dense textbooks teenagers are often asked to read, these attitudes are hardly surprising.

Like many other educators, I don't believe history has to be taught this way. I'm convinced that infusing social studies with quality literature can help to counteract teenagers' negative feelings about history, as well as provide them with portraits of people different from themselves. By presenting vivid settings, engaging characters, and compelling problems, historical fiction and autobiographies can often bring social studies to life for adolescents. As Mary Burke-Hengen (1995) puts it, literature "can help us understand our history and our society as well as our places in it" (p. 55).

Before beginning my doctoral studies, I taught sophomore English at Noble High School in Berwick, Maine. I collaborated with my social studies teammate Susan Hackett to develop an American studies curriculum that covered the period from 1800 to 1945. We began the school year with an integrated unit on nationalism in early nineteenth-century America. Susan dealt with history and art, whereas I introduced students to classic essays, stories, and poems from that time period. Unfortunately, most of the works we read were written by white men: Washington Irving, James Fenimore Cooper, Henry David Thoreau, and Edgar Allan Poe, to name a few.

Concerned that my students, who were almost all white, were not being exposed to literature written by multicultural authors, I decided to make *Narrative of the Life of Frederick Douglass,* a classic written by an African American, the focus of our next unit. Organized around the essential question, "How do we get from nationalism to a nation divided?" the unit explored the decades before the eruption of the Civil War. I wanted students to see the abolition movement through the lens of someone who had personally suffered from slavery, and I was convinced that students would enjoy the adventure and drama of Douglass's story once they were immersed in it.

Nonetheless, I knew that Douglass's book, like much early American literature we had studied, would be difficult for the weaker readers in my heterogeneously grouped classes. The archaic language, unfamiliar sentence patterns, and different historical context could prevent some of them from considering the ideas I wanted to discuss.

Borrowing from ideas in Joan Kaywell's (1993) *Adolescent Literature as a Complement to the Classics,* I decided to pair the *Narrative* with a piece of more accessible young adult (YA) fiction. I chose Gary Paulsen's *Nightjohn,* a YA novel set in the same historical period, as a way to introduce students to some of the issues, including justice, prejudice, and the power of literacy, raised by the *Narrative.* In the next few pages, I will discuss how I used the simpler and shorter *Nightjohn* to support and illuminate *Narrative of the Life of Frederick Douglass.* I will describe a number of classroom activities, as well as share my students' responses—and my own—to these two texts.

Experiencing the Texts

First published in 1845, *Narrative of the Life of Frederick Douglass* is the best known of all slave narratives, the genre that Henry Louis Gates (1987) says gave "birth to the Afro-American literary tradition" (p. x). In the *Narrative,* Douglass tells the story of his early life on a Maryland plantation. For a time, he leads a relatively easy life, comparatively speaking, as a house servant in Baltimore. His mistress, Mrs. Auld, even begins to teach him to read—a move that is expressly forbidden by her husband, who eventually puts a stop to it. Back on the plantation, Douglass is sent to a notorious slave breaker named Covey. He refuses to submit, besting Covey in a fight that Douglass calls the "turning point" of his life as a slave, which "rekindled within me the few expiring embers of freedom, and revived within me a sense of my own manhood" (p. 104).

From this point, it is only a matter of time before Douglass eludes his captors. In a move that disappoints teenage readers looking for adventure, he omits the specific details of his escape, saying that he wants to protect those who aided him and leave the route open for others to follow. In the North after his escape, he meets prominent abolitionist William Lloyd Garrison, who convinces him to join the formal antislavery movement and sponsors the writing of the *Narrative.*

Paulsen's book has a hero with an equally strong and independent spirit. Nightjohn is the nickname of an escaped slave who, unlike Douglass, returns to the South to teach reading in secret. When John arrives at the Waller plantation, he begins to teach twelve-year-old Sarny the alphabet, letter by letter. Waller, the master, catches Sarny scratching a word in the dirt, and he whips Mammy, the old woman who cares for Sarny, because she refuses to reveal the girl's teacher. To spare Mammy more pain, John admits the crime to Waller, even though he knows that the penalty, "according to the law, is removal of an extremity" (p. 74). After losing both his big toes, John leaves the plantation for a short while. Upon his return, he leads Sarny to a night school where a number of slaves are learning to read and write, and she begins to help him, sharing with the others the few letters she knows.

I decided to begin the unit by reading *Nightjohn* aloud to all of my classes. Pared to the visceral essentials, the text is short—fewer than 100 pages—and the first-person narrative, told from Sarny's point of view, sounds much like speech. I wanted to give my students a sense of how written dialect should sound. This "inner ear," so to speak, would help them to read Alice Walker's *The Color Purple* later in the year. In addition, it would help to immerse them in the rich slave culture of the time. To supplement my own somewhat feeble attempts at dramatization, I also showed my classes an excellent laserdisc on the life of abolitionist Sojourner Truth, in which an actress delivers Truth's stirring "Ain't I a Woman?" address.

Over a period of several days, I read *Nightjohn* aloud, stopping periodically to discuss the story, answer questions, and allow students to write responses in their reader's journals. Although we talked extensively about *Nightjohn* when we finished reading it, that was hardly the end of our discussion of the book. It came up regularly as we worked our way through Douglass's *Narrative.*

After we read the first few pages of the *Narrative* together, students were assigned to read the rest of it on their own in three big chunks. (I did record myself reading the Douglass text, and I made that audiotape available to a number of students who needed more support. Half a dozen of them even brought me their own tapes to make personal copies.) We discussed each of those sections in detail. I expected that students' prior knowledge of some of the themes and issues of the *Narrative* would make it easier for them to negotiate the more complicated text independently, and this seemed to be the case. Three significant themes surfaced in both of the books: the power of literacy, the definition of activism, and the nature of courage. Each of these will be discussed in turn.

Considering the Power of Literacy

Literacy plays a large role in the power struggles in both *Nightjohn* and the *Narrative.* John risks his life by returning to the South to teach slaves to read. When Sarny asks why reading is so important, John replies, "'Cause to know things, for us to know things, is bad for them. We get to wanting. . . . They thinks we want what they got" (p. 39). Douglass writes that learning to read was a "grand achievement, and I prized it highly. From that moment, I understood the pathway from slavery to freedom" (p. 59). The white people in both books are sharply aware of literacy's power to stir independence. Both Waller, the master in *Nightjohn,* and Douglass's master Mr. Auld have a great deal invested in keeping the slaves ignorant.

When my students first learned that slaves were forbidden to read or write in most southern states, a couple of them jokingly said, "Cool! I wouldn't have to do any English homework." Because their initial definition of reading included only novels and textbooks, many kids didn't immediately understand why this law was a powerful tool in white southerners' campaign to keep slaves subordinate. Accordingly, they didn't understand why characters in either book were willing to risk so much for learning.

To illustrate this idea in a concrete way, I asked small groups of students to generate lists of everything that people read and write in contemporary society. When the groups had exhausted the possibilities, we began to make a class list on chart paper. Eventually, this list ran to several sheets, with items ranging from the driver's manual to food ingredients, from a rent agreement to a college application. The sheer scope of the list helped some kids to realize how much literacy permeated their daily lives, even if they didn't consider themselves readers or writers in an academic sense. "Wow, I didn't realize how much I couldn't do if I couldn't read!" one boy said.

Beyond giving students a keener understanding of the issues in the two texts, this reconception of literacy helped a few students to think about why they needed an education, and, even more specifically, a language arts education. Although it certainly didn't convince all of my disaffected students of the value of school (or my class, for that matter), the activity and the resulting discussion did serve to focus attention on the issue in a new and different way.

When I collected journals the next day, one student's response forced me to think more deeply about the importance of literacy in my own life. Josh had written me a note: "Ms. Chandler, would *you* risk your life to be able to read? Would you be willing to cut off your toes?" I didn't know the answer then, and I still don't, but I've been thinking about it ever since. What could be a better question prompted by literature than one that even the teacher can't forget?

Considering the Definition of Activism

For me, it's impossible to think about literacy in these two texts without also thinking about narrative as social activism. This was a hard concept for my students to grasp, but an important one. For them, activism meant picketing or demonstrating or registering voters; they saw writing as a passive, solitary activity rather than a dynamic, social endeavor. They also tended to see texts as divided into two kinds—primarily for entertainment or for information. The idea that they might be designed to persuade or influence an audience did not come immediately to their minds.

When I asked my students why they thought Douglass decided to write his own story, they struggled with the question. "How should we know? We never talked to him," the class skeptic said with scorn. After a while, however, they began to consider several ideas, which varied in sophistication:

- Maybe he needed money to buy back the other members of his family.
- Maybe he wanted to blow the whistle on the people who had mistreated him.
- Maybe he wanted to show that blacks could be as literary and sound as educated as whites.

Eventually, they decided that Douglass wanted to provide powerful evidence to bolster the efforts of the abolition movement. They were able to identify elements in the *Narrative* that were probably designed to elicit the most outrage in readers: Douglass's grandmother left alone in the woods to die, the brutal shooting of a slave in the river, Douglass's own aunt being whipped because she resisted the advances of a white man.

At this point, I drew Sojourner Truth's speech and Harriet Beecher Stowe's *Uncle Tom's Cabin,* from which we had read excerpts, back into the discussion. We talked about the differences in tone, style, and intended audience for each of the three texts. In order to help students connect to the present, I reread them the dedication at the beginning of *Nightjohn:* "to the memory of Sally Hemings, who was owned, raised, and subsequently used by Thomas Jefferson without benefit of ever drawing a single free breath." We speculated about Paulsen's purpose in writing a novel with such an unusual dedication and discussed the race relations and tensions in 1993.

Then we began to brainstorm occasions in our own time when people use texts—oral or written—as a way to push for change in society. One student mentioned petitions. Another student brought up the letters to the editor that students in a neighboring town had written during a recent controversy over hats in school. Someone else mentioned Maya Angelou's poetry. Writing might not have been the first tool they thought of for fighting injustice, but at least it was in the quiver of options after our discussion.

Considering the Nature of Courage

Because my students were almost all white, it was hard for them, no matter how much they sympathized with Sarny or Frederick Douglass, to put themselves in the black characters' places. Had they lived in those times, they would have been privileged by the color of their skin, which meant that they read the texts differently than the ethnically diverse students I taught in Boston during my internship. I discovered that some of my students from Noble High School were considering the implications of this fact when I assigned them two chapters from Harriet Beecher Stowe's *Uncle Tom's Cabin* to compare with Douglass's *Narrative.* The excerpts discussed the 1850 Fugitive Slave Act, which required escaped slaves to be returned from free soil and made it impossible for white northerners to keep slavery at arm's length.

As we talked about the difference between morality and legality, one girl raised her hand. Referring to a Stowe character who violates the Fugitive Slave Act, she said, with a little sadness in her voice, "I like to think that I'd have been a Mrs. Byrd if I had lived back then. But I don't think I would have been. I think I would have ignored what was going on around me if it didn't have to do with me—or worse, I might have been like Mrs. Auld [Douglass's mistress], after she got mean."

My room went quiet for a moment, as students considered for themselves where they might have fallen on the spectrum of courage and compassion. We didn't discuss those thoughts, nor did I want to. The literature had already worked its magic; there was no need to break the spell.

Although it was important for students to ponder how they would have behaved in these historical situations, it was even more important for them to think about how the issues resonated in their own lives. For what would they be willing to make a sacrifice? When and why might they be called to make decisions with potentially unpopular consequences? How had they handled these ethical dilemmas in the past, and how might they handle them in the future? These were sticky questions, and some students resisted engaging them. Others thought long and hard but remained silent during discussions; I could see in their faces or read in their journals that they were wrestling with the answers, but they were not ready or willing to share those ideas. A few brave students told stories or offered opinions.

Many students admired Frederick Douglass because he stood up for himself. He also stood up for others. As time went on, it became clear that numerous tenth graders had been in situations where they had to defend themselves, gaining self-confidence just like Douglass did in his fight with Covey the slave-breaker. Unfortunately, my kids also told stories of times when they had stood silently by when a homophobic group baited an effeminate-looking boy or when a powerful pair of girls shredded the self-esteem of a younger one who didn't wear the right clothes. I learned something about human nature from those discussions, and I think my students did, too: it is easier to risk ridicule for your own right to be different than it is to stand up for *someone else* who is different.

Considering the Implications of Teaching These Texts

In relatively homogeneous Berwick, Maine, the differences that divide people are rarely ethnic or racial ones. Although I want very much for my students to read literature written by and about people from different cultural groups, I often need to convince them first that this is necessary. Then, without whitewashing the differences, I need to help kids find parallels and intersections between these groups and their own experiences. Most of my students don't see the connections on their own, and sometimes they resent my assigning literature that pushes them outside of their comfort zone.

It's important for me to breathe life into the history that my students have inherited, but it's just as important to help them think about the future and their place in it. Sadly, discussions about multicultural issues often run less smoothly than conversations about characters who more closely resemble the readers in my classes. I don't give up, though: I wait, I listen, and I prod. I trust authors like Frederick Douglass and Gary Paulsen to help me do my job.

References

Burke-Hengen, Mary. 1995. "Telling Points: Teaching Social Studies with Literature." *Building Community: Social Studies in the Middle School Years.* Eds. M. Burke-Hengen and T. Gillespie. Portsmouth, NH: Heinemann.

Douglass, Frederick. 1960. *Narrative of the Life of Frederick Douglass: Written by Himself.* Cambridge, MA: Belknap Press.

Gates, Henry L. 1987. *The Classic Slave Narratives.* New York: Mentor.

Kaywell, Joan, ed. 1993. *Adolescent Literature as a Complement to the Classics.* Norwood, MA: Christopher-Gordon.

Paulsen, Gary. 1993. *Nightjohn.* New York: Delacorte.

Walker, Alice. 1983. *The Color Purple.* New York: Washington Square Press.

19 Teaching about China, Chinese Culture, and Chinese Americans through Literature Exploration and Interdisciplinary Instruction

Alyce Hunter
West Windsor Plainsboro (NJ) Middle School

The purpose of infusing facts, ideas, and images of China into the literature/reading curriculum and interdisciplinary instruction at West Windsor Plainsboro Middle School is to help all students at this culturally diverse school—where approximately one-third of the seventh and eighth graders are of Asian heritage—understand the ways in which people in the world and in the United States are diverse and yet united by values, practices, and traditions. The goals of instruction are to focus on the important facts and trends in the history and culture of China, to teach strategies and processes of literary and cultural analysis, and to emphasize techniques that help middle-level learners understand and eliminate stereotypes of Chinese and Chinese Americans.

Combined with a reading/writing workshop approach to instruction, language arts teachers use traditional Chinese text in translation, classic novels, and multicultural young adult literature to develop in students a multicultural perspective that acknowledges and respects the dignity and worth of all human beings. Literature study and language arts experiences are viewed as multicultural education that is based on the premise that diversity is a positive element because it enriches the nation and provides people with opportunities to relate to each other. Such multicultural education tries to acquaint students with the uniqueness of cultures so that they come to view other cultures as meaningful and as worthy of respect as their own. Other goals of this type of instruction are to give learners the skills, attitudes, and concepts for cross-cultural competency and to reduce discrimination caused by the lack of communication and understanding between and among groups.

Following the seminal work of Atwell in *In the Middle* (1987), language arts teachers at West Windsor Plainsboro Middle School use a student-centered workshop approach. Adopting and adapting Atwell's strategies, they utilize such techniques as mini-lessons, group sharing, conferencing with oneself and others, editing conferences, and student-to-student and student-to-teacher dialogue journals. The assumptions about literacy and literacy experiences that underlie these techniques and this approach include providing opportunities for learners to read, discuss, and write about a variety of literary selections; to generate meanings based on their own prior experience and reading; and to learn about literary texts and how writers create meaning through texts. Reading and writing are taught and learned as complementary skills and processes.

Multicultural educational experiences involve providing individual and group opportunities to help learners understand multiple aspects of the Chinese culture, including literature, art, music, and societal symbols and characteristics. Students read in translation the short story "The Story of Miss Li" by Po Hsing-Chien. It tells of a young nobleman's love for a woman of lesser status who tricks him into giving her all of his money. According to Confucian tradition and teaching, when the young man disobeyed his father to be with this woman, he broke the sacred bond of fidelity to his father. The young man is afraid to return to his father and becomes a vagrant. Years later Miss Li sees him, takes him in, and nurses him back to health. When the young man's father hears of her noble actions, he acknowledges and embraces them both. This story is analyzed as a way to focus on similarities in Chinese and American cultures. While reading, students identify in writing the many different human relations and instances of romance in the story. During discussion guided by the teacher, they are challenged to consider the universal human emotions portrayed in "The Story of Miss Li." Then they consider this story as representative of a work written originally in Chinese and then translated.

This examination of the role of the translator leads to the studying of translated Chinese poetry to gain an understanding and appreciation of the Chinese culture. Using sources such as *Sunflower Splendor: Three Thousand Years of Chinese Poetry*, *The Poems of Mao Tse-Tung*, and

The Open Boat: Poems from Asian America, the teacher selects samples of poems that are developmentally appropriate to seventh and eighth graders. Then the learners are challenged through such activities as reading Nellie Wong's poem "How a Girl Got Her Chinese Name," which explains how Nellie's American teacher anglicized her Chinese name of Nah Lei (Where or Which Place) and subsequently her parents gave her a different Chinese name—Lai Oy (Beautiful Love). They write their own poem based on a clash between their personal, family, or cultural heritage and today's society. Students also read a teacher-prepared packet of Chinese poetry, write about a specific poem that "speaks" to them personally, and compare with a peer partner various translations of the same poem.

Using a reading/writing workshop approach, they read and analyze the classic novel *The Good Earth* and the young adult novels *Forbidden City* and *Dragonwings.* Objectives for the student letters, journal responses, and literary circle discussions are to understand the characteristics of the Chinese family structure in the different historical periods depicted in these books, to examine how family relationships reflect the political conditions of each time, and to understand the values and beliefs embedded in the family structure depicted in this literature. Many middle-level students find *The Good Earth,* the classic story of the deterioration of the love and life of Wang Lung and O-Lan, a difficult read. Yet they are able to write insightful comments individually and in cooperative groups when asked to explain the irony of the title of the novel and list the human relations that exist in the novel. Students categorize these relationships according to the five Confucian relationships and discuss whether or not they think these characters are living up to the Confucian and societal expectations for behavior. The young adult novels *Forbidden City* and *Dragonwings* are easily understood by middle-level students. *Forbidden City* is the thrilling and suspenseful tale of a Canadian father and seventeen-year-old son who witness the idealism and harshness of the Tian An Men Square uprising of 1989. Students can be asked to comment upon the many meanings of the book's title. They also like to discuss how Alex's perceptions of food, culture, and events are colored by his own background. *Dragonwings,* which is very accessible for basic skills and remedial readers, tells of Moon Shadow's coming from China to San Francisco in 1903 to live with his father, whom he has never met. It provides historically accurate insight into the Chinese American community of that time and into the San Francisco earthquake. This book can be used with learners who are recent immigrants to help them realize the universalities of their own personal experience. Also, based on Windrider's dream, students construct kites of their own design. An annotated bibliography of materials is available in our middle school media center for both teacher and students to learn more about China, Chinese, and Chinese Americans. This listing includes sources on religion, foods and arts, tales old and new, social life and customs, science, reference, history and geography, and novels. Nonprint materials as well as magazines are also listed.

The concept of interdisciplinary curriculum as an organizational structure that emphasizes student concerns and elicits facts, topics, and strategies from different subjects is considered important at West Windsor Plainsboro Middle School. Interdisciplinary instruction is teaching so that learners see and internalize the logical relationships of similar concepts, skills, and attitudes that exist across traditionally discrete subject areas. Interdisciplinary experiences involve communication and coordination between language arts and social studies teachers to identify relevant skills, knowledge, and concepts. A plan entitled "The Chinese Family: A Historical Perspective" requires learners to work in small groups to develop family life simulations based upon social status and a period of history selected from a matrix. This matrix is a time line of dynasties and significant events and concepts during each dynasty's time period. For example, the Yang Dynasty, which lasted from 1279 through 1368, is described by these sentences: "Mongols conquer China. Drama flourishes. Peking Opera becomes popular. Marco Polo visits China." Using a historical workshop approach that involves the selection of a specific dynasty and the development of essential questions, students' research and studies lead to presentations on a typical family life through dramatization, a family album, an exchange of letters among family members, or some similar product. Language arts competency for the one-act plays is judged by considering how well learners use dialogue, develop characterization, demonstrate content knowledge, and present clear and logically developed ideas. A play-writing chart that requires participants to identify the setting, characters, conflict or problem, and the plot before they begin to write is provided by the language arts teacher.

Viewing and analyzing films on China is another effective and enjoyable interdisciplinary way for middle-level learners to enhance their understanding of Chinese culture. Appropriate films include the following: *The Good Earth,* a black-and-white film that closely follows the book as the story of a peasant family fighting hardship and famine; *My Favorite Concubine,* a film with many parts that are not suitable for middle-school students, but selected clips appropriately show the role of the Chinese theater in appreciating Chinese culture and art; *Yellow Earth,* a film in Chinese that presents learners with the scenic beauty of China and challenges them to understand plot through actions and characterization; and *The Story of Qui Ju,* a 100-minute film that is rated PG and portrays the story of a woman's quest for justice in modern-day China. Assignments based on these films require learners to integrate their knowledge of Chinese culture and to extend knowledge of local government and the justice system in China. They work cooperatively to explain what they had learned from these films about the court system in China, the one-child policy and its acceptance, the differences between rural and urban life in contemporary China, and the role of the extended family. Students prepare written reports and present them to their classmates. Learners rewrite the ending of a film and explain to their peers the advantages and disadvantages of their new ending.

Interdisciplinary teaching and learning about China, Chinese culture, and Chinese Americans can be expanded into the curricula of mathematics and science also. Students can learn to use an abacas to compute and then compare its speed of calculation and accuracy of results with speed and results from pencil and paper computation and from the use of calculators. Science connections can be made by considering the Chinese art of acupuncture and its relation to anatomy.

The inclusion into middle-level language arts curriculum of multicultural resources, such as translations and young adult literature, challenges teachers to be reflective and introspective about their own learning and teaching. Effective multicultural education should help students understand the totality of a culture and develop decision-making and social skills. At West Windsor Plainsboro Middle School, particular attention is given to the studying of China, Chinese, and Chinese Americans as a way to help all learners relate to and appreciate the cultures of their own and their classmates' ancestors.

References

Atwell, Nancie. 1987. *In the Middle: Writing, Reading, and Learning with Adolescents.* Portsmouth, NH: Heinemann.

Barnstone, Willis K., and Ko Ching-Po, eds. 1972. *The Poems of Mao Tse-Tung.* New York: Harper & Row.

Bell, William. 1990. *Forbidden City.* New York: Doubleday.

Buck, Pearl. 1965. *The Good Earth.* New York: Harper & Row.

Hongo, G. ed. 1985. *The Open Boat: Poems from Asian America.* New York: Anchor.

Hsing-chien, P. 1998. "The Story of Miss Li." *Anthology of Chinese Literature, Vol. 1: From Early Times to the Fourteenth Century.* Ed. Cyril Birch. New York: Grove Press.

Liu, Wu-chi, and Irving Lo, eds. 1975. *Sunflower Splendor: Three Thousand Years of Chinese Poetry.* Bloomington: Indiana University Press.

Yep, Laurence. 1975. *Dragonwings.* New York: HarperCollins.

20 Dramatic Encounters: Experiencing Multicultural Literature

Jeffrey D. Wilhelm
University of Maine

Filling the Spaces between People

"Drama is about filling the spaces between people with meaningful [emotional] experiences. . . . Out of these we can build reflective processes" (Heathcote 1984, 97).

Imaginative literary experiences can provide students with a unique and powerful way of knowing about people, cultures, and situations very distant from them in background, time, and place. The same is true, in a more immediate and physical way, of story-based drama activities, which can provide deeply felt, personally lived experiences. The compelling nature of drama, like that of literature, is this very potential it holds for students to engage in a "lived through experience" (Heathcote 1984).

This "living through" is not something students will necessarily do as they read, especially if the topic of their reading is distant to them in time, space, or personal experience. They may have problems activating their background knowledge; personally connecting to the story and the experiences of characters; and comprehending the rich action, feelings, conflicts, values, and meanings implicit in the story. Drama, however, can be integrated with challenging reading experiences, such as those about different cultures. Dramatic activity provides a particularly effective bridge to difficult-to-access meanings because students can physically and emotionally experience—both as themselves and as the Other they read about—the situation and consequences of another time, place, and cultural situation.

My own students were helped greatly by drama as they pursued personal inquiry projects related to the study of culture and to the study of civil rights. Throughout these units, their inquiry was pursued in large part through the reading of multicultural literature.

Through dramas based on their reading, they were helped to recognize their commonalities and differences with people from these different cultural situations. They were helped to fully evoke the world of story and to personally experience what had happened to others. Because of these intense experiences, they were able to reflect and consider their reading experiences as part of their inquiries. Through drama, they not only learned important information but added an ethical, humane, and personal dimension to their understanding. They achieved new understanding and became something new themselves in the process.

Cecily O'Neill (1995) has written often and convincingly of this "liminal quality" of drama. Liminality defines a time and space "betwixt and between" one context of meaning and action and another. O'Neill writes that during drama work, students are "literally on the threshold (the *limen* in Latin). . . . [They] are neither what they have been or what they will be. They are caught up in a process of separation, transition, and transformation" (p. 66). In the liminal state, people "play" with the familiar to defamiliarize it, and "play" with the unfamiliar to make it part of their experience.

My friend Brian Edmiston (1993) argues that when readers talk or write about stories, they are always outside the world of story and are not helped to directly experience it. In drama, however, readers must go "inside" the story as they adopt the perspectives of characters, empathize with them, critique them, and try to understand them. Without this kind of engagement, the drama cannot be created and sustained. This is certainly what we found when Brian joined me last year to help infuse drama into my integrated studies classroom. Heathcote (1984) uses the phrase "now and imminent time" to describe the feeling students have during dramas that the experience is happening now rather than in the past. All three of these researchers have documented how drama helps readers to feel they are in the middle of events that really concern them because, during a drama, people are imaginatively in the same world as the world of the story.

All this is why drama is a powerful way to experience and explore multicultural literature; it helps us to use that literature to journey toward new understandings about other people.

Integrating Drama and Reading Multicultural Literature

As a middle school teacher, I worked very closely with my social studies partner, Paul Friedemann. We were striving, over the course of several years, to co-construct an inquiry-based integrated curriculum that infused the use of storytelling, story reading, drama, and art through all of our work. During our projects we welcomed other adults and educators into our classrooms, and one of our favorite visitors and friends was the drama educator Brian Edmiston. So powerful were our experiences with Brian that during this past school year he agreed to work with us on a regular basis.

It was an exciting time. Blending the reading of multicultural stories with drama activities that asked students to observe and appreciate other cultures, to enter into the experiences of people from those cultural groups, and to manipulate those situations to explore possibilities for change proved to be a powerful combination. This combination enlivened the students' reading and enlightened their thinking.

As students in American schools become increasingly diverse, the use of multicultural literature in classrooms becomes increasingly important not only for the students from different cultural groups, who can express pride as they contribute to their classmates' understanding of their heritage, but for all of our students. A primary justification for the use of multicultural literature is that it helps all students to experience and understand different cultural backgrounds and perspectives, which can positively inform how they live and interact in an increasingly pluralistic society (e.g., Yokota 1993). We found that using drama with the reading of multicultural literature can support the constructing of such understanding.

What follows is a story of how multicultural literature and story-based drama activities were blended into a semester of integrated social studies and language arts units. During this semester we pursued two extended units: one was a cultural journalism unit and the second was a unit on civil rights and citizenship. Both units culminated with a documentary project, during which students asked and pursued the answers to their own research questions.

One hundred twenty-five seventh-grade students were involved in these units. They made up a middle school "house" that included all of the school's EEN (exceptional educational needs) labeled population at this grade level. These students, labeled ED (emotionally disturbed) and LD (learning disabled), numbered seventeen. The school itself serves a midsized midwestern town and a large outlying rural area. The population of the school is approximately 80 percent white, with small but growing populations of East Asian, Hmong, Chicano, and Eastern European immigrants.

The Cultural Journalism Unit

During the first unit, groups of students worked collaboratively to build background knowledge about different cultural groups that are part of the great mosaic of American culture. After some introductory activities to help them explore the "culture" of our own town, school, and peer groups, students developed research questions about a particular cultural group and pursued these questions through reading of primary and secondary sources, fiction and nonfiction; interviewing cultural informants; conducting electronic searches; viewing videos; listening to music; studying art and artifacts; preparing and eating traditional foods; and much more. Finally, they created hypermedia documents to represent their new understandings to their classmates and a community audience including parents, elementary school learning buddies, and the local senior citizen center. The completed projects were shared publicly during a learning fair held at the school.

To begin their work, learning groups read folktales, poetry, songs, and other traditional materials from the culture they had chosen. Once research questions had been decided upon, a more focused reading agenda was pursued by the group and its individual members.

One group of five boys chose to study African American culture. After several revisions, Troy, Anthony, Joe, Tom, and Stan agreed on their question: "What did African Americans do to survive in the face of injustices, from slavery times to the present?"

This group pursued shared readings of several books, using the paired reading (Copperman 1986) and literature circle (Daniels 1994) techniques. This list included Julius Lester's *The Last Tales of Uncle Remus,* Virginia Hamilton's *The People Could Fly,* Patricia McKissack's *Christmas in the Big House, Christmas in the Quarters,* and Mildred Taylor's *Roll of Thunder, Hear My Cry.* In addition, individual members of the group read other books independently and shared their reading with other members during book club meetings. Walter Dean Myers's *The Mouse Rap,* Julius Lester's *To Be a Slave,* and Patricia McKissack's *The Dark Thirty* were read, as were poems and spirituals from collections like *Lift Every Voice and Sing, Pass it On, The Dream Keeper and Other Poems,* and Ashley Bryan's collection *All Day, All Night: A Child's First Book of African-American Spirituals.*

The boys shared their readings and understandings with other classmates through the use of tableau drama and symbolic story representations. In tableau drama, students freeze their bodies into a picture of a particular scene. They can do this after a short role-play in which students act out a scene and then freeze a snapshot of its climax. Other possibilities include displaying a variety of scenes to narration, much like a slide show, and having the narrator tap individuals in the frozen scene who then "come to life" to report on their views and feelings or to be interviewed by the class.

This group used tableau drama to show how slaves created a community of implicit resistance with their secret meetings and covert acts of resistance as recorded in *To Be A Slave.* They also enacted scenes from *Roll of Thunder, Hear My Cry* about the Logans, a family of color trying to save their farm and maintain their considerable dignity in the face of the Depression, mortgage foreclosures, Klan night riders, burnings, and other acts of overt racism. The boys' drama work showed the Logans using the notion of family as a place where they were all safe and supported, and using their brains and creativity against the physical intimidation of Mr. Simms, Mr. Granger, and the night riders. They would act out short scenes (such as Cassie Logan's humiliation at the hands of the Simmses and her later revenge on Lillian Jean Simms), freeze at a climactic moment, and then provide a caption or commentary for the frozen photo or "tableau."

After this latter scene with Lillian Jean, Troy provided the caption: "Cassie whales on Lillian Jean and finally gets her revenge! But she has to make sure no one will ever find out so the family won't be hurt. So she's holding Lillian Jean's secrets over her!" In this tableau the group showed their understanding that the family's safety was more important than individual acts of revenge. It also demonstrated, as the group articulated, that the family's acts of resistance "had to be really smart, really tricky." They couldn't rely on "brute strength or anything, because then they would just get crushed. The whites were stronger . . . so they had to use their smarts."

The group made use of symbolic story representations (SSR) (cf. Enciso, 1992) as they chose different traditional tales to present to each other. (For more information about this technique, see Wilhelm 1996a and 1996b.) When using SSR they found or created cutouts that symbolically represented important characters, objects, settings, cultural values or ideas, and a moral or central focus of the story. They also created a cutout of themselves as reader. The cutouts were then used to both dramatize the story and their reading of the story. The reader cutout was used to show where they were in the story; who they connected to; and what they were thinking, feeling, noticing, and doing as they read. At some point in the story, they reported on the central focus or meaning of the story and tried to provide at least a tentative answer why this story was of importance to the culture that preserved and told it.

Interestingly, during his SSR performance, Tom reported that Anansi (the spider of a West African folktale) was "a lot like the Logans [from *Roll of Thunder*]—tricky and smart. He tells stories to remember the past so he'll know how to deal with new situations. That's what this story means: learn from experience . . . be careful and smart and you can outsmart people who are trying to hurt you." To represent this central focus, Tom created a thought bubble which he attached to the spider cutout that represented Anansi.

The dramas throughout this first unit seemed to help students to take on the roles of ethnographers, participant-observers of the culture who studied stories as artifacts to look for and explain significant patterns of behavior.

Civil Rights and Citizenship Unit

The civil rights and citizenship unit began with a process drama that Brian Edmiston conceived and he and I created with students, called "The Space Traders Drama." The drama work was based on the story "The Space Traders" from Derek Bell's (1992) collection *Faces at the Bottom of the Well*, and it was designed to help students experience and examine issues of prejudice and civil rights.

In process drama, students create their own unscripted dramas. In this case the students actively and collaboratively thought through the story and its implications as they made, shaped, and appreciated a dramatic event suggested by the text. Process dramas do not reenact story events, but create events on the "edges of text" that fill textual gaps, follow story possiblities, explain story events, and follow student interests.

To begin the drama, we told students that the United States was suffering a grave financial crisis, and we asked them, as a group of senators, to brainstorm what kinds of things the government spent money on. A list was compiled on the chalkboard, and the senators classified the items on the list into general categories, such as the military, welfare, education, parks, public services, and prisons. Committees were then formed and asked to rank the areas of expenditure in terms of importance and to compose a proposal for eliminating the least valuable budget item. After proposals were made and debated, in three of my classes the senators decided to eliminate welfare, and in another two classes they decided to eliminate the prison system.

When it was decided to cut welfare in his class, Tom justified his vote by explaining, "They're lazy" and Joe by "They should get a job."

Tom explained in his drama diary that "It's not our responsibility to help people who won't help themselves. As a senator I have to protect the hard-working people of this country and teach the lazy ones a lesson."

At this point, the Space Trader, played by Brian Edmiston, entered the drama, offering gold, chemicals to clean the environment, and knowledge to solve all of the country's problems—in exchange for the least valued members of society. This was exactly what happened in Bell's story, except that the Space Trader offered his riches in exchange for all Americans of African descent. In this class the least valued members of society were the welfare recipients, designated as such by the senate. When asked by a "senator" what the aliens would do with the welfare recipients, the Space Trader told them, "It is none of your concern."

At this point the Space Trader story had acted as a "pre-text" for the story that we now created together dramatically. What we pursued from this point was spontaneous, and operated on the "edges of text" because we did not follow the story any longer, but explored the logic of it in our own "drama world." As we did so, we explored issues of civil rights and social justice.

The students, in their roles as senators, now debated whether to accept the Space Trader's offer, and "voted with their feet" to form a continuum of opinions from those who were completely for accepting the offer to those who were completely against it. Most of the students voted for accepting the offer. Anthony, when asked by a radio interviewer about the possible fates of the welfare people at the hands of the Space Traders, replied that "It doesn't matter if they die; they're worthless anyway." Tom offered that "If they had a job and worked like they're supposed to, then they wouldn't have to go with them [the Space Traders]."

Over the next few days of the drama, students took on a variety of other roles. First, they became the welfare recipients, imagining step by step how they came to be on welfare, why they couldn't find a job, how they were treated, and how they felt about their situation. They were taken to a detention center to await deportation with the aliens. They wrote letters to the "Senate" and to their families and friends, describing their feelings and thoughts. They then embarked on their journey into outer space and imagined the best and worst that could happen to them by using the tableau drama technique. On the last day of the drama, they once again became senators, debating again whether the welfare recipients should be sent to outer space. This time the classes decided—almost unanimously—not to accept the offer.

Anthony said that "I've changed my mind. You can't decide for other people. Even if we need the money we can't make them go—they're people too." Jenny, a girl from the boys' class, wrote that "At first, I thought that the aliens could take our prisoners or the welfare people because we didn't need them. Then after I thought about it I kind of changed my mind. You can't put a price on a person's life. It was very prejudiced for me to do that. Maybe it was a mistake and they regret it and then it would be too late for them. Maybe they couldn't help not getting a job. We were all being too selfish and too quick to decide."

The drama here and the ones that followed in this unit allowed the students to engage in phenomenological research. The phenomenologist enters into and participates in the experience of people in different situations; in this case the students lived the lives of those who suffered from prejudice and a lack of guaranteed rights. A discussion of fundamental human rights, and how these are different from earned privileges, was pursued and student groups composed manifestos of rights all people should enjoy.

Drama to Pursue Understanding

After pursuing some shared readings, the students had the chance to form new groups and choose a research question about a topic regarding civil rights here in America. Their findings were to be represented in a video documentary to be presented to the class at the end of the school year.

Though many of the student groups reformed and chose to pursue topics like gun control or the history of women's rights—topics that did not have to do with particular cultural groups—many students chose to study a civil rights topic that was important to the group they had previously studied, for example, the Japanese internment camps during World War II. This was true of our five boys, who grouped together again and decided to pursue research on the breaking of the color lines in professional baseball.

As in the previous unit, students moved from shared whole-class readings to shared small-group readings to individual readings. Their drama work was based on the readings they completed in their group and was based on and made use of the information (stories, pictures, graphs, maps) they had collected as a group and as individuals.

The group read *Teammates* by Peter Golenbock and *Grandma's Baseball* by Curtis Gavin. *Teammates* is the story of how Pee Wee Reese stood up for the stoic Jackie Robinson, who was enduring racist slurs from fans and players alike. *Grandma's Baseball* regards a grandfather who played in the Negro Baseball League before integration of the major leagues. Three of the boys read *Black Diamond,* by the McKissacks, a nonfiction book packed with photographs. Two of the boys read Walter Dean Myers's *Mop, Moondance and the Nagasaki Knights,* and Joe read *Stealing Home* by Mary Stolz. Tom and Stan convinced the group to do their research on Hank Aaron as they read various biographies of this baseball great. Their original research question was "Who is Hank Aaron?"

The group vigorously pursued their research and wrote first drafts of their video scripts. At this point the group expressed dissatisfaction with their scripts ("Boring!"), their question, and how they were framing and understanding their topic. The group quickly changed their question to "How did Hank Aaron get so good at baseball?" But they soon recognized that their scripts were basically reports listing facts (e.g., he and his brother would hit bottle caps with broom handles, toss burning rags back and forth, cut school to play baseball, watch Negro League games).

Using process drama, the students created unscripted meaning as they worked within the provided drama frame. In the dramas, Brian Edmiston and I extended the students' thinking by asking them to enter into the experience of being a black ballplayer. What was it like in the Negro League? What were the costs and benefits of leaving the Negro League for the majors? What was Aaron's experience as a black ballplayer in a profession dominated by whites? How did the hate mail the boys had read about affect Hank and his family? In order to answer these questions, the students played the parts of sportswriters, Negro League teammates, white minor league and major league teammates, baseball fans, Hank, his family, and people who would write hate mail.

In one scene, Hank—played by Tom—decided that he did not want to put up with the racism he suffered in the major leagues. He was interviewed by Brian Edmiston, playing a sportscaster, who asked "How do you want to be remembered? How will this decision affect how you will be remembered?" Hank then went to visit his Negro League teammates, who advised him to "grit it out, so the rest of us might get a chance [to play in the Majors]" and "you can't give them the satisfaction of thinking they chased you out." In another scene, played out as Hank neared Babe Ruth's home run record, the family opened hate mail that included death threats and discussed whether Hank should go to the ball park that night.

During and after the drama, the boys negotiated a series of new research questions designed to get at "what it was like for him," as Anthony put it. They asked "how did his life change when he went to the majors?" and "how did his life change when he broke the home run record?" Because they wanted to include all of the important changes Hank endured, they eventually settled on this research question: "What did Hank Aaron have to do off the ballfield to become great?"

These dramas helped the students to apply what they had discovered to their own lives, to make judgments and critical evaluations, and to begin thinking about how individuals and groups might intervene and change situations. As such, the dramas became a form of both phenomenological and action research, in which they experienced situations from their reading and cast about for actions that would improve the situation they found themselves in. Stan spoke on several occasions about how white players like Pee Wee Reese (who stood up to racism) and players of color like Jackie Robinson and Hank Aaron had changed history through their courage. "I was surprised by what I found out. I thought he [Aaron] would be a national hero—he is to some, but not to everybody—because he's black and *that's it* and that's the only reason. I don't think that's fair." Asked how one could help change prejudicial attitudes, Stan said, "You have to stand up and speak your mind. You have to be fair yourself." He also explained that doing dramas and making videos "could help people see better."

Anthony, demonstrating how his group realized the importance of Hank's inner experiences, explained that "we realized that the most important things he had to put up with and get over were things like fighting through prejudice. If he couldn't do that then he could never be a great ballplayer. He did both and that's why he's great." Tom said the following: "The dramas made me realize that the research question about what he had to do was . . . well we kind of thought we knew. I kind of thought it just had to do with practice, but now I see it had to do with being black and being great at baseball. It was overcoming prejudice and discrimination. [The library work and reading] was easy, the dramas and like . . . understanding [the inner experience of Hank] well . . . that's what was really hard."

Multicultural Readings and Drama

Blending the reading of multicultural literature with drama activities that asked students to observe and appreciate other cultures, to enter into the experiences of people from those cultural groups, and to manipulate those situations to explore possibilities for change proved to be a powerful combination that enlivened the students' reading and enlightened their thinking.

Tom, who after initially resisting drama work became quite a spokesman for it, had this to say: "School is about facts—mostly boring facts; drama is about making facts exciting because you add the feelings. . . . Drama takes facts and asks how they might have been different or how the facts might affect you or someone else and how all that would feel. That's why I like drama." And that is why drama is an invaluable technique for those who teach to help students gain an understanding of their world and the people who inhabit it.

Acknowledgment

The author wishes to acknowledge the contributions of Paul Friedemann in team-teaching the described units, and Brian Edmiston for conceiving and helping to implement much of the drama work that is detailed here.

References

Bell, Derrick. 1992. *Faces at the Bottom of the Well: The Permanence of Racism.* New York: Basic Books.

Bryan, Ashley, illus. 1991. *All Night, All Day: A Child's First Book of African-American Spirituals.* New York: Atheneum.

Copperman, Paul. 1986. *Taking Books to Heart: How to Develop a Love of Reading in Your Child.* Reading, MA: Addison-Wesley.

Daniels, Harvey. 1994. *Literature Circles: Voice and Choice in the Student-Centered Classroom.* York, ME: Stenhouse.

Edmiston, Brian. 1993. "Going Up the Beanstalk: Discovering Giant Possibilities for Responding to Literature Through Drama." *Journeying: Children Responding to Literature.* Eds. K. Holland, R. Hungerford, and S. Ernst. Portsmouth, NH: Heinemann.

Enciso, P. 1992. "Creating the Storyworld: A Case Study of Young Readers' Engagement Strategies and Stances." *Readerstance and Literary Understanding: Exploring the Theories, Research, and Practice.* Eds. J. Many and C. Cox. Norwood, NJ: Ablex Publishing Co.

Gavin, C. 1990. *Grandma's Baseball.* New York: Crown.

Golenbock, Peter. 1990. *Teammates.* San Diego: Harcourt Brace

Lester, Julius. 1968. *To Be A Slave.* New York: Dial.

———. 1994. *The Last Tales of Uncle Remus.* New York: Dial.

Hamilton, Virginia. 1993. *The People Could Fly: American Black Folktales.* New York: Knopf.

Heathcote, Dorothy. 1984. *Dorothy Heathcote: Collected Writings on Education and Drama.* Eds. L. Johnson and C. O'Neill. Portsmouth, NH: Heinemann.

Hoose, Phillip. 1993. *It's Our World Too!* New York: Little, Brown.

Hughes, Langston. 1994. *The Dream Keeper, and Other Poems.* New York: Knopf.

McKissack, Patricia. 1992. *The Dark Thirty: Southern Tales of the Supernatural.* New York: Knopf/Borzoi Books.

———.1994. *Christmas in the Big House, Christmas in the Quarters.* New York: Scholastic.

McKissack, Patricia, and Frederick McKissack, Jr. 1994. *Black Diamond: The Story of the Negro Baseball Leagues.* New York: Scholastic.

Myers, Walter D. 1990. *The Mouse Rap.* New York: HarperCollins.

———. 1995. *Mop, Moondance and the Nagasaki Knights.* Boston: Houghton Mifflin.

O'Neill, Cecily. 1995. *Drama Worlds: A Framework for Process Drama.* Portsmouth, NH: Heinemann.

Stolz, Mary. 1992. *Stealing Home.* New York: HarperCollins.

Taylor, Mildred. 1976, 1997. *Roll of Thunder, Hear My Cry.* New York: Viking Penguin.

Wilhelm, Jeffrey. 1996. *Standards in Practice: Grades 6–8.* Urbana, IL: NCTE.

———. 1997. *You Gotta Be the Book: Teaching Engaged and Reflective Reading with Adolescents.* New York: Teachers College Press and NCTE.

Yokota, J. 1993. "Issues in Selecting Multicultural Children's Literature." *Language Arts* 70.3: 156–167.

21 Science and English: Connecting with Multicultural Young Adult Literature

Amy Hackett
Mott Middle College High School
Flint, MI

As teachers in a high school with a large at-risk student population and located on a community college campus, my colleagues and I are involved in helping our students get a "fresh start" and experience success in their personal and academic lives. One of the ways we do this is through team teaching in interdisciplinary courses. As a science teacher, I have been fortunate to team with an English teacher for the last two years in a course we call "Earth and Space." We integrate specific scientific topics and concepts by reading related fiction, nonfiction, and poetry. For example, when we are learning about space, we read Gore Vidal's play *Visitor from a Small Planet.* Based upon the scientific concepts they are studying and the play, the students imagine that they are visitors from another planet who have come to Earth. They then write letters back to their leader describing life on Earth. Another example occurs during the unit on ecology when we provide students with an article to read and respond to about the plight of cougars in California as their habitats are being destroyed. We found that these integrated science and English experiences provide our students with opportunities to respond creatively and criticially in subject areas that many of them have previously considered dull and boring. We also discovered that our students are more involved and more successful when we use this approach.

Based upon these experiences, I decided that I want to find even more ways of integrating science and English. Reflecting upon the demographics of my student population, I decided to become familiar with multicultural young adult literature that could be related to various topics in science. As I read, I created the following Idea Bank. This

Idea Bank is designed to identify books that have elements that can be discussed in conjunction with various units in a science class. For example, we have used *The Plague* by Jean Ure to discuss the spread of diseases. We examine epidemics and the students apply their scientific knowledge to judge the realism of the book.

Idea Bank: Bridging Science and Multicultural Literature

General Science

For students who do not like science or who have a history of failure in science courses, books such as the following ones help them to see the real-life applications of this study and its importance in people's lives. For example, *Standing Tall* includes biographical sketches of Hispanic scientists.

Curtis, Christopher Paul. 1997. *The Watsons Go to Birmingham—1963.* New York: Bantam Doubleday Dell.

Levitin, Sonia. 1987. *The Return.* New York: Atheneum.

Naidoo, Beverly. 1990. *Chain of Fire.* New York: HarperCollins.

Palacios, Argentina. 1994. *Standing Tall: The Stories of Ten Hispanic Americans.* New York: Scholastic.

Paulsen, Gary. 1985. *Dogsong.* New York: Simon & Schuster.

Pitts, Paul. 1994. *Crossroads.* New York: Avon.

Schami, Rafik. 1992. *A Hand Full of Stars.* New York: Puffin.

Taylor, Mildred. 1990. *Mississippi Bridge.* New York: Dial.

Health and Health-Related Issues

The study of health and health-related issues may be one of the most important and immediately practical aspects of the curriculum for adolescents. Too often, however, this study is greeted with yawns and a lack of concern. The following list of books helps to personalize information and issues and provides students with a way of making connections with their own lives. For example, *It Happened to Nancy* is a sensitive first-person account of a young woman with AIDS. Her age and experiences provide high school students with a chilling awareness that AIDS can happen to anyone.

Anonymous. 1994. *It Happened to Nancy: A True Story from the Diary of a Teenager.* Ed. Beatrice Sparks. New York: Avon Flare.

Castaneda, Omar S. 1993. *Among the Volcanoes.* New York: Dell.

Crutcher, Chris. 1987. *The Crazy Horse Electric Game.* New York: Bantam Doubleday Dell Books for Young Readers.

———. 1993. *Staying Fat for Sarah Byrnes.* New York: Bantam Doubleday Dell Books for Young Readers.

Kent, Deborah. 1992. *Why Me?* New York: Scholastic.

Naidoo, Beverly. 1984. *Journey to Jo'Burg: A South African Story.* New York: HarperCollins.

Namioka, Lensey. 1994. *April and the Dragon Lady.* San Diego: Harcourt Brace.

Nixon, Joan Lowery. 1994. *Land of Promise.* New York: Dell.

Paulsen, Gary. 1990. *The Crossing.* New York: Bantam Doubleday Dell Books for Young Readers.

Robert, Willo Davis. 1988. *Sugar Isn't Everything: A Support Book, in Fiction Form, for the Young Diabetic.* New York: Simon & Schuster.

Soto, Gary. 1994. *Jesse.* San Diego: Harcourt Brace.

Temple, Frances. 1992. *Taste of Salt: A Story of Modern Haiti.* New York: Orchard.

Ure, Jean. 1993. *Plague.* New York: Puffin.

Williams-Garcia, Rita. 1995. *Like Sisters on the Homefront.* New York: Dutton.

Wolff, Virginia Euwer. 1994. *Make Lemonade.* New York: Scholastic.

Woodson, Jacqueline. 1994. *I Hadn't Meant to Tell You This.* New York: Delacorte.

Plant Life

In each of the following books, the importance of vegetation to the character's survival is dramatically demonstrated.

Castaneda, Omar S. 1993. *Among the Volcanoes.* New York: Dell.

Hobbs, Will. 1989. *Bearstone.* New York: Simon & Schuster.

Pitts, Paul. 1988. *Racing the Sun.* New York: Avon.

Earth Science and Ecology

Among the many applications in earth science and ecology are those that involve the water cycle. Several of the books in the following list incorporate water as an integral part of the setting. For example, the ocean in *Blue Skin of the Sea,* the rapids in *Downriver,* the swamps in *Which Way Freedom?*, and the flooding in *Plain City* provide students with opportunities to examine the role and importance of water in everyday life. Through the use of this literature, students are able to go beyond mere facts and figures to gain an understanding of the importance of the preservation and protection of the earth and the implications of its misuse in people's lives.

Curtis, Christopher Paul. 1997. *The Watsons Go to Birmingham—1963.* New York: Bantam Doubleday Dell.

Hamilton, Virginia. 1993. *Plain City.* New York: Scholastic.

Hansen, Joyce. 1992. *Which Way Freedom?* New York: Avon Camelot.

Hobbs, Will. 1989. *Bearstone.* New York. Simon & Schuster.

———. 1991. *Downriver.* New York: Atheneum.

Hughes, Monica. 1993. *The Crystal Drop.* New York: Simon & Schuster Books for Young Readers.

Levine, Ellen. 1995. *A Fence Away from Freedom.* New York: Putnam.

Namioka, Lensey. 1994. *April and the Dragon Lady.* San Diego: Harcourt Brace.

Nixon, Joan Lowery. 1993. *Land of Hope.* New York: Dell.

Paulsen, Gary. 1985. *Dogsong.* New York: Simon & Schuster.

Salisbury, Graham. 1997. *Blue Skin of the Sea.* New York: Bantam Doubleday Dell Books for Young Readers.

Staples, Suzanne Fisher. 1995. *Haveli.* New York: Random House.

22 Multicultural Literature and Mathematical Connections: Bridges to Span Mathematical Understanding in a Diverse World

David K. Pugalee
University of North Carolina at Charlotte

Reading provides a means by which young adults make sense of their own world. It is an experience which sets a stage for the reader to explore their own feelings and beliefs as well as those of the characters. It is this vibrant interaction between different emotional planes which makes printed material one of the most powerful communicative media. Teachers have many opportunities to promote this type of reading, which maximizes this powerful potential while building on the students' present literacy skills. One such opportunity can be constructed by building links between literature and other subjects. These connections between literature and other disciplines create a unique window for meaningful inquiry.

Such connections are being forged in current efforts to reform the mathematics curriculum. Elementary schools have long recognized the importance of such connections and have developed books, sometimes referred to as "trade books," which make mathematical connections through ingenious and entertaining stories and illustrations. These resources serve an important function in instilling an excitement about reading while creating enthusiasm about mathematics by investigating the subject via interesting contexts. One of the goals of these efforts should be to infuse the student with the skills necessary to contemplate the mathematics which they might encounter in their own reading as they grow older.

In a broader context, making mathematical connections to our larger world through literature entails the development of a sense of appreciation for the cultures and contributions of others. The complex nature of our social interactions stands as a reminder that we have failed to dispel stereotypes and build an understanding and appreciation of other cultures. The challenge for all of us is to make the most of opportunities for learning. In making mathematical connections, the use of literature with multicultural ideas can be utilized to accomplish goals of mathematics instruction while also providing occasions to learn about other cultures.

Approaches in Implementation

Once again, bear in mind that multiple approaches for inclusion of literature should be used so that it becomes part of the curriculum, a vital link in the learning process. Not every piece of literature can provide both the depth and breadth of content which clearly addresses all of the values and goals desired by the teacher. Yet, as each piece of literature is explored, the foundation builds for realization of these goals and values. The intent is to prevent conveying a fragmented approach to the use of multicultural literature in the classroom, particularly the mathematics class. Creativity becomes a driving force for the teacher as methods are explored and revised. The following paragraphs present some alternatives and experiences; however, these ideas should in no way be viewed as a comprehensive discussion of techniques for implementing multicultural literature in the mathematics classroom.

Extending Examples from Trade Books

Trade books are a good way for the beginning teacher to implement literature into a math class; however, the teacher will hopefully develop a comprehensive program which gives literature an important role in the classroom agenda. Some children's books have an appeal to young adult and even adult audiences. *Math Curse,* by John Scieszka and Lane Smith, has already become a popular seller, especially among adults. The character of the book is a girl who faces mathematics in every aspect of her life. It is a light and fun-filled production which can be used to spark interest and enthusiasm while also serving to dispel some of the stereotypes of the math whiz.

Although many of the examples found in *Math Curse* are explicitly stated, there are some gems which are hidden in the story. For example, the teacher, Mrs. Fibonacci, is named after a leading mathematician of the Middle Ages. This "name dropping" presents one opportunity to study numbers and sequences. Fibonacci numbers present a wide range of investigations at various levels of ability. Students find gratification in finding natural occurrences of Fibonacci numbers. Some examples include the spirals in sunflowers seeds, pinecones, and the petals in a flower. I have found the sequence a natural way to reinforce functions and discuss relationships between this sequence and Pascal's triangle or the golden ratio. Exploration with Fibonacci numbers is one activity which provides rich experiences for all grade levels.

Another experience occurs during lunch, in which there are pizzas cut into eight equal slices and apple pies cut into six equal slices: "And you know what that means: fractions." The experience is followed with some multiple-choice questions. The food idea continues with a challenge to "estimate how many M&Ms you would eat if you had to measure the Mississippi River with M&Ms." These examples demonstrate that the book is one of those rare productions which transcends the boundaries of age.

Such books can provide warm-up exercises or can serve as an extended class project. Imagine the research; conjecturing; planning; problem solving; and, yes, fun involved in an exercise such as the M&M problem in the foregoing paragraph. This book provides a lighthearted introduction to some of the difficult math themes that I and many other teachers have found to be important investigations from the middle grades through high school. Trade books provide quick and easy ways to establish a link between math and literature. In using trade books the teacher becomes a decision maker in determining the extent of related mathematical problems and projects.

Constructing Exercises from Informative Text

Many types of literature contain a wealth of information. Such types of reading are prime locations for finding examples which have mathematical relevance. Such texts, however, are much more constricting in that fewer individuals may find the information to be of personal interest. In such cases, teachers may select various types of assignments which are somewhat self-directed in nature. Students may be asked to write a report or summary which might be shared with the class or they may become involved in small-group explorations built around common interests.

There are many books which can supplement inquiries into the history of mathematics. An interesting diversion to the usual historical themes is to consider the role of mathematics in a particular aspect of one's life. An interesting and very informative book, though probably written for younger audiences, is *Celebrate: A Book of Jewish Holidays.* This book presents an easily comprehended synopsis of the meaning of each of the major Jewish holidays. Particularly striking is the extent to which numbers and geometry reinforce those beliefs—from three-cornered cookies of Purim to the round loaves of Rosh Hashanah, which symbolize the circularity of the year. Then there are lessons in proportions and measurement which are easily extended from stories of Jonah and the whale told as part of Yom Kippur. In another text, *Africa Counts,* students might explore the relationships of numbers and patterns in African culture. An activity which students find especially interesting is comparing and contrasting the time systems which emerge from these studies of different cultures.

A powerful activity which continues from these investigations is to have students write or discuss how cultures use geometry. I find that this is a wonderful way to get students to think about different shapes. "Why are igloos and teepees round?" is a nice follow-up question which I have used in order to direct the discussion. I follow up with a problem in which I give them a piece of string which I have cut to 48 units (the block on grid paper serves as the unit). I then ask them to figure out what shape gives the largest area. Many are surprised to learn that the circle provides the greatest area. Of course, there are some aerodynamic reasons for using round housing which might also emerge from discussions and literature. A nice companion piece is *The Village of Round and Square Houses* (Grifalconi 1987). Activities such as these provide a springboard for other math topics, including pi, rational numbers, number theory, and geometry. These types of activities allow students to develop a broader sense of community while also relating events to mathematics. The teacher can develop various types of activities and questions to supplement the investigation to meet specific content objectives which might be important. What is of great value is that students are learning and working together in discovering other cultures and developing important process skills which will help them investigate mathematics in future situations.

Using Excerpts and Passages to Structure Investigation

A teacher may encounter particular examples which make great mathematics lessons. In such cases a stage is set which will likely encourage students to explore the text on their own time. In any case, the activities will reinforce the goals for mathematics instruction while at the same time clarifying values from a multicultural perspective. This allows for the students to visualize connections of mathematics into other subjects and parts of their lives without putting excessive time demands on the teacher to have the class involved in reading an entire work. In settings where the teacher can collaborate with others, the reading may be picked up as part of another course or used during structured reading times.

Several such pertinent examples can be found in Mary Lyons's *Letters from a Slave Girl.* A recipe for crackers presents a good measurement activity as well as an exercise in language. Students could search for answers to meanings of terms such as "1 pony glass of sugar" and "4 good pinches of salt." How much butter is "butter the size of an egg"? The main character's grandmother, Gran, was able to sell the crackers for "a few coppers." This presents many directions for the mathematics lesson to diverge: measurement, graphing, proportions, profit and expense concepts, etc. Such information provides potential learning episodes for students at varying levels of ability.

Another excerpt which provides students with an opportunity to get involved in some extended inquiries is a reward notice offering $100 for the return of Harriet Jacobs, a runaway slave. Students will be challenged in finding various ways to estimate the value of that reward in today's monetary terms. Students often figure out that the cookies being sold for a few pennies would today cost at least fifty cents. Although it is a somewhat simplistic approach, students generally use proportional reasoning to argue that the reward would be at least $2500. Of course, there are complicated economic principles which are used to make more accurate estimates. In discussing these students' reaction to the problem with a high school economics teacher, he replied that this is a great project idea for his own classes. Here lies the power of using literature in mathematics class. Students are presented with instances where the power of mathematics becomes instrumental in helping them truly understand the story. One hundred dollars may not seem as important on initial inspection, but when this value is questioned and compared to today's values, the story attains a greater meaning. The mathematics teacher may design any number of structures for the use of such pieces of literature. The delight comes in presenting mathematics in meaningful and relevant contexts which accomplish more than mathematics instruction by enriching students' lives with other perspectives.

Bridging Inquiry with Content

English is one of the foundations of American education. Students will be involved in such instruction for each year of their school experience. By becoming aware of what is being read in English classes, mathematics teachers can look for ways to build links between the two classes through literature. Dialogue between the involved teachers becomes central in meshing such instructional practices. English teachers can quickly relate instances from their literary selections which have mathematics applications. The mathematics teacher can then design ways to bring those elements into mathematics instruction.

Consider a selection by William Least Heat Moon which appeared in *The Atlantic Monthly.* This story could easily be part of a reading selection for a high school English class. The selection presents the perspective of a Native American on one of the great forces of nature, the wind. This piece, though not full of mathematical content, provides students with an occasion to question what they read. The writer talks of a part of Kansas referred to as "Tornado Alley." In the discussion, he states that such a tornado belt can average 250 tornadoes a year. Later, he relates that people in Kansas have sighted 1747 tornadoes since 1950. The ensuing mathematical discussion can focus on what it means to find an average. Do the numbers presented here really support each other? What if there are some months when the likelihood of a tornado increases by 200 percent or 300 percent? Given these numbers, how many tornadoes might be expected in those months? How many would be left for the remaining months? The inquiry could lead to a data collection project of actual records. The data could be arranged in graphs and charts. Mathematical functions which could provide reasonable projections of future tornado activity could be derived from the data. The small inclusion of a piece of mathematics has sparked a journey into another culture and into how mathematics is intricately linked to understanding one natural phenomenon which shapes that society.

Discovering Possibilities from Personal Reading

A desired outcome of such programs is to have students read for themselves and become aware of the intricate nature of mathematics in our world. Personal readings, on the other hand, present a challenge for the teacher who hopes to reconnect individual reading with the class. One possibility for accomplishing this objective is to have students keep a personal log or book journal of their personal reading and the role of mathematics in that literature.

For example, a student may avidly be reading *Sticks* by Joan Bauer, which details the ambitious struggle of Mickey Vernon, who with the capable assistance of Joseph Alvarez sets out to become a force in the world of pool. The story builds a sound argument for scientific and mathematical approaches to a sport which often fails to recognize the importance of these natural forces. The struggle to become "Mickey Vernon, pool champion of the world" entails a knowledge of vectors and angles. Other math themes included in the story include estimation, percentages, and measurement. Through the use of a journal, a student could record instances where mathematics becomes important in the stories which they are personally reading. Teachers could ask students to summarize such instances and provide a brief description of how the mathematics is applied. The student might also be asked to discuss the characters in the story and the roles which they played in developing the story. I have found that students who are involved in journaling are more acutely aware of their thinking processes as they engage in solving mathematical problems (Pugalee 1996). Other teachers who have also used various forms of journaling in mathematics have found that writing improves students' metacognitive processes. Additionally, such reflections heighten the students' level of awareness of the multicultural nature of our society as well as the importance of mathematics in our everyday lives.

Conclusion

As literature increases students' exposure to different worldviews, they will begin to develop the values which are essential in creating an understanding of our diverse world. The teacher can also heighten such experiences while engaging the students in deliberations about mathematics. Young adult literature contains many such opportunities. Mathematics teachers can provide the guidance and structure necessary to shape students' thinking so that it becomes natural to consider the roles of various cultures in shaping our lives. Additionally, students will emerge from such experiences having developed a sense of the importance of mathematics as well as the skills necessary to contemplate answers to the queries which ensue from literary excursions.

References

Bauer, Joan. 1996. *Sticks.* New York: Delacorte.

Grifalconi, A. 1987. *The Village of Round and Square Houses.* Boston: Little, Brown.

Gross, Judith. 1992. *Celebrate: A Book of Jewish Holidays.* New York: Grosset & Dunlap.

Heat Moon, William Least. 1994. "Wind." *Reading and the Writing Process.* Eds. Susan Day, Robert Funk, and Elizabeth McMahan. New York: Macmillan College.

Lyons, Mary E. 1992. *Letters from a Slave Girl: The Story of Harriet Jacobs.* New York: Simon & Schuster.

Pugalee, David K. 1997. "Connecting Writing to the Mathematics Curriculum." *Mathematics Teacher.* 90(4):308–310

Ruddell, Robert B., and Martha Rapp Ruddell. 1995. *Teaching Children to Read and Write: Becoming an Influential Teacher.* Needham Heights, MA: Allyn & Bacon.

Scieszka, Jon, and Lane Smith. 1995. *Math Curse.* New York: Viking Children's Books.

Zaslavsky, Claudia. 1995. *Africa Counts: Number and Pattern in African Culture.* New York: Lawrence Hill.

IV Reflecting Our Lives

Part I of this volume presented chapters representative of the "who" of multicultural young adult literature, whereas Parts II and III dealt with the "how." In this final section we invite the reader to step back to see the field of multicultural young adult literature in a broad context—the "what" and "why" of the field. Ted Hipple, Betty Poe, Mary Harmon, and Diana Mitchell reflect on various aspects and implications of using multicultural young adult literature. In his chapter, Hipple raises pertinent questions about the issue of multiculturalism. Poe presents a broad curricular perspective that is sensitive to wide-ranging cultural perspectives. Harmon advocates a meaningful "inclusion" of multicultural authors and works in the classroom. In the concluding chapter, Mitchell, drawing on her long career as a former high school teacher, makes the essential case for literature making a difference in students' lives.

23 Puzzlements from a Pooper: or Much Confusion about "Multicultural"

Ted Hipple
University of Tennessee

Doggerel from my high-school days: When one of our group of rowdies demurred about joining the rest of us in what was probably an illicit activity—a cigarette behind the gym, skipping sixth period—we sang to him or her: "Every party needs a pooper, that's why we invited you. Party pooper, party pooper."

Story 1: Some years and degrees later I was back in a high school, this time supervising a student teacher in Jacksonville, Florida, as part of my work as a professor at the University of Florida. Two new factors made that school different from what it had been a year or so earlier: the state had mandated total desegregation of public schools so that each school had to be within five percentage points of the black-white racial makeup of the district as a whole. Thus, this formerly almost all-white school now had a student body about 35 percent African American. And, also new, the school had an elective program in English, with a large array of courses students could choose to take.

My student teacher taught an American literature elective and showed me the American poetry unit she and her directing teacher had put together. It had the expected poets from the nineteenth century and, from the twentieth, Robinson, Frost, Sandburg, and cummings. "Where," I asked in all innocence, "are Langston Hughes, Paul Laurence Dunbar, Countee Cullen?"

"Oh," I was quickly told by the directing teacher, "we have a Black Literature elective that takes care of that kind of literature." I visited this elective class and found two white students, twenty-three African American.

Back on campus and still annoyed with this curricular and classroom segregation, I wrote an essay for *English Journal* entitled "Let's

Take the Black out of Black Literature" and sent it off, rather confident that the editor would accept it, just as he had taken six or eight previous manuscripts I had sent him. My thesis was that some literature by African American authors is so good that it deserves a place in any American literature course. Though formerly the editor had responded quickly to my submissions, on this one I heard nothing for months and finally wrote him. He returned the manuscript with a short note: "Not only am I not going to publish your piece, I hope no one does. And I'm going to make it more difficult for you to get it published." I looked at the essay and discovered that he had scrawled heavy pencil marks up and down each page. The paper would have to be retyped.

It was and I sent it off a few months later to a new *English Journal* editor, Stephen Tchudi, who accepted it within days of receiving it and published it shortly thereafter in *English Journal,* February 1974.

Question: Why did these two editors think so differently about what might have been called at that time (though it wasn't) "multicultural literature"?

Story 2: A few years ago I was teaching an adolescent literature course and using Bruce Brooks's *The Moves Make the Man,* a novel that prominently features an African American teenage male. In that same course I passed around a copy of Don Gallo's NCTE publication *Speaking for Ourselves,* in which authors wrote short autobiographical statements and included a picture. When one of my students saw the picture of Brooks, he blurted out, "My God! I thought he was black."

Question: Is a white man who writes about people of color automatically suspect?

Story 3: At an NCTE convention a few years ago I overheard two fellow conferees talking about a panel they were going to that included Walter Dean Myers. "He is," said one, "a really fine black writer." I inferred, perhaps unfairly, that the emphasis was on "black" and wondered what the speaker might have thought had I changed her sentence to "Walter Dean Myers is a really fine writer who happens to be black." Or if I had told her I was going to a session with Robert Cormier, "a really fine white writer," or one with Sue Ellen Bridgers, "a really fine woman writer."

Question: Would Myers's *Glory Field* or *Somewhere in the Darkness* be viewed differently if Myers were white?

What, you may be wondering, is the point of this rambling introduction, particularly that party pooper business? Simply put, I want to raise a few issues about the subject of this worthwhile book, multicultural literature. And I may be viewed as a party pooper for doing so.

Though I have not seen the other essays in this volume, my hunch is that they may be more positive than not about this topic and I'd rather their authors weren't mad at me for raining on their highly legitimate parade. Still . . .

When I decided to submit something for this book, my plan was to write on British novelist Aidan Chambers, in my judgment one of the absolutely best writers for young adults anywhere, but not, as it happens, as well known or as highly regarded in the United States as in other parts of the English-speaking world. I was going to try to do something about that, discussing his considerable talents, advocating that his novels be more widely read, recommending classroom practices. But then I paused. How, I asked myself, could Chambers, a white male who writes mainly about white males, be considered multicultural enough for a collection like this one? Well, it is a different culture, England, after all, I rationalized. And the Chambers novel I was intending to focus on, *Dance on My Grave,* has, as its central characters, two gay teens; whether fairly or not, homosexuality is commonly regarded as a culture different from the mainstream one.

But my arguments didn't signify. The more I thought about it, the more conflicted I became. Just what does "multicultural" mean? Cynically I thought of Inspector Renault's famous line in the movie *Casablanca:* "Round up the usual suspects." Do we, in our attempts to make our literature curriculum multicultural, round up a Myers novel, a Virginia Hamilton or Mildred Taylor, drag out Laurence Yep and Gary Soto, try to squeeze in Amy Tan, wonder if Ishiguro and V. S. Naipaul are too hard? Do we confound "multicultural" and "multiethnic"?

Questions followed, ones I couldn't answer. Are Jane Austen and Terry McMillan writing about the same culture, exploring, as they both do, romance among men and women, from a woman's point of view? What is the relationship between Charles Dickens, who writes of poverty in nineteenth-century London, and Richard Wright, who writes of poverty in twentieth-century Chicago? Where to peg Alan Paton's classic *Cry, the Beloved Country,* an echo in form and content, by Paton's own admission, of John Steinbeck's *The Grapes of Wrath?* One culture here? Or two?

Indeed, I wondered, moving from literature to speech, is culture somewhat like idiolect—highly individualized even if amenable to being grouped under some heading labeled "dialect"? We observe that the speech of an African American in Atlanta may be rather different from that of an African American in Harlem and much more like that of a white American in Atlanta, just as the Harlem African American talks a lot like a white person from Westchester County.

Or take economics. A few years back, wealthy Japanese businessmen were buying resorts all over the place in California. Clearly attuned to the art of the deal, are they culturally more akin to millionaire developer Donald Trump or the Tokyo custodian who cleans their offices back home?

Carried to what is perhaps an extreme beyond its merits, this notion may suggest that every person is a culture unto himself or herself. Custom and convenience may suggest groupings of individuals under labels like "Hispanic" or "Chinese," but do these terms obscure individuality? Or, moving in the other direction, is it likely that one individual is a member of many cultures simultaneously? A Korean grandfather who lives in Queens, owns a deli in Brooklyn, attends a Methodist church in Manhattan, and plays golf in the suburbs—what is he? What *are* he?

Concerns about these issues and adolescent literature, when centered on schoolhouse pedagogy, became even more muddied. Do we—should we—choose literature *because* it is by or about someone of a minority ethnicity? Does Rosa Guy get selected before Katherine Paterson? If we do choose what we teach based on the minority status of its author or its characters, is literature writ large the first loser, our students the second? On the other hand isn't it important for students to read literature written by good authors whose ethnicity they share? Many teacher educators are quick to cite the value of having African American teachers teach African American youngsters. Would it not follow that these same students could profit from reading literature by African American authors or about African American characters? But then to what extent is classroom practice shaped by obeisance to or fears about political correctness? Where does a Hirschian taxonomy of cultural literacy fit into the mix?

And, once it is selected, how do we teach the literature? Should we focus on the features we usually explore—language, plot, themes, character development, tone? Or emphasize the author's race, with the attendant risk of mistaking biography for literary study? Should we try to discover cultural (ethnic?) identifiers in the literary work, much as we used to hunt for obscure symbols? Or do all of the above?

In sum, I remain uncertain about what I am with respect to this complex subject of multicultural adolescent literature. Arrogant sophist? intellectual gadfly? muddled fool? party pooper? politically incorrect? Regarding the last charge, I should perhaps add that I am a yellow-dog Democrat, drive a foreign car, enjoy Beaujolais and Brie. But about the central focus of this book I am in a puzzlement, to use the felicitous phrase of the King of Siam character from *The King and I* (and, by the way, what culture[s] was he a part of?).

What I do know about myself, returning to the topic I was going to write about, is that I like Aidan Chambers. His four novels for adolescents—*Breaktime, Dance on My Grave, N.I.K.,* and *The Toll Bridge*—are magnificent, outstanding examples of language carefully chosen, plots skillfully imagined, characters adroitly drawn; and culture, however described, provocatively explored. But that's another essay for another time. For now, please read Chambers; you'll be glad you did.

Suggested Readings

Chambers, Aidan. 1979. *Breaktime.* New York: HarperCollins.

———. 1982. *Dance on My Grave.* New York: HarperCollins.

———. 1987. *NIK: Now I Know.* New York: HarperCollins.

———. 1992. *The Toll Bridge.* New York: HarperCollins.

Myers, Walter Dean. 1992. *Somewhere in the Darkness.* New York: Scholastic.

———. 1996. *The Glory Field.* New York: Scholastic.

24 Weaving Many Cultures into the Curriculum

Elizabeth A. Poe
Radford University

One of the exciting developments in the field of young adult literature has been the proliferation of literature representing a variety of cultural perspectives. This expansion, coupled with the power of literature to transport readers beyond themselves and their own personal experiences, makes it possible for young adults to gain insight into the lives of people from diverse backgrounds. Such insights promote understanding of human commonalities as well as cultural differences. Rather than promote multicultural awareness by creating units on specific ethnic groups or devoting a week or month to a particular racial group, literature that speaks about the variety of cultures comprising America can be woven across the curriculum continuously.

One way to help students develop multicultural understanding is to offer them young adult literature with characters and/or situations that are both familiar and unfamiliar. Characters or situations readers can identify with enable them to enter stories where they meet and learn from characters and situations outside their personal experiences. Will Hobbs's *Far North* and Jacqueline Woodson's *I Hadn't Meant to Tell You This* are examples of books which offer such opportunities. In *Far North,* Gabe Roberts is an Anglo from Texas; Raymond Providence, his roommate in their Canadian boarding school, is a Dene Indian. When they are stranded in the Yukon wilderness, both Gabe and Raymond learn from Johnny Raven, an elder in the Dene tribe. Marie in *I Hadn't Meant to Tell You This* is a middle-class black teen, and her classmate Lena is a lower-class white teen. The girls are initially drawn to one another because each has lost her mother. Racial identity may be a reason readers bond with a particular character in novels such as these, but social status, family situations, and personal characteristics also offer possibilities for connection. Having connected with one character, the reader can share the experiences of both characters as they increase their mutual understanding. Sometimes the understanding is completely personal, but sometimes it involves insight into another's cultural circumstances.

Multicultural awareness can also be sparked by encouraging students to read books about contemporary teens from ethnic or racial groups different from the reader's. Feelings or experiences common to adolescence may enable the reader to identify with a protagonist and create an interest in that character's culture. If the character develops an interest in his or her own cultural identity, the reader can vicariously enter into the heritage of another group. Such an interest may lead to further reading of historical fiction or nonfiction related to that ethnic group. For example, Cloyd Atcitty in Will Hobbs's *Beardance* is curious about his heritage as a Ute Indian. As he learns more about his ancestry, readers who have come to care about him will increase their knowledge of this Native American tribe. Students may want to expand this information by reading other fiction and nonfiction about the Utes.

Interest in historical incidents may also be generated when readers become emotionally involved with a novel's characters. After reading *The Watsons Go to Birmingham—1963* by Christopher Paul Curtis or *Spite Fences* by Trudy Krisher, students may wish to study the civil rights movement. They can step back in history and deepen their understanding of circumstances that shaped the need for this social change by reading books such as *Roll of Thunder, Hear My Cry* by Mildred D. Taylor, *Nightjohn* by Gary Paulsen, *Many Thousand Gone: African Americans from Slavery to Freedom* by Virginia Hamilton, or *Slave Dancer* by Paula Fox. Sheila Gordon's *Waiting for the Rain* could provide a similar impetus for learning about apartheid in South Africa. Cynthia Voigt's *David and Jonathan* can do the same for the Holocaust.

When the curriculum allows for individual reading, perhaps through a reader's workshop or independent reading program, students may encounter books that evoke personal growth in a multitude of areas. If the classroom or school library includes an abundance of young adult literature with multiethnic characters and experiences, it is likely that adolescents will expand their cultural awareness. Teachers, librarians, and parents who can talk with teens about these books and the readers' experiences with them further increase the chances for multicultural understanding.

Although insights occur through individual reading, literature circle experiences also facilitate multicultural awareness. Literature circles can be designed around broad, overarching concepts, topics, or themes that encompass the breadth of human experience. By working in small groups and sharing their learning with the large group, students are able to focus on one or two books as well as learn about the general topic. Successful literature circles depend upon literature that is, first and foremost, interesting to young adult readers. Each book offered must be a potentially engaging story of literary quality worthy of classroom study. Allowing students to select the books they read and beginning discussions with each reader's individual experience with that book demonstrates that all students are valued members of the learning community. Acknowledging individual worth is an important step toward recognizing the value of diversity. Such a reader-response approach also guards against the study of the book becoming rote and pedantic.

A broad topic such as immigrant experiences addresses multiculturalism directly because it provides opportunities to examine a common experience among various cultures within American society. This topic would work well in a social studies class or as a social studies/ language arts interdisciplinary unit. Many students will be curious about the immigration stories of their ancestors or the ancestors of their friends. Others may identify with the stories of more recent immigrants. Those whose ancestors did not immigrate to America have certainly been affected by the immigration of others. Therefore, immigration is a topic which should enable students to discover similarities as well as differences among the many cultures of our society.

There are numerous books suitable for a unit on the immigrant experience. Kathryn Lasky tells the story of some of America's first English immigrants in *Journey to the New World: The Diary of Remember Patience Whipple.* Twelve-year-old Mem, as she is called, traveled aboard the Mayflower and lived in the Puritan settlement of Plymouth. The mid-nineteenth-century story of Peggy O'Driscoll, who leaves Ireland for America, is chronicled by Marita Conlon-McKenna in *Wildflower Girl. Dragonwings,* by Laurence Yep, introduces readers to the plight of early twentieth-century Chinese immigrants. Rifka, in Karen Hesse's *Letters from Rifka,* is a Jewish girl who escapes from Russia with her family but must immigrate to America alone. *Land of Hope,* the first in Joan Lowery Nixon's "Ellis Island" series, tells the story of another Jewish girl, Rebekah Levinsky, who leaves Russia for a new life in the United States. *Land of Promise* follows Rose Carney, a fifteen-year-old Irish farm girl who immigrates to Chicago, and *Land of Dreams* is the story of Kristen Swenson, who emigrates with her parents from Sweden to Minnesota. The latter half of the twentieth century also figures in immigration stories. *Kiki: A Cuban Boy's Adventures in America,* by Hilda Perera, is the story of a Cuban refugee who immigrates to America in the 1960s. In *Children of the River,* Linda Crew tells the story of Cambodian refugee Sundara. *Journey of the Sparrows,* written by Fran

Leeper Buss with Daisy Cubias, relates how illegal aliens Maria and her brother flee El Salvador, are smuggled over the border in a wooden crate, and find help in Chicago.

Nonfiction/informational works can supplement the study of fiction in topical literature circles. Brent Ashabranner's informational works, for example, speak effectively to young adults about the experiences of immigrants in the United States. *The New Americans: Changing Patterns of U.S. Immigration* traces the history of early American immigration, identifies some patterns among immigrants, and discusses issues relevant to this portion of American society. *Into a Strange Land: Unaccompanied Refugee Youth in America,* coauthored by Melissa Ashabranner, tells the stories of Asian refugees who came to America after the Vietnam War. *An Ancient Heritage: The Arab-American Minority* describes Arab-American immigration experiences. *The Vanishing Border: A Photographic Journey along Our Frontier with Mexico* contributes information about immigration work along the U.S./Mexican border. *Our Beckoning Borders: Illegal Immigration to America* takes a closer look at the problems involved with illegal immigration. In *Still a Nation of Immigrants,* Ashabranner focuses on our newest immigrants, who come primarily from Asia and Latin America. In addition to discussing circumstances facing current immigrants, Ashabranner looks at the effect of immigration on the United States as a multicultural nation.

Several publishing houses have produced series concerned with immigration. Rosen Publishing Group has published *In Their Own Voices,* a series of informational works about teenage refugees from Bosnia-Herzegovina, Cambodia, Haiti, Iran, Nicaragua, Russia, and Vietnam. In each sixty-four page volume, a variety of teens tell why they had to leave their country, how they escaped, and what life has been like for them in the United States. Silver Burdett's New Discovery Books series on immigration, Footsteps to America, includes books entitled *Asian Indian Americans, Chinese Americans, Dominican Americans, Korean Americans, Vietnamese Americans,* and *West Indian Americans.* Written by Alexandra Bandon, each of these informational books provides a historical perspective about the immigrants' original country, describes what life has been like for this group in America, and includes personal narratives from immigrants.

Diversity within geographic regions is another broad concept that lends itself to interdisciplinary study. Beginning with a common reading, such as Carolyn Meyer's *Rio Grande Stories,* students can explore the variety of cultures that coexist and mingle within an area of the country. *Rio Grande Stories* would be an effective way to begin such a unit because it tells the story of middle school students researching various aspects of the many cultures in Albuquerque, New Mexico. Projects based on their research as well as process notes are compiled in a class publication. Along with learning about the Native American, Hispanic, African American, Jewish, and Anglo people who live in this region, readers are given a blueprint for a Heritage Project they could conduct in their own community and/or geographical region. Their investigations may be conducted individually or in a literature circle format. This type of Foxfire approach can help students in any part of the country understand the wealth of cultural diversity surrounding them.

One way to include multicultural literature in an English curriculum is to select a literary motif and offer novels with characters from many racial groups that fit this pattern. The journey—which commonly serves as a structure for stories involving quests, bravery, self-discovery, and storytelling—works well for this purpose. *The Odyssey* by Homer is the Western prototype of journey stories. As Odysseus travels by ship, trying to return to Ithaca after the Trojan War, he encounters many hardships and shows much bravery. Some of the danger he faces, however, results from his desire to have strange experiences. Will Hobbs's *Downriver* is also a tale of bravery, but it too involves poor judgment on the part of its characters. Jessie and the others let Troy persuade them to steal a raft and take an illegal trip down the Grand Canyon's Colorado River. Jessie and her comrades learn about themselves from this foolhardy adventure.

Huck and Jim, in Mark Twain's *Huckleberry Finn,* also take an illegal raft trip. They encounter adventures and Huck ends up discovering unsettling aspects of his own character. In Gary Paulsen's *The Car,* Terry Anders makes a road trip, even though he is too young to drive, and connects with two hippies who turn his journey into a life-changing quest for knowledge and wisdom. *Walk Two Moons* by Sharon Creech is Salamanca's quest for information about the death of her mother. As Salamanca drives cross-county with her grandparents, they tell each other stories. In the end these stories help Salamanca discover more than she had originally planned. The multileveled tales told as they travel make this journey reminiscent of Chaucer's *Canterbury Tales* because characters from various cultures are involved in these excursions from a variety of perspectives.

Structuring the study of several novels around a common theme, such as "knowing our family's past helps us understand ourselves," can also raise multicultural awareness in an English class. Young adult novels that speak to this theme might include *The Joy Luck Club,* by Amy Tan, in which four American-born daughters learn of their Chinese American mothers' struggles in China; Jane Yolen's *Briar Rose,* the disguised story of how Becca's grandmother suffered in Poland during the Holocaust; and *The Glory Field,* Walter Dean Myers's comprehensive treatment of one African American family's survival and triumph from slavery to the present. Hadley Irwin's *Kim-Kimi,* the story of a Japanese American teen's search for her Japanese heritage, leads Kimi to discover the injustice her father's family endured during World War II. Kim's father died when she was young, but in Bruce Brooks's *Midnight Hour Encores,* Sib's mother deserted Sib and her father. After a cross-country trip to meet her mother, Sib begins to understand the importance of her relationship with her father. Like the other characters in the books suggested for this unit, Sib discovers much about herself. In each of these books, a young person's identity is shaped by knowledge of one or more parent. Because this is a universal situation, the specific instances hold intriguing possibilities for exploring similarities and differences among cultural experiences.

Whether approached through thematic units, literature circles, or individual reading, a firm commitment to providing as many perspectives as possible is imperative if students are to grow beyond their own experiences. Of course, there are many ways to group books to provide this breadth of perspective and at the same time enable students to read on a developmentally appropriate level. Fortunately, we have excellent resources to assist in the selection of literature, making the representation of many cultures throughout all areas of the curriculum a distinct possibility. Let us all continue to read widely and deeply and encourage our students to do the same.

Suggested Readings

Ashabranner, Brent. 1983. *The New Americans: Changing Patterns in U.S. Immigration.* New York: Dodd.

———. 1987a. *The Vanishing Border: A Photographic Journey along Our Frontier with Mexico.* New York: Dodd, Mead.

——— and Melissa Ashabranner. 1987b. *Into a Strange Land: Unaccompanied Refugee Youth in America.* New York: Putnam.

———. 1991. *An Ancient Heritage: The Arab-American Minority.* New York: HarperCollins.

———. 1993. *Still a Nation of Immigrants.* New York: Dutton.

———. *Our Beckoning Borders: Illegal Immigration to America.* New York: Dutton.

Bandon, Alexandra. 1994a. *Chinese Americans.* Parsippany, NJ: New Discovery.

———. 1994b. *Korean Americans.* Parsippany, NJ: New Discovery.

———. 1994c. *Vietnamese Americans.* Parsippany, NJ: New Discovery.

———. 1994d. *West Indian Americans.* Parsippany, NJ: New Discovery.

———. 1995a. *Asian Indian Americans.* Parsippany, NJ: New Discovery.

———. 1995b. *Dominican Americans.* Parsippany, NJ: New Discovery

Brooks, Bruce. 1986. *Midnight Hour Encores.* New York: HarperCollins.

Buss, Fran Leeper, with Daisy Cubias. 1993. *Journey of the Sparrows.* New York: Dell.

Cerar, K. Melissa. 1995. *Teenage Refugees from Nicaragua Speak Out.* New York: Rosen.

Chaucer, Geoffrey. 1960. *The Canterbury Tales.* Trans. Neville Coghill. New York: Penguin.

Conlon-McKenna, Marita. 1991. *Wildflower Girl.* New York: Holiday House.

Creech, Sharon. 1994. *Walk Two Moons.* New York: HarperCollins.

Crew, Linda. 1989. *Children of the River.* New York: Bantam Doubleday Dell.

Curtis, Christopher Paul. 1997. *The Watsons Go to Birmingham—1963.* New York: Bantam Doubleday Dell.

Fox, Paula. 1991. *The Slave Dancer.* New York: Dell.

Gordon, Sheila. 1989. *Waiting for the Rain.* New York: Bantam.

Hamilton, Virginia. 1993. *Many Thousand Gone: African Americans from Slavery to Freedom.* New York: Knopf.

Hesse, Karen. 1992. *Letters from Rifka.* New York: Holt.

Hobbs, Will. 1991. *Downriver.* New York: Atheneum.

———. 1993. *Beardance.* New York: Atheneum.

———. 1996. *Far North.* New York: Morrow.

Homer. 1992. *The Odyssey.* Trans. Robert Fitzgerald. Illus. Barnaby Fitzgerald. New York: Everyman's Library/Knopf. (For a more accessible edition, see Barbara Lionie Picard, reteller. 1952. *The Odyssey.* Illus. Joan Kiddell-Monroe. Oxford: Oxford Press.)

Irwin, Hadley. 1987. *Kim-Kimi.* New York: McElderry.

Krisher, Trudy. 1994. *Spite Fences.* New York: Delacorte.

Lasky, Kathryn. 1996. *Journey to the New World: The Diary of Remember Patience Whipple.* New York: Scholastic.

Meyer, Carolyn, ed. 1994. *Rio Grande Stories.* San Diego: Harcourt Brace.

Myers, Walter Dean. 1996. *The Glory Field.* New York: Scholastic.

Nixon, Joan Lowery. 1993. *Land of Hope.* New York: Dell.

———. 1994. *Land of Promise.* New York: Dell.

———. 1995. *Land of Dreams.* New York: Dell.

Paulsen, Gary. 1994. *The Car.* San Diego: Harcourt Brace.

———. 1995. *Nightjohn.* New York: 1995.

Perera, Hilda. 1992. *Kiki: A Cuban Boy's Adventures in America.* Trans. Warren Hampton and Hilda Gonzalez. New York: Pickering.

She, Colleen, ed. 1995. *Teenage Refugees from China Speak Out.* New York: Rosen.

St. Pierre, Stephanie. 1995. *Teenage Refugees from Cambodia Speak Out.* New York: Rosen.

Tan, Amy. 1996. *The Joy Luck Club.* New York: Ivy.

Taylor, Mildred. 1976, 1997. *Roll of Thunder, Hear My Cry.* New York: Viking Penguin.

Tekavec, Valerie, ed. 1995a. *Teenage Refugees from Bosnia-Herzegovina Speak Out.* New York: Rosen.

———. 1995b. *Teenage Refugees from Haiti Speak Out.* New York: Rosen.

Twain, Mark. 1885. *The Adventures of Huckleberry Finn, Tom Sawyer's Comrade.* Illus. Edward Windsor Kemble. New York: Webster.

Voigt, Cynthia. 1992. *David and Jonathan.* New York: Scholastic.

Wapner, Kenneth. 1995. *Teenage Refugees from Vietnam Speak Out.* New York: Rosen.

Woodson, Jacqueline. 1994. *I Hadn't Meant to Tell You This.* New York: Delacorte.

Yep, Laurence. 1975. *Dragonwings.* New York: HarperCollins.

Yolen, Jane. 1993. *Briar Rose.* New York: Tor.

Zamenova, Tatyana. 1995. *Teenage Refugees from Russia Speak Out.* New York: Rosen.

References

Berger, Laura Standley, ed. 1993.*Twentieth-Century Young Adult Writers.* Detroit: St. James Press.

Christenbury, Leila, ed. 1995. *Books for You: An Annotated Booklist for Senior High Students.* Urbana, IL: NCTE.

Harris, Violet, ed. 1992. *Teaching Multicultural Literature in Grades K–8.* Norwood, MA: Christopher-Gordon.

Herz, Sarah K., with Donald R. Gallo. 1996. *From Hinton to Hamlet: Building Bridges between Young Adult Literature and the Classics.* Westport, CT: Greenwood.

Lindgren, Merri V., ed. 1991. *The Multicolored Mirror: Cultural Substance in Literature for Children and Young Adults.* Written in cooperation with the Cooperative Children's Book Center, University of Wisconsin–Madison. Fort Atkinson, WI, Highsmith.

Poe, Elizabeth Ann, and Susanne L. Johnston. 1993. *Focus on Relationships: A Reference Handbook.* Santa Barbara: ABC-CLIO.

Rochman, Hazel. 1993. *Against Borders: Promoting Books for a Multicultural World.* Chicago: American Library Association.

25 Moving from the Merely Mentioned to the Multicultural

Mary R. Harmon
Saginaw Valley State University

The move toward multicultural perspectives and classroom activities permeates the literature of teaching and learning. Excited by new materials and approaches as well as by the outlooks and stories of persons whose voices have been ignored or silenced, many of us have worked hard in our classrooms toward the inclusion of texts by a diversity of writers and speakers. As we proceed, I'd like to insert a note of caution for consideration, not to slow progress or discourage those eager for change, but to ensure that in our desire to create more diverse classrooms, we and our students do not fall victim to what I call "mentioning—exclusion by means of inclusion" despite all of our best intentions.

In their *The Politics of the Textbook* (1991), Michael W. Apple and Linda K. Christian-Smith describe *mentioning* and its effects. They suggest that mentioning results in non–dominant culture authors' outlooks, selections, and dialects being included in classroom instruction but not examined and developed in depth or given any real cultural value. Rather, their value may be denigrated or denied, thereby positioning dominant culture authors, their modes of expression, and their works as the standards or the norms against which all others are measured. Sometimes mentioning occurs when selected bits and pieces of non–dominant culture authors' works, outlooks, and dialects are integrated into the dominant tradition by bringing them into close association or equating them with the values of the dominant group (Apple and Christian-Smith 10). In such instances, important cultural differences or values will be erased. In effect, then, mentioning excludes non–dominant culture authors, their works, values, and modes of expression from the classroom mainstream even while appearing to include them.

Recently, Arthur Applebee observed literature classrooms across the United States and found that "works by women make up only 16 percent of the reading students are asked to do for English courses in grades 7–12, and works by non-white authors less than 7 percent" (1992, 32; 1993, 60–77). My recent examinations of high school American literature anthologies revealed that not only are the works of women and writers of color seriously underrepresented in current textbooks; at times, through their own language use in their nonselection portions, anthologies send mixed messages and/or discriminatory and negative messages about dialectal language variants, women, uneducated persons, and various ethnic groups (Harmon 1993, 1997). Such studies suggest that, instead of creating classrooms where the works of a wide diversity of authors and perspectives enjoy an integrated representation, too often even well-intentioned teachers work in classrooms where such works, authors, and outlooks are merely mentioned and sometimes inadvertently devalued.

Creating a Multicultural Climate

We can move from the mentioned to the multicultural by making a lifelong commitment to creating truly multicultural classrooms, confident that in doing so we serve all our students' best interests. In such classrooms, we can eliminate mentioning and its exclusionary effects. Recognizing mentioning is the key to countering it. We must examine our teaching and professional materials and avoid or supplement those which give only limited or token attention to multicultural works and authors. As we fully integrate multicultural works into our classrooms and discuss them in depth for their literary merit, we will move beyond those "tack-on" or "birthdays and holidays" approaches which point to multicultural and women's works and voices as isolated, "different," "other," or nonmainstream. Avoiding overly general or *essentialist* statements which dismiss the value of differences will help counter mentioning: saying that Alice Childress or Virginia Hamilton is *the voice* of the African American community is as inaccurate as saying that Robert Cormier or Chris Crutcher is *the voice* of the Anglo community. We can check our school libraries and book sales and advocate for widely diverse reading materials for our students' selection; we can expose our students to literary works written in a variety of dialects and assist them to value dialectal differences and varied modes of expression.

Pairing and Thematic Teaching

As we work to present our students with a well-integrated and wide variety of authors, genres, dialects, voices, and settings, we can move from mentioning by constructing thematic units and linking cross-time and cross-cultural pairings. Instead of taking chronological or genre studies approaches to literary exploration, an increasing number of us teach thematically—that is, we and/or our students select works from different genres and time periods and from a wide variety of perspectives organized in varying degrees around a theme, such as "Dreams and Dreamers," "A Search for a Home (room, place, identity) of One's Own," "Parents and Children," "Aging," "Competition and Cooperation," "Biases and Prejudices," and "Growing Up in America." As thematic units are constructed, care is taken to choose themes which, by their nature, do not virtually exclude one gender or ethnic group and to select works which ensure that many sides of and perspectives on the chosen theme are examined. A unit on "Families" can be broadened in scope to explore culturally determined differences in the importance of family roles and kinship and to examine a variety of family groups in addition to the intact, nuclear family of mother, father, and children. Units which provide readers with the experiences and perspectives of primarily one gender or ethnic group—as often do many units on "Individualism," "War," "Initiation," "Sports," and "The West"—limit many students' engagement and self-perception and can be enriched to ensure that varied voices and views are read and discussed. Among the resources available to aid teachers in the construction of multicultural thematic units, Eileen Iscoff Oliver's *Crossing the Mainstream* (1994) provides many suggestions for and examples of truly inclusive literature units.

Cross-cultural and cross-time pairings assist those teachers who are directed by their schools to work within a chronological framework. Reading excerpts from Miriam Starkey's *The Devil in Massachusetts* along with Cotton Mather's accounts of the Salem Witchcraft trials adds a twentieth-century woman's view of those occurrences. Brown and Stephens augment this pairing by suggesting the use of Ann Rinaldi's *A Break with Charity* and Arthur Miller's *The Crucible* (Brown and Stephens 1995, 257). Selections from William Least Heat Moon's *Blue Highways* could be paired with United States settlers' accounts of Native Americans, as could N. Scott Momaday's *The Way to Rainy Mountain.* Throughout their recent *Teaching Young Adult Literature: Sharing the Connection,* Brown and Stephens offer many suggestions for pairing, or "bridging," as they call it. Whaley and Dodge, in their *Weaving in the Women* (1993), also present ideas for cross-time and cross-cultural pairings, and they give readers many other practical suggestions for ensuring greater cultural and gender balance, thus countering mentioning in chronological courses such as American and British literature.

Pairing can also help us avoid stereotyping and essentialist approaches and statements. To teach Toni Morrison's *The Bluest Eye* as Claudia's story as well as Pecola's gives readers an example of a young African American woman, who, sensitive to the lessons of her upbringing, can manipulate language on several levels and can both reflect on and take responsibility for her life. Teaching it along with Alice Childress's *Rainbow Jordan,* Ntozake Shange's *Betsy Brown,* and/or Andrea Lee's *Sarah Phillips* gives students a variety of perspectives on growing up as African American women in the United States. Placing Reginald McKnight's "The Kind of Light That Shines on Texas" next to Richard Wright's "The Man Who Was Almost a Man" or "The Man Who Saw the Flood" similarly may broaden a student's range of awareness. Comparing and contrasting the tones and contents of Langston Hughes's "The Negro Speaks of Rivers" and Nikki Giovanni's "Ego Tripping" would alert students to the fact that ethnic pride takes variant forms. Linking the creation, fall, and redemption poem that runs throughout Leslie Marmon Silko's *Ceremony* to other creation, fall, and redemption stories would make for lively class discussion and comparative analysis. One of the many strengths of Amy Tan's *The Joy Luck Club,* Sandra Cisneros's *Woman Hollering Creek,* and McKnight's short story collection *The Kind of Light That Shines on Texas* is that these works all present so many varied narrators, situations, dialects, and characters that, for the thoughtful reader, stereotyping and essentialism are next to impossible. And all three texts work well to call into question students' preconceived attitudes toward gender, ethnicity, and/or social class.

Switching Perspectives: Empowering Silent Voices

Yet another way to move from mentioning to creating a multicultural climate—even in classes where a traditional curriculum is mandated—is to examine and discuss the roles (or lack of roles) given to women and minority persons in the selections read for the class and to expose and ask students to explore the works' subtextual commentary on women and persons of color. Following Nancy R. Comely's example (1992), I asked my students to read Ernest Hemingway's "Indian Camp," and record everything Nick, the young protagonist, learns about women and Native Americans in the story—these lessons being subtextual in nature—as he observes his father deliver a Native American woman's baby. Among my students' responses were the following: he learns that women's screams of pain in childbirth are "not important"; he learns that Native American men cannot "take it"; and he learns that a Native American woman who reacts to the pain of an unanesthetized breach birth can be dismissed as "squaw bitch." Some students, then, rewrote the story from the perspective of the Native American woman, a character who, except for her cries of pain (which are unimportant according to Nick's father), is given no voice in the story. Similarly, when using Marvel's "To His Coy Mistress," I ask students to contextualize and consider the Coy Mistress's dilemma and to compose a reply to her suitor from her point of view, thereby giving the silent mistress a voice to respond to her attempted seduction.

As we move from mentioning and commit to classrooms where a wide variety of works by a wide range of voices speak to one another and to our students, resources exist to help us. Among some of the recent best are Whaley and Dodge's *Weaving in the Women* (1993), Oliver's *Crossing the Mainstream* (1994), and Brown and Stephens's *Teaching Young Adult Literature: Sharing the Connection* (1995), as well as collections like Moore's *I Know Some Things: Stories about Childhood by Contemporary Writers* (1992), Lauter's *Heath Anthology of American Literature* (1994), and Beaty and Hunter's *New Worlds of Literature* (1994). Volumes 1 through 3 of Joan F. Kaywell's (ed.) *Adolescent Literature as a Complement to the Classics* (1996) highlight pairings and thematic approaches. *English Journal* regularly features articles which both annotate suggested multicultural texts for use in the 7–12 classroom and describe the practical aspects of multicultural pedagogy.

With such resources at our disposal, our own eagerness to move toward truly inclusive classrooms, and our own enthusiasm and appreciation for diverse perspectives and modes of expression, we, as English language arts teachers, *can* make a difference. We can expose and counter mentioning as we work toward achieving not only classrooms where diversity is seen as a strength but also a nation that values the strength and vitality that multicultural diversity provides.

References

Apple, Michael W., and Linda K. Christian-Smith, eds. 1991. *The Politics of the Textbook.* New York: Routledge.

Applebee, Arthur N. 1993. *Literature in the Secondary School: Studies of Curriculum and Instruction in the United States.* Urbana, IL: NCTE.

Applebee, Arthur N. 1992. "Stability and Change in the High School Canon," *English Journal.* pp. 27–32.

Beaty, Jerome, and J. Paul Hunter, eds. 1994. *New Worlds of Literature: Writings from America's Many Cultures.* New York: Norton.

Brown, Jean E., and Elaine C. Stephens. 1995. *Teaching Young Adult Literature: Sharing the Connection.* Cincinnati: Wadsworth.

Comley, Nancy R. 1992. "Father Knows Best: Reading around 'Indian Camp.'" *Gender Issues in the Teaching of English.* Eds. Nancy Mellin McCracken and Bruce C. Appleby. Urbana, IL: NCTE.

Harmon, Mary R. 1993. *A Study of Sociolinguistic Texts and Subtexts as Found in Five High School American Literature Anthologies.* Unpublished Dissertation. Ann Arbor, MI: University Microfilms.

Harmon, Mary R. (In press)."Gender/Language Subtexts as Found in Literature Anthologies: Mixed Messages, Stereotypes, Silence, Erasure." *The Proceedings of the Seventeenth Annual Conference of the Organization for the Study of Communication, Language, and Gender.* Cresskill, NJ: Hampton Press.

Kaywell, Joan F., ed. (1993, 1995, 1996). *Adolescent Literature as a Complement to the Classics,* Volumes 1–3. Norwood, MA: Christopher Gordon.

Lauter, Paul, ed. 1994. *The Heath Anthology of American Literature.* Volumes 1–2. Lexington, MA: D.C. Heath.

Moore, Lorrie, ed. 1993. *I Know Some Things: Stories about Childhood by Contemporary Writers.* Boston: Faber & Faber.

Oliver, Eileen Iscoff. 1994. *Crossing the Mainstream: Multicultural Perspectives in Teaching Literature.* Urbana, IL: NCTE.

Whaley, Liz, and Liz Dodge. 1993. *Weaving in the Women: Transforming the High School English Curriculum.* Portsmouth, NH: Heinemann.

26 Connecting with Students through Multicultural Young Adult Novels

Diana Mitchell

"This is the first novel I've ever been assigned to read that I have absolutely loved!"

"I told my parents they *had* to read this book."

"I read this book through my other classes. I couldn't put it down!"

The book my tenth-grade American literature students were responding to was Walter Dean Myers's *Fallen Angels.* They pounced on that novel and read it in big gulps. They entered the classroom talking about the book and wanted to talk about it even more in class. This kind of overwhelmingly positive response caused me to do some serious thinking about why students read this book so eagerly and how I could incorporate more experiences like this into my classes.

This chapter will focus on both of those questions. First, it will examine the reasons young adult literature works in the class and why the use of multicultural young adult literature makes sense. Then it will turn to ways that multicultural young adult literature can be incorporated into the language arts class. Several methods will be described, followed by an in-depth look at how to use a young adult, multicultural novel as a whole-class book. This discussion will focus on one particular novel *Toning the Sweep.* Included in the activities described to use with the novel are suggestions for discussing the racial issues that are a part of many of these multicultural books.

Why Young Adult Literature Connects with Students

Contemporary Language Makes the Books Immediately Accessible

Fallen Angels was written in the language of today. No one had to explain to my students what the language was saying; they did not have to leap across language barriers to get into the heart of the book. I did not have to explain antiquated vocabulary words or unusual language structures. Because there were no language roadblocks, the students plunged into the story and got to its essence quickly. They were not asked to patiently wade through the unfamiliar, swamplike territory of vocabulary lists and explanations of what the book meant before they were engaged.

The Action in Contemporary Young Adult Novels Begins Immediately

Most teens read to see what happens in a story and to figure out why people behave as they do. Reading *Fallen Angels,* they wanted to know who would crumble under stress, who would cope effectively with their fear, and who would survive. Because teens are part of a generation that grew up with television "stories," they have high expectations for books. A book must quickly grab their interest or they view it as "boring" and unworthy of their time. They are not usually willing to wait around and keep reading in spite of teacher admonitions that the book "will get really good."

Young adult authors know their audiences and write to engage them. I once heard Lois Duncan, a prolific and popular young adult author, speak on this issue. She said that authors no longer have the luxury of describing the lace curtains or what a room looks like; they know they have to capture the attention of their readers on the first page. Young adult novels are written to do this. The authors of these books respect where their readers are coming from and work to live up to their readers' expectations. They don't assume that they can change the nature of their readers; instead they work with their readers by using their writing skills to pique reader interest.

The Issues Are Relevant to Student Lives

Teens are willing to deal with almost any kind of issue as long as they can see how it applies to them or their world. When an issue or theme in a novel touches them or moves them or speaks to them, they become involved in that book and want to talk about it and look deeper into it. Too often, we teachers have to do the work of uncovering themes and issues for teens and show them how they can relate to teens' lives. It is often difficult not to sound patronizing as we patiently explain connections to teen lives that they did not see themselves. By using young adult novels, we let the books do the work for us, since the literature speaks for itself. Students sense that we respect what they know and are willing to work with them, not impose adult ideas of what they should be interested in and what they should know.

In contrast to most novels we ask our students to read in high school literature classes, *Fallen Angels* is a book that encourages students to immediately respond and to interact with the characters and the issues. They could understand why Richie felt so responsible for being a role model for his younger brother; they could understand the fear the soldiers felt about going into battle because they could see what the conditions surrounding those battles were like in Vietnam. The friendship and even the antagonism that developed because of the hostile environment made sense to them.

Although the war was removed from their lives, the issues and emotions present in the book were ones they could relate to. These were not just abstract issues dealt with intellectually and interpreted by the teacher, but issues made real through the language of the book.

Young Adult Literature Bridges the Gap between School and Our Students' Lives

In our students' lives today, they see people out of work and people struggling to keep their heads above water. They see teens in their school succumbing to drugs or gangs or alcohol or promiscuous sex. They talk to other students who have very real home problems. They worry about being accepted. They wonder what will happen to them and how they'll be able to succeed. I once had a student whom we would call "at risk" today. He was from a poor home, no one in his family had ever graduated from high school, and his mother had just died. He told me, "I don't want to be no bum." He knew, however, that the odds were not in his favor. To use literature that is far removed from the interests or concerns of these students is just another way of telling them that school is not real; that it has nothing to do with anything they'll ever face; that it's just something they have to get through.

As English language arts teachers we have this wonderful opportunity to directly connect what we do in school with the lives of these students. Through the literature we select for our classes, we can ease the alienation so many students feel in school today.

My students responded strongly to the characters in *Fallen Angels* because they were like people they knew and understood. The main characters were teens from urban areas, some who had just graduated from high school, who believed that going into the army was a way out of their current life into something better. Since almost all teens believe that what they do after high school has to be better than high school, the novel provided a reality check for them and a departure point for some intense discussions. They also liked the honesty in the novel: one of the main characters, Peewee, said exactly what he was thinking. Racial issues were discussed freely, and students liked the sense that important issues were actually being talked about, not covered up. Because of Peewee's comments, they too wondered about the disproportionately high numbers of minority soldiers who saw front-line duty. They too thought about whether they'd prefer someone of their own race "covering their back" if they were in combat.

Young Adult Literature Reflects the Racial, Class, and Family Compositions of Our Students

With the burgeoning lists of titles of young adult literature being published each year, it is easy to find books that reflect the racial, class, and familial compositions of our students. Part of the reason my students responded so strongly to *Fallen Angels* was that it reflected their backgrounds. The soldiers and officers were black and white, rich and poor, and from two-parent and single-parent families just like members of my class. Reading books whose characters make visible the racial or economic or familial aspects of who students are affirms and validates that aspect of students' lives. When students can see themselves in the literature used in school, they don't feel marginalized because they feel they are at the heart of what is being dealt with.

Why Multicultural Literature Makes Sense in the Classroom

For over twenty years I taught in an urban school district with a multiethnic population. The high school I taught in the last twelve years was made up of almost 60 percent students of color, mainly African Americans, with some Latinos and Southeast Asians. I became acutely aware of the need to broaden the works I chose to teach when a Latino boy asked me, "When are we going to read about people like me?" Thus it makes sense to me to use multicultural literature such as *Fallen Angels*. It not only allows students to see themselves in novels but also to get a much more complete view of who lives in this world.

I have sometimes heard teachers say that they don't "have" to use multicultural literature because they have no students of color. I wish they would rethink that view, for it seems to me that when there are no students of color present, the need is even greater to use multicultural literature. How else will students learn the worth of the views and the literature of people who don't look like them? How else will students learn that they can be enriched through contact with other cultures? How else can we validate the literature written by others besides Anglo men?

Just because the faces of our students do not include many different shades does not mean that all the students in our classes are the same. We have to remember that our students come to us from many backgrounds and experiences. Some have had a strict religious upbringing; others have traveled widely; still others have relatives in Texas or Hanoi or Tennessee. My job, it seems to me, is to open up my classroom to the voices of many. Whether all of our students represent only one racial group or have all been raised in the same town, within those students lie the voices of many. They vary in the way they view the world, in the way they view adults such as teachers and preachers, and in the way they view others who don't look like they do. Thus every class is a diverse class made up of students with different views on authority, on religion, on the importance of education, on what is most important in their lives, and on whether they view others with trust or distrust. So I try to use literature that reflects the ethnic background of the class, but also literature that shows people the students might not know otherwise. I feel they need to know that their world is not the whole world, that others who are different also make contributions and experience the same human emotions that they do.

I don't want students to think that any race or religion or social group is monolithic. I want them to know that there are diverse views in any grouping of people. When we look at any kind of literature, I want my students to realize that any one author does not speak for a whole group.

Using Multicultural Young Adult Literature

Collections of Short Stories

In approaching multicultural literature, I usually try to integrate it into the themes or units we are dealing with in class. Somehow singling out literature as "ethnic" seems to be saying to students that now we're going to look at "them"—the different ones. Thus I prefer to find other ways to incorporate this literature. One way I've done this is to start by using some of the exciting new collections of short stories that focus on themes teens can relate to. Don Gallo's *Join In: Multiethnic Short Stories* is organized around the themes of "Expectations," "Friendships," "Dilemmas," "Connections," and "Confrontations" and includes stories concerned with studying for the PSATs, wanting to be an Asian rapper, and dealing with racial slurs. Laurence Yep's *American Dragons: Twenty-Five Asian American Voices* has stories that deal with a young girl who has to decide if it's okay to be a math whiz and a girl who no longer wants to be the Chinese Shirley Temple of her mother's dreams. The themes focused on in this collection are "Identity," "In the Shadow of Giants," "The Wise Child," "World War II," "Love," and "Guides." For teachers working to gather material for units on any of these themes, many of these short stories would fit the bill and work well with students.

With Other Novels

Another way I've included multicultural young adult literature in the class is to use a novel as a companion to another novel. I have used *Fallen Angels* with *The Red Badge of Courage* and linked the themes and issues. *The Great Gatsby* could be paired with a young adult novel that deals with striving after the American Dream, such as *Finding My Voice* by Marie G. Lee.

We can also give our students a more accurate idea of what was happening in the time period we are addressing by bringing in young adult literature that presents a different view of the same time period. In American literature it would work to use *Wolf by the Ears,* by Ann Rinaldi, when dealing with pre-Revolutionary literature. This historical novel is written from the point of view of the young woman rumored to be the daughter of Thomas Jefferson and his slave Sally Heming. A novel set between the Revolutionary War and the Civil War is Carolyn Meyer's *Where the Broken Heart Still Beats*. It is the story of Cynthia Ann Parker, who was abducted by Cherokees as a young girl, grows up and marries into the tribe, has three children, and is then "reclaimed" by her own family. Hostilities against Native Americans are very clear in this novel, which deals with a woman who can no longer accept the white man's ways.

As Part of a Thematic Unit

Often I'll find several books on one theme and give students the choice about which one they'll read. One time we looked at the question,

"What do we owe our families?" After writing about their own views on this issue, students selected one of the following books: *Shabanu* (Pakistani), by Suzanne Fisher Staples; *April and the Dragon Lady* (Chinese), by Lensey Namioka; *Glory Field* (African American), by Walter Dean Myers; *Where the Broken Heart Still Beats* (Native American), by Carolyn Meyer; and *White Peak Farm* (Anglo), by Berlie Doherty.

On the theme of "wanting to know where we came from," which focused on the desire to know who our parents are, we used the following: *A Little Love* (African American), by Virginia Hamilton; *Denny's Tapes* (African American), by Carolyn Meyer; *Molly by Any Other Name* (Japanese), by Jean Davies Okimoto; *Somewhere in the Darkness* (African American), by Walter Dean Myers; and *Arena Beach* (Anglo), by Donna Staples.

On the theme of "Dealing with parents/stepparents," we used *Plain City* (African American), by Virginia Hamilton; *Shizuko's Daughter* (Japanese), by Mori Kyoko; *Jesse* (Mexican American), by Gary Soto; *Songs from Home* (Anglo), by Joan Elizabeth Goodman; *April and the Dragon Lady* (Chinese), by Lensey Namioka; and *Wish You Were Here* (Anglo), by Barbara Shoup.

When we've dealt with the theme of "having relationships outside of our race or background," students have read *I Hadn't Meant To Tell You* (African American and Anglo), by Jacqueline Woodson; *Children of the River* (Cambodian and Anglo), by Linda Crew; *The Roller Birds of Rampur* (Indian and Anglo), by Indi Rana; *Shadowman's Way* (Native American and Anglo), by Paul Pitts; and *The World of Daughter McGuire* (African American and Italian), by Sharon Dennis Wyeth.

As a Whole-Class Novel

Sometimes we will use one of these novels as a whole-class book. One novel I've used this way is *Toning the Sweep,* by Angela Johnson. I loved this short novel because so much was packed into so few pages. The mother/daughter relationship between Emily's mother and grandmother, has to be worked out and the issues of dealing with the racial hatred that caused her grandfather's death have to be dealt with, but the issue at the heart of the book is the impending death of the grandmother, who wants to die in her own way. Much of the novel focuses on Emily's learning how to cope with all of these issues while she stays in the beautiful desert where her grandmother lives.

I loved the descriptions of the desert and the fact that the grandmother was such an independent character. Although the main characters are African American and the grandmother moved from the South because of racial violence, this book largely focuses on relationships, not on racial issues.

Beginning a Whole-Class Novel

I felt my students might like the book because in high school it's easier to be friends with a grandparent than a parent, and a grandmother was featured prominently in the novel. We started by writing grandparent stories. To get the creative juices flowing, I brought in the collection that Nikki Giovanni edited called *Grand Mothers*. After writing their own stories, we moved to swapping "can you top this" stories about the colorful or eccentric grandparents they had written about.

I felt it was important that students understand the tenor of the times in the South and in the country in the 1960s. To help students understand this in a more personal way, I asked them to interview their parents or grandparents about what they remembered about those times in the South. Some students brought taped interviews in; others wrote them up. Some of the students' grandparents lived in the South at that time and had vivid memories of the sit-ins at restaurants. Some remembered living in small towns where racism was very evident. Others talked about living in the North at the time and remembering Violet Liuzzo, a white woman from Detroit, who was murdered when she went south to participate in Civil Rights activities. Now that students had thought about some of the issues in the novel, we were ready to start.

While Reading the Novel

Since *Toning the Sweep* is a short novel, students read it quickly. I asked them to write responses in their literature logs as they read and to bring in questions they wanted to discuss. In their literature logs, which they can choose to share in their discussion groups, I also asked them to relate their lives and experiences to what happens in the book through such questions as the following:

> Have you ever refused to do something in school you were asked to do? Explain. Compare your behavior to Emily's.
>
> Mama hated her big feet when she was a teen. What about your appearance would you like to change? Explain.
>
> When you daydream, where do you go in your head? Create a story of drifting off and going somewhere else.
>
> At twelve what made you sad?

Share some of your memories of your family pictures or videos.

"Daddy says everybody has one [a story] and their stories are all a part of us." What kind of family stories does your family tell over and over?

Have you ever taken pictures that you've especially liked? Describe the best and worst pictures ever taken of you.

What are the hardest rules for you in school? Which ones are hardest for Emily?

Who is the friend you've known the longest? How do you account for staying friends so long?

"Mama says they didn't have a clue about raising me." Ask your parents how they know how to raise children. What could you as a teenager tell someone about raising children ?

Emily knows Ole is dying. Explain why you think it would be easy/hard to be around a dying person. What do you think it would be like?

Emily could hear her mother say, "Stealing is stealing and there ain't no way around it." What kind of things do the adults in your life say to you about life? How do you respond?

Most of the work in class was done in small groups. If students didn't feel they could generate enough discussion through responses and questions and they wanted the security of a structure, I often gave them ways to get started. One day I might ask them to focus on characters. I tell them to talk about who they like, who they don't understand, what they'd like to say to a character, and what they wished characters had said to each other. Sometimes I ask them about specific things about characters. For this novel I asked them to describe all the kinds of things Emily liked about her grandma and how they found out those things. I also asked them if they had ever known anyone like the aunts who lose every bit of control they have and roll across the floor.

Other times I might ask them to focus on events or the plot line. Did the events seem realistic? Would they have reacted differently to an event in the book? Why do they think the character reacted to the event the way she did?

Sometimes we'll focus on issues. We make a list on the board before we break into small groups so each group will have an abundance of material to work with. When they talk about themes and issues, I ask them to consider what the author wants them to think about the issue. I might pose questions like the following: What do you think Angela Johnson is saying about the process of dying? What statement might she be making about mother/daughter relationships? What do you think she's saying about racism?

Another day I might ask students in small groups to focus on the book itself. Did the plot structure seem workable? Did any events seem out of place or contrived? Did it move well or were there some parts that lagged? What did they notice about the language and words used?

Dealing with Difference through Novels

I also believe that difference must be dealt with in the classroom. I don't think we can be repetitive in our approach to difference and talk about all we read only in terms of it. But as frequently as we deal with theme and plot and setting and characters, we need to think about ways we can broaden our discussions of characterization to include a look at the way characters are being portrayed along ethnic, social, and gender lines. The suggestions that follow deal only with racial implications but could just as easily be reworked to help students take a look at gender and social representation. I often give students a shortened list of the following questions so they can include some of these issues in their discussions and in their responses in their literature logs.

1. What are minorities/majorities disapproved of for doing?
2. Compare minority/majority families. How are the fathers portrayed? The mothers? What's expected of each of them? What are they criticized for?
3. Look at how majority/minority women are characterized. What's expected of them?
4. In groups, students can discuss relationships shown. What characteristics are shown as positive for a male in a relationship with a female and vice versa? Are expectations the same for majority/minority members?
5. Is there a difference in what races gain status for (e.g., sports, competitiveness, relationships)?
6. How does the author want you to view members of the races portrayed?
7. How would the character have changed if the author had assigned him or her a different race?
8. How does the author characterize the different races? Look at the characters' speech, their appearance, their actions, or what others say about them.
9. How does the language in the story reinforce/refute racial stereotypes?

10. What about the character is paid most attention to? Does this vary among races?
11. Which characters seem to have the most interesting plans for the future? Does this vary by race?
12. Compare the races represented in the literature read in terms of the following personality characteristics: active/passive; selfless/selfish; rational/emotional; stable/unstable; courageous/afraid; risk taker/complier; aggressive/nonaggressive; challenging/obedient; low need for friendship / high need for friendship; competitive/nurturing (frequently viewed as opposites in society).
13. Which of the main character's experiences were related to the character's race?
14. Which of the main character's experiences are similar to ones you have had? Why do you think this is true?
15. Which of the main character's experiences will you probably never have? Why?

After the Novel

I usually like to end a novel with some kind of all-class or group project. For this novel, students could stage a talk show in which they interviewed the characters and got their opinions on such issues as dealing with death, relationships, and dealing with hate. We always stage these kinds of productions and students often wear clothing that is somehow evocative of the character. Other students chose to make videos, since so much of the story showed Emily videotaping snippets of her grandmother's life to remember her after she died. Students either interviewed their elders on their thoughts about death and racism or put together a video of still shots about what they would like others to remember about their life so far.

As another kind of culminating activity, I create a list of options that include writing, drama, and art. I ask students to choose from the following or invent one of their own.

> What would you like to say to a character? Write this in the form of a letter. (You could tell Ole what you think of her decision to discontinue chemotherapy or ask her more about leaving the South or ask Mama about her relationship with Ole.)
>
> Write from the point of view of a character saying the things he or she never got the chance to say to another character. (You could write what Mama would have to say to her father or what Ole would say to her husband.)

Write an essay or story on issues brought up in the book (e.g., death of a family member, an incident of racial hatred, or older people who feel free to act as they wish).

Create a poetic or artistic response. (Write several poems about characters or themes or places in the book. If you are artistic, draw a picture of how you visualize something in the book such as Ole's house or the desert or Ole driving her car.)

Respond using photos and poems. Bring in a photo of a person or event that evokes lots of memories for you. Write a poem about the picture.

Write about something that was alluded to but not fully developed in the novel or add a chapter or scene. (Write the funeral scene. Who would speak? What would they say? Write a new chapter showing what Ole would have done if she had stayed in the South after the murder of her husband.)

Read through several poetry books and select a poem that would mean a lot to a specific character. Find poems for several of the characters, and on the back of the poem write why you think this poem suits the character.

In Conclusion

When I use multicultural literature in my classroom, I try to make sure that discussions cover a full range of topics, including the issue of race. I don't avoid discussions of differences; I welcome them. School is one of the few places that adults have access to teen thinking through discussions, and often teens need an adult viewpoint or even someone to challenge their thinking. The language arts class seems like a good place to do this, because not only are we dealing with the differences among people, we are also dealing with the humanness of all people and all the things we have in common as human beings. If we use young adult literature that reflects the composition of our country, we can provide our students with experiences with groups of people they have never met. We can also give them the thrill of seeing someone like themselves in books and of realizing they are not invisible in the work and materials of the language arts class.

References

Crew, Linda. 1991. *Children of the River.* New York: Bantam Doubleday Dell.

Doherty, Berlie. 1990. *White Peak Farm.* New York: Orchard.

Gallo, Don. ed. 1995. *Join In: Multiethnic Short Stories by Outstanding Writers for Young Adults.* New York: Bantam Doubleday Dell.

Giovanni, Nikki. 1994. *Grand Mothers.* New York: Holt.

Goodman, Joan Elizabeth. 1994. *Songs from Home.* San Diego: Harcourt Brace.

Hamilton, Virginia. 1985. *A Little Love.* New York: Berkley Books.

Johnson, Angela. 1994. *Toning the Sweep.* New York: Scholastic.

Kyoko, Mori. 1993. *Shizuko's Daughter.* New York: Fawcett Juniper.

Lee, Marie G. 1992. *Finding My Voice.* New York: Dell.

Meyer, Carolyn. 1987. *Denny's Tapes.* New York: McElderry.

———. 1992. *Where the Broken Heart Still Beats: The Story of Cynthia Ann Parker.* San Diego: Harcourt Brace.

Myers, Walter Dean. 1988. *Fallen Angels.* New York: Scholastic.

———. 1992. *Somewhere in the Darkness.* New York: Scholastic.

———. 1994. *Glory Field.* New York: Scholastic.

Namioka, Lensey. 1994. *April and the Dragon Lady.* San Diego: Harcourt Brace.

Okimoto, Jean Davies. 1993. *Molly by Any Other Name.* New York: Scholastic.

Pitts, Paul. 1992. *The Shadowman's Way.* New York: Avon.

Rana, Indi. 1994. *The Roller Birds of Rampur.* New York: Fawcett.

Rinaldi, Ann. 1993. *Wolf by the Ears.* New York: Scholastic.

Shoup, Barbara. 1994. *Wish You Were Here.* New York: Hyperion.

Soto, Gary. 1994. *Jesse.* San Diego: Harcourt Brace.

Staples, Donna. 1993. *Arena Beach.* Boston: Houghton Mifflin.

Staples, Suzanne Fisher. 1995. *Haveli.* New York: Random House.

Woodson, Jacqueline. 1994. *I Hadn't Meant to Tell You This.* New York: Delacorte.

Wyeth, Sharon Dennis. 1994. *The World of Daughter McGuire.* New York: Delacorte.

Yep, Laurence. 1993. *American Dragons: Twenty-five Asian American Voices.* New York: HarperCollins.

Annotated Bibliography of Fiction

Bosse, Malcolm. 1996. *The Examination.* New York: Farrar, Straus & Giroux.

Two brothers set out for Beijing, where one is to take the government exams for a scholar. Their adventures on their journey rival the exploits of Tom Sawyer and Huckleberry Finn.

Brooke, William. 1995. *A Brush with Magic.* New York: HarperCollins.

This is the fanciful tale of Liang, an orphan boy, who can bring to life anything he paints with his magic brush.

Chang, Margaret. 1990. *In the Eye of War.* New York: McElderry.
This is the story of the final days of the Japanese occupation of China during World War II as seen through the experiences of a ten-year-old.

DeJong, Meindert. 1956, 1987. *The House of Sixty Fathers.* New York: Harper Collins. An adventure tale of an accidental sea journey from Japan to China by a teenage boy.

Fritz, Jean. 1984. *Homesick: My Own Story.* New York: Dell/Yearling.
Fritz's fictional account of her childhood in China during the 1920s.

Namioka, Lensey. 1994. *April and the Dragon Lady.* San Diego: Harcourt Brace.
A "generation gap" story about a Chinese American teenager and her grandmother.

Neville, Emily. 1991. *The China Year.* New York: HarperCollins.
A New York teenager spends a year in China when her father accepts a teaching position in Beijing.

Paterson, Katherine. 1995. *Rebels of the Heavenly Kingdom.* New York: Puffin.
Story of rebellion in nineteenth-century China as a young boy and girl engage in activities to overthrow the Manchu government.

Yee, Paul. 1989. *Tales from Gold Mountain: Stories of the Chinese in the New World.* New York: Macmillan.
Short stories about the immigrants who built the transcontinental railroad, panned for gold, and settled the western United States

Yep, Laurence. *Child of the Owl* (1990 HarperCollins), *Dragon's Gate* (1993 HarperCollins), *Mountain Light* (1997 HarperCollins), *The Serpent's Children* (1996 HarperCollins), and *The Star Fisher* (1997 Puffin).
A variety of novels about China and Chinese immigrants to the United States.

V Learning More about Young Adult Literature

As we work with teachers to help expand their curricula to include a diversity of books and authors, we are always asked for resource lists. This section devotes two chapters to providing teachers with sources of information to learn more about the field in general or about specific books and authors. In the first chapter, Dee Storey provides information about biographical, bibliographical, and electronic sources to benefit both teachers and students. The concluding chapter presents a listing of all of the young adult titles we have included in this book, with brief annotations.

27 A Source Guide for Locating Multicultural Literature for Young Adults

Dee Storey
Saginaw Valley State University

Several organizations representing different philosophies, goals, and audiences provide an accumulated body of information regarding multicultural literature. The following bibliography is an overview of children's and adolescent multicultural literature that is available pertinent to trends, issues, authors, illustrators, and awards. The sources cited are current publications. For a historical perspective, educators may wish to consult volumes or editions that were published before 1990.

Defining Multicultural Literature

Sims, Rudine. 1982. *Shadow and Substance: Afro-American Experience in Contemporary Children's Fiction.* Urbana, IL: NCTE.

Sims defines multicultural literature, reacts to the issues of author authenticity, and creates a context for change.

Presenting Authors and Illustrators

Cummings, P., ed. 1992. *Talking with Artists.* New York: Simon & Schuster.

Conversations with fourteen illustrators, including Tom Feelings and Leo and Diane Dillon.

Cummings, P., ed. 1995. *Talking with Artists: Volume Two.* New York: Macmillan.

Conversations with eleven illustrators, including David Wisiewski and Sheila Hamanaka.

Rollock, Barbara. 1992. *Black Authors and Illustrators of Children's Books: A Biographical Dictionary.* 2nd edition. New York: Garland.

Silvey, Anita. 1995. *Children's Books and Their Creators.* Boston: Houghton Mifflin.

Something about the Author. 1971–1997. (91 volumes). Detroit, MI: Gale Research.

Biographical information about illustrators is also available within this source.

Bibliographies for Children's and Adolescent Literature Specifically Multicultural in Focus

Bishop, Rudine, ed. 1994. *Kaleidoscope: A Multicultural Booklist for Grades K–8.* Urbana, IL: NCTE.

Helbig, Alethea, and Perkins, A. 1994. *This Land Is Our Land: A Guide to Multicultural Literature for Children and Young Adults.* Westport, CT: Greenwood.

Lindgren, M. V. 1991. *The Multicolored Mirror: Cultural Substance in Literature for Children and Young Adults.* Fort Atkinson, WI: Highsmith.

Marantz, Sylvia, and Kenneth Marantz. 1994. *Multicultural Picture Books: Art for Understanding Others.* Worthington, OH: Linworth.

Miller-Lachmann, Lyn. 1991. *Our Family, Our Friends, Our World: An Annotated Guide to Significant Multicultural Books for Children and Teenagers.* New Providence, NJ: R. R. Bowker.

Rochman, Hazel. 1993. *Against Borders: Promoting Books for a Multicultural World.* Chicago: American Library Association.

Thomas, Rebecca. 1996. *Connecting Cultures: A Guide to Multicultural Literature for Children.* New Providence, NJ: R. R. Bowker.

General Bibliographies with Subheads Specific to Multicultural Issues, Characters and Settings

Lima, Carolyn. 1993. *A to Zoo: Subject Access: Children's Picture Books.* New Providence, NJ: R. R. Bowker.

Book Links. Chicago, IL: A Booklist Publication of the American Library Association.

Children's Books in Print. 1997. New Providence, NJ: R. R. Bowker.

Subject Guide to Children's Books in Print. 1997. New Providence, NJ: R. R. Bowker.

Children's Catalog. New York: H. W. Wilson.

Freeman, Judy. 1990. *Books Kids Will Sit Still For: The Complete Read-Aloud Guide.* 2nd Edition. New York: R. R. Bowker.

Gillespie, John, and C. Naden, eds. 1994. *Best Books for Children: Preschool through Grade 6.* 5th Edition. New Providence, NJ: R. R. Bowker.

Roser, Nancy, ed. 1993. *Adventuring with Books: A Booklist for Pre-K–Grade 6.* Urbana, IL: NCTE.

Wurth, Shirley, ed. 1992. *Books for You: Booklist for Senior High Students.* 11th Edition. Urbana, IL: NCTE.

Awards and Other Honors

A partial listing of awards:

Australian Multicultural Children's Literature Awards: Office of Multicultural Affairs in the Department of the Prime Minister and Cabinet for cultural diversity and social harmony.

Carter G. Woodson Award: National Council for the Social Studies to promote and celebrate ethnic minorities and race relations that are portrayed sensitively and accurately.

Coretta Scott King Award: American Library Association to celebrate African American authors and illustrators.

Notable Children's Trade Books: the National Council for the Social Studies. The annual list of notable books exemplifying the 10 strands of social studies understanding is announced in the April/May issue.

Sydney Taylor Body of Work: Association of Jewish Libraries/ National Foundation for Jewish Culture for literature that has stood the test of time and portrays and displays positive Jewish values.

Sydney Taylor Book Award: Association of Jewish Libraries/ National Foundation for Jewish Culture for the portrayal of positive Jewish values.

Specific Awards cited in:

Brown, Muriel W., and R. Foudray. 1992. *Newbery and Caldecott Medalists and Honor Book Winners: Bibliographies and Resource Material through 1991.* New York: Neal-Schuman Publishers.

Children's Books: Awards and Prizes. 1996. New York: Children's Book Council.

Jones, Delores B. 1994. *Children's Literature Awards and Winners: A Directory of Prizes, Authors, and Illustrators.* 3rd Edition. Detroit, MI: Gale Research.

Teaching Multicultural Literature

Beaty, Janice. 1996. *Building Bridges with Multicultural Picture Books for Children 3–5.* New York: Macmillan.

Brown, Jean, and E. Stephens. 1996. *Exploring Diversity: Literature Themes and Activities for Grades 4–8.* Englewood, CO: Teacher's Idea Press.

Diamond, Barbara J., and Moore, M. A. 1995. *Multicultural Literacy: Mirroring the Reality of the Classroom.* White Plains, NY: Longman.

Finazzo, Denise A. 1997. *All for the Children: Multicultural Essentials of Literature.* Albany, NY: Delmar.

Harris, Violet E. 1993. *Teaching Multicultural Literature in Grades K–8.* Norwood, MA: Christopher Gordon.

Hayden, Carla D., ed. 1993. *Venture into Cultures: A Resource Book of Multicultural Materials and Programs.* Chicago: American Library Association.

Samway, K. D. 1995. *Literature Study Circles in a Multicultural Classroom.* York, ME: Stenhouse.

Stephens, Elaine C., J. E. Brown, and J. E. Rubin. 1995. *Learning about the Holocaust: Literature and Other Resources for Young People.* North Haven, CT: Shoe String Press.

Professional Journals

ALAN. A Journal of the Assembly on Literature for Adolescent Literature of the National Council of Teachers of English.

English Journal. Urbana, IL: NCTE.

The Horn Book Magazine. Boston: The Horn Book.

Interracial Books Bulletin. New York: Council on Interracial Books for Children.

Language Arts. Urbana, IL: NCTE.

The New Advocate. Norwoood, MA: Christopher Gordon.

Social Education. Washington, D.C.: National Council for the Social Studies.

Social Studies. Washington, D.C.: Helfdref Publications.

Social Studies and the Young Learner. Washington, D.C.: National Council for the Social Studies.

Book Review Journals

Booklist: Chicago: American Library Association.

The Bulletin of the Center for Children's Books. University of Illinois Graduate School of Library and Information Science. Champaign, IL: University of Illinois Press.

Children's Literature Review. Detroit, MI: Gale Research.

Internet Sources

Leu, Donald, and Diadiun Leu, D. 1997. *Teaching with the Internet: Lessons from the Classroom.* Norwood, MA: Christopher Gordon.

Chapter 10: "Increasing Multicultural Understanding."

Chapter 5: "Using the Internet for Language Arts and Literature."

Polly, Jean A. 1996. *The Internet Kids Yellow Pages—Special Edition.* Berkeley, CA: Osborne–McGraw-Hill.

Annotated Bibliography

Ruth Copp, Dallas Fischer, Alyce Hunter, Kent Sikora, and Erin C. Sullivan with Karen Selby

Abells, Chana Byers. 1986. The Children We Remember. New York: Greenwillow.

Abells has created a photographic essay of Jewish children before, during, and after the Holocaust using photographs from Yad Vashem in Jerusalem. The small amount of text is simple and direct.

Adler, David. 1995. *We Remember the Holocaust.* New York: Holt.

This is an account of the Holocaust that includes personal accounts of life in Nazi death camps. It also gives a chronology of the Holocaust.

Anderson, Mary. 1980. *The Rise and Fall of a Teen-Age Wacko.* New York: Atheneum.

This book describes the problems for a Jewish teen of moving from a mostly Jewish urban environment to a non-Jewish rural environment.

Angelou, Maya. 1970, 1997. *I Know Why the Caged Bird Sings.* New York: Bantam.

An eloquent retelling of her youth as only Maya Angelou can do. The reader experiences the pain and joy of trying to grow up while being tossed between her grandmother in the poor South and her parents on the West Coast during the 1930s and 1940s.

———. 1993. *Life Doesn't Frighten Me.* New York: Stewart, Tabori & Chang.

A touching poem with vivid illustrations that lend a reality to her work.

———. 1995. *Phenomenal Woman: Four Poems Celebrating Women.* New York: Random House.

These poems, which are among Angelou's most acclaimed work, set aside traditional standards of feminine beauty and attractiveness in order to instill and celebrate a sense of self-confidence and inner strength in unstereotyped female identity.

Anonymous. 1994. *It Happened to Nancy: A True Story from the Diary of a Teenager.* Ed. Beatrice Sparks. New York: Avon Flare.

An autobiographical presentation of a young female's struggle with AIDS.

Arrick, Fran. 1983. *Chernowitz!* New York: Signet.

Ninth-grader Bobby Cherno, called Chernowitz by the anti-Semitic local bully Emmett, sees acts of anti-Semitism escalate as others follow Emmett's lead. Bobby vows revenge and learns the difficulties of facing prejudice.

Ashabranner, Brent. 1983. *The New Americans: Changing Patterns in U. S. Immigration.* New York: Dodd, Mead.

This is a history of immigration to the United States with a discussion of the changes in immigrants' countries of origin as well as difficulties and successes encountered by immigrants.

———. 1987a. *The Vanishing Border: A Photographic Journey along Our Frontier with Mexico.* New York: Dodd, Mead.

This book examines the effects on Mexico and the United States of sharing a 2,000 mile border.

———and Melissa Ashabranner. 1987b. *Into a Strange Land: Unaccompanied Refugee Youth in America.* New York: Putnam.

This is the story of Southeast Asian children who came to the United States after the Vietnam War.

———. 1991. *An Ancient Heritage: The Arab-American Minority.* New York: HarperCollins.

Ashabranner chronicles the history of Arab-American immigrants in the United States and reveals the diversity within the Arab-American minority.

———. 1993. *Still a Nation of Immigrants.* New York: Dutton.

Ashabranner examines the effect of rising levels of immigration on the United States and discusses recent immigrants, mainly from Asia and Latin America, and the problems and contributions of these immigrants.

———. 1996. *Our Beckoning Borders: Illegal Immigration to America.* New York: Dutton.

Ashabranner presents reasons people risk illegal immigration as well as ideas about solving the problem of illegal immigration.

Asher, Sandy. 1982. *Summer Begins.* New York: Bantam.

Summer, a Christian, needs a topic for her eighth-grade paper and decides to research the feelings of non-Christians who must be a part of the school's Christmas program. Summer doesn't seek or expect the many different reactions and learns a lot about herself and people of religions other than hers.

———. 1983. *Daughters of the Law.* New York: Dell.

Ruthie, in deciding whether or not to be Bat Mitzvahed, wrestles with her aunt's wish that she observe the Jewish rite of passage ceremony versus her deceased father's hatred for organized religion.

Bandon, Alexandra. 1994a. *Vietnamese Americans.* Parsippany, NJ: New Discovery.

One in a series, this book relates historic reasons given for emigrating from Vietnam, reasons for immigrating to the United States, the prejudices and opportunities encountered in the United States, and information about Vietnamese lifestyles and culture.

———. 1994b. *West Indian Americans.* Parsippany, NJ: New Discovery.

One in a series, this book relates information about prejudices and opportunities encountered as well as information about lifestyles and culture.

———. 1995. *Asian Indian Americans.* Parsippany, NJ: New Discovery.

One in a series, this book relates historic reasons given for emigrating from India, reasons for immigrating to the United States, the prejudices and opportunities encountered in the United States, and information about East Indian lifestyles and culture.

Bauer, Joan. 1994. *Squashed.* New York: Bantam Doubleday Dell Books for Young Readers.

Sixteen-year-old Ellie must overcome a variety of adversities in her attempt to grow the largest pumpkin in Iowa. Along the way she acquires two unforeseen benefits: a stronger relationship with her father and the attention of a young man with whom Ellie shares many common interests.

———. 1996. *Sticks.* New York: Delacorte Press.

Ten-year-old Mickey, a math genius, prepares for the most important pool championship of his life with the assistance of his grandmother, his best friend, and his dead father's best friend.

———. 1995. *Thwonk.* New York: Delacorte Press.

Remember the old adage, "Be careful what you wish for—it may come true." This is what happens to A.J., a struggling young photographic artist with a history of heartwrenching love episodes, when a cupid doll comes to life and offers her romantic assistance.

Bell, Derrick. 1992. *Faces at the Bottom of the Well.* New York: Basic Books.

The burdens of racism cannot change until whites' position in society is threatened. Even the poorest of white people look down upon the black faces who seem to be at the bottom of society's well. It seems this author's message is that we must work together to end racism.

Blair, Cynthia. 1988. *Crazy in Love.* New York: Fawcett.

Sallie and Rachel are close friends, but when Rachel is attracted to Sallie's boyfriend, Saul, the friendship is tested. Rachel is caught between the values of her Jewish heritage and dating Saul.

Blume, Judy. 1970. *Are You There, God? It's Me, Margaret!* New York: Bradbury.

Margaret, a sixth grader whose parents are of different faiths, grapples with common concerns of many adolescents including what type of relationship she should have with God.

Bode, Janet. 1989. *Different Worlds: Interracial and Cross-Cultural Dating.* New York: Franklin Watts.

A presentation of the difficult and complex issues involved in interracial and cross-cultural dating among teens. The issues discussed range from peer pressure to parental reaction to psychological motivation.

———. 1989. *New Kids on the Block: Oral Histories of Immigrant Teens.* Danbury, CT: Franklin Watts.

Young immigrants discuss the emotional and psychological difficulties they encounter as they leave their homelands and try to adjust to their new life in an unfamiliar culture.

———. 1991. *Beating the Odds: Stories of Unexpected Achievers.* Illus. Stan Mack. New York: Franklin Watts.

A presentation of various young adults who have not merely overcome seemingly impossible difficulties (e.g., poverty, drug abuse, sexual abuse) and survived, but demonstrated success in doing so.

———. 1992a. *Kids Still Having Kids: People Talk about Teen Pregnancy.* Illus. Stan Mack. New York: Franklin Watts.

A presentation of various case studies and interviews which focus on teen pregnancy and teen mothers. Topics include adoption, abortion, parenting, foster care, and sex instruction.

———. 1992b. *The Voices of Rape: Healing the Hurt.* New York: Laurel Leaf.

First-hand accounts of both rape victims and rape offenders. Discussions include such issues as the physical, psychological, and legal aspects and ramifications of rape.

———. 1993. *Truce: Ending the Sibling War.* New York: Laurel Leaf.

A dicussion of the occasionally strained relationships of siblings, focusing on various means with which to end conflicts and improve relationships.

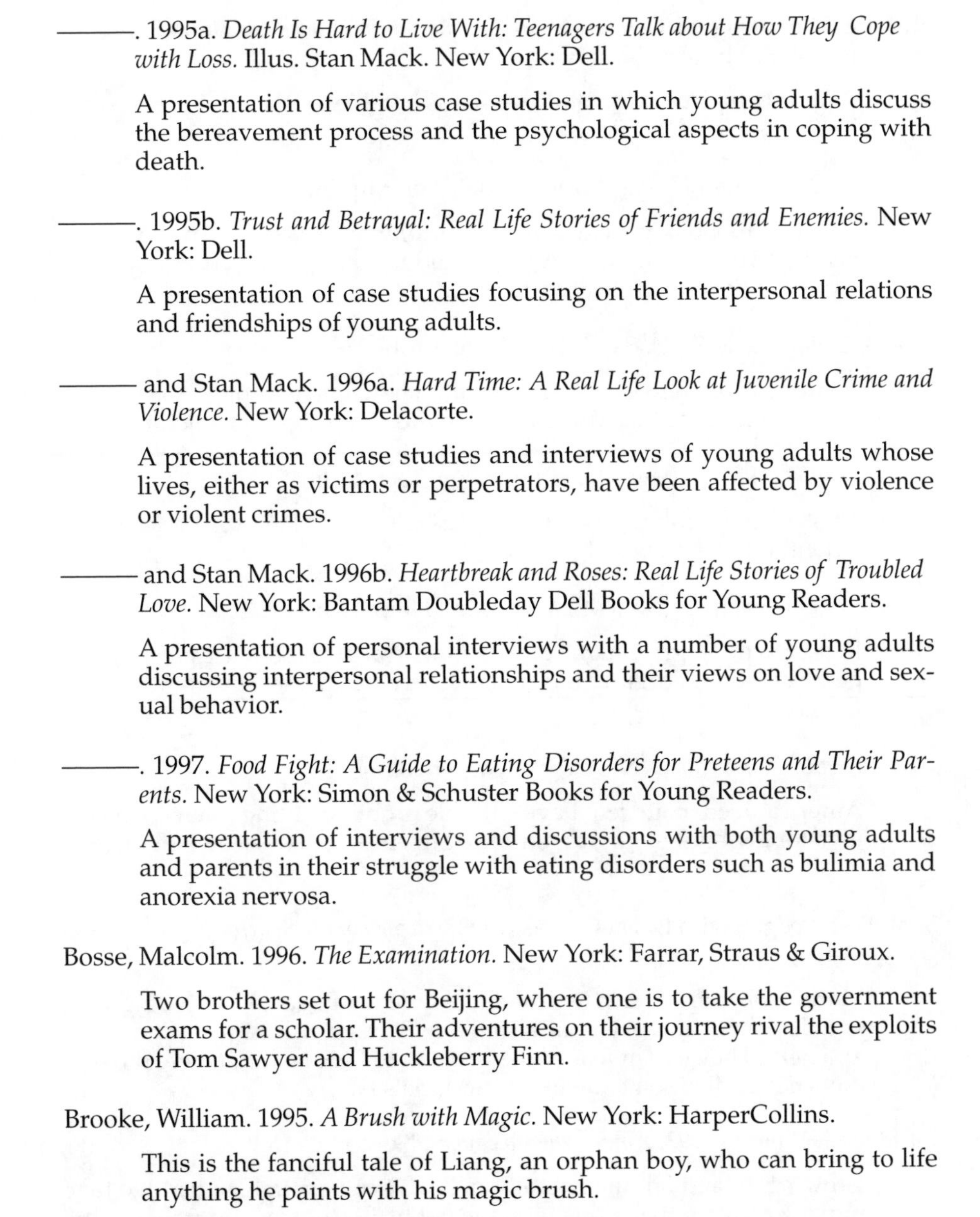

———. 1995a. *Death Is Hard to Live With: Teenagers Talk about How They Cope with Loss.* Illus. Stan Mack. New York: Dell.

A presentation of various case studies in which young adults discuss the bereavement process and the psychological aspects in coping with death.

———. 1995b. *Trust and Betrayal: Real Life Stories of Friends and Enemies.* New York: Dell.

A presentation of case studies focusing on the interpersonal relations and friendships of young adults.

——— and Stan Mack. 1996a. *Hard Time: A Real Life Look at Juvenile Crime and Violence.* New York: Delacorte.

A presentation of case studies and interviews of young adults whose lives, either as victims or perpetrators, have been affected by violence or violent crimes.

——— and Stan Mack. 1996b. *Heartbreak and Roses: Real Life Stories of Troubled Love.* New York: Bantam Doubleday Dell Books for Young Readers.

A presentation of personal interviews with a number of young adults discussing interpersonal relationships and their views on love and sexual behavior.

———. 1997. *Food Fight: A Guide to Eating Disorders for Preteens and Their Parents.* New York: Simon & Schuster Books for Young Readers.

A presentation of interviews and discussions with both young adults and parents in their struggle with eating disorders such as bulimia and anorexia nervosa.

Bosse, Malcolm. 1996. *The Examination.* New York: Farrar, Straus & Giroux.

Two brothers set out for Beijing, where one is to take the government exams for a scholar. Their adventures on their journey rival the exploits of Tom Sawyer and Huckleberry Finn.

Brooke, William. 1995. *A Brush with Magic.* New York: HarperCollins.

This is the fanciful tale of Liang, an orphan boy, who can bring to life anything he paints with his magic brush.

Brooks, Bruce. 1986. *Midnight Hour Encores.* New York: HarperCollins.

Sixteen-year-old Sib, a musician like her parents, discovers more about herself and her relationship with her father after a trip to meet the mother who abandoned her when she was born.

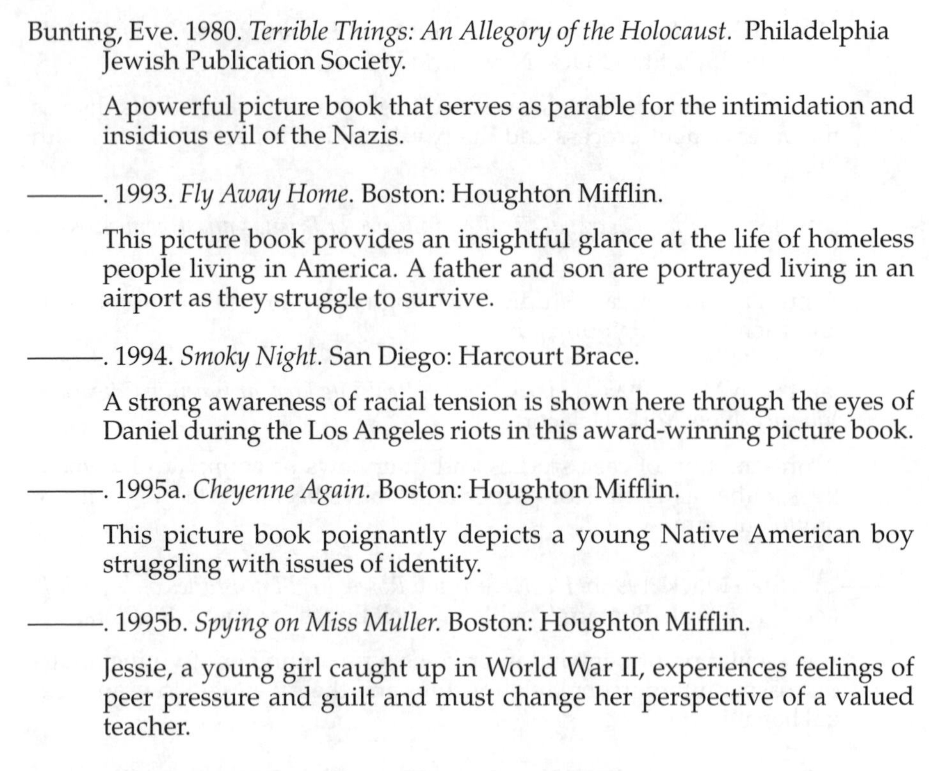

Bunting, Eve. 1980. *Terrible Things: An Allegory of the Holocaust.* Philadelphia Jewish Publication Society.

A powerful picture book that serves as parable for the intimidation and insidious evil of the Nazis.

———. 1993. *Fly Away Home.* Boston: Houghton Mifflin.

This picture book provides an insightful glance at the life of homeless people living in America. A father and son are portrayed living in an airport as they struggle to survive.

———. 1994. *Smoky Night.* San Diego: Harcourt Brace.

A strong awareness of racial tension is shown here through the eyes of Daniel during the Los Angeles riots in this award-winning picture book.

———. 1995a. *Cheyenne Again.* Boston: Houghton Mifflin.

This picture book poignantly depicts a young Native American boy struggling with issues of identity.

———. 1995b. *Spying on Miss Muller.* Boston: Houghton Mifflin.

Jessie, a young girl caught up in World War II, experiences feelings of peer pressure and guilt and must change her perspective of a valued teacher.

———. 1996. *Going Home.* New York: HarperCollins.

Americanized children have trouble understanding their parents' love for a seemingly outdated Mexican culture in this colorful picture book.

Buss, Fran Leeper, with Daisy Cubias. 1993. *Journey of the Sparrows.* New York: Dell.

Maria and some of her family illegally leave El Salvador, hiding in a wooden crate, and eventually settle in Chicago, where they find hope and help. They live in fear of deportation to El Salvador, where the soldiers have killed some members of Maria's family.

Castaneda, Omar S. 1993. *Among the Volcanoes.* New York: Dell.

Growing up and finding oneself can be difficult enough, but add to that nursing an ill mother along with the political struggles and upheaval of contemporary Guatemala, and life can at times seem overwhelming.

Cerar, K. Melissa. 1995. *Teenage Refugees from Nicaragua Speak Out.* New York: Rosen.

Teenage refugees from Nicaragua tell why and how they left home and how they have adjusted to life in the United States in this volume in a series of "In Their Own Voices" books.

Chaikin, Miriam. 1979. *I Should Worry, I Should Care.* New York: Harper & Row.

Just before World War II, Molly and her family move from Manhattan to Brooklyn, and Molly is sad to leave her old friends but curious about the new neighborhood.

Chang, Margaret. 1990. *In the Eye of War.* New York: McElderry.

This is the story of the final days of the Japanese occupation of China during World War II as seen through the experiences of a ten-year-old.

Cisneros, Sandra. 1994. *The House on Mango Street.* New York: Random House.

Vivid sketches of people and places from her childhood.

Clifford, Eth. 1985. *The Remembering Box.* Boston: Houghton Mifflin.

Nine-year-old Joshua learns about his Jewish heritage from his grandmother's stories about the items in her "remembering box."

Coerr, Eleanor. 1993. *Sadako.* New York: Putnam.

The aftermath of the atomic bomb is one of suffering for Sadako, who contracts leukemia as a result of exposure to radiation. As she lies in the hospital dying, she busies herself folding one thousand paper cranes, wondering if the legend of healing is true.

Conlon-McKenna, Marita. 1991. *Wildflower Girl.* New York: Holiday House.

In the 1850s, thirteen-year-old Peggy leaves Ireland for Boston in search of work and opportunity.

Creech, Sharon. 1994. *Walk Two Moons.* New York: HarperCollins.

Thirteen-year-old Salamanca tells stories to her grandparents on a car trip from Ohio to Idaho, where she hopes to see her mother and talk her into returning. In the storytelling process, Sal tells part of her own story, too.

Crew, Linda. 1989. *Children of the River.* New York: Boston Doubleday Dell.

After fleeing Cambodia and the Khmer Rouge Army, Sundar Sovan is torn between the American way of life and maintaining the cultural traditions of her family.

Crutcher, Chris. 1987. *The Crazy Horse Electric Game.* New York: Bantam Doubleday Dell Books for Young Readers.

Willie Weaver is an aspiring young athlete who becomes both physically and emotionally disabled as the result of a boating accident. Embittered and alienated, he leaves home and eventually finds himself in an alternative education program, where he is able to redefine his physical and emotional balance.

———. 1993. *Staying Fat for Sarah Byrnes.* New York: Bantam Doubleday Dell Books for Young Readers.

Sarah has learned to use sarcasm and her wits as a means of coping with the horrifying scars she received at the early age of three. As the truth of Sarah's scars begin to come to light, it is her best friend Eric who helps her deal with both the truth and pain of her abused childhood.

Curtis, Gavin. 1990. *Grandma's Baseball.* New York: Crown.

In this delightful picture book, Grandma comes to live with a young boy's family after her husband dies. Grandma seems grumpy, but when he begins to play with a baseball that sits on Grandma's dresser, the boy learns a great deal more about his Grandma.

DeJong, Meindert. 1956. *The House of Sixty Fathers.* New York: Harper & Row.

An adventure tale of an accidental sea journey from Japan to China by a teenage boy.

Doherty, Berlie. 1990. *White Peak Farm.* New York: Orchard Books.

The story of a British family who owns a sheep farm, each member having dreams that many times do not coincide with the family's expectations. It's the family, though, that holds them together.

Dorris, Michael. 1992. *Morning Girl.* New York: Hyperion Books for Children.

A story of two Arawak Indian siblings whose relationship is typical of any brother and sister. They are of a community whose people have great respect for one another and their environment; many things change, though, when Christopher Columbus makes his discovery.

Filipovic, Zlata. 1995. *Zlata's Diary: A Child's Life in Sarajevo.* New York: Viking Penguin.

This is the story of a young girl's survival in war-torn Bosnia. It is gripping in its honest appraisal of a country whose leaders sought a path of self-destruction.

Finkelstein, Norman H. 1993. *Remember Not to Forget: A Memory of the Holcaust.* Illus. Lois and Lars Hokanson. New York: Morrow/Mulberry.

This book introduces young readers to the Nazi extermination of six million Jews during World War II.

Fisher, Leonard Everett. 1980. *A Russian Farewell.* Portland, OR: Four Winds Press.

In the early part of this century, a Jewish family from the Ukraine escapes to the United States to avoid religious persecution.

Fox, Paula. 1991. *The Slave Dancer.* New York: Dell.

In 1840, thirteen-year-old Jessie is kidnapped from New Orleans and is forced to play his fife on a slave ship so that the slaves can dance and exercise in their cramped ship quarters to stay in shape and, therefore, make a profit when sold by the slave traders.

Freedman, Russell. 1994. *Kids at Work: Lewis Hine and the Crusade against Child Labor.* Boston: Houghton Mifflin.

A photographic essay recording the efforts of teacher and photographer Lewis Hine to raise public awareness about the evils of child labor.

Fritz, Jean. 1984. *Homesick: My Own Story.* New York: Dell/ Yearling.

Fritz's fictional account of her childhood in China during the 1920s.

Gallo, Don, ed. 1995. *Join In: Multiethnic Short Stories by Outstanding Writers for Young Adults.* New York: Bantam Doubleday Dell.

Characters from varying ethnic backgrounds—Japanese, Cuban, Lebanese, African American, and Chicano, to name a few—come to life in stories about young adult issues: friendship, prejudice, happiness, and pain.

Gerber, Merrill Joan. 1990. *Handsome as Anything.* New York: Scholastic.

Rachel, a senior in high school, is searching for the right guy. One of the topics in this book is dating outside of one's faith.

Giovanni, Nikki. 1994. *Grand Mothers.* New York: Holt.

Stories about grandmothers and their contribution to our lives are shared by several female authors, such as Gloria Naylor, Kyoko Mori, Mary Elizabeth King, and Gwendolyn Brooks, in this collection of poems and short stories.

Girion, Barbara. 1980. *Like Everybody Else.* New York: Scribner.

Seventh-grader Samantha is at odds with her mother over her elaborate arrangements for Samantha's Bat Mitzvah. Samantha learns a lot about herself in the process of planning and discussing the Bat Mitzvah with her mother.

Glenn, Mel. 1989. *Squeeze Play: A Baseball Story.* New York: Clarion.

Jeremy, a sixth-grader whose teacher requires attendance at after-school baseball games, is helped to deal with the teacher, insecurity about playing baseball, and the teasing of classmates, by kindly Mr. Janowicz, a Holocaust survivor.

Golenbock, Peter. 1990. *Teammates*. San Diego: Harcourt Brace.

Jackie Robinson was the first black player in major league baseball. This story tells of his struggle with prejudice and his acceptance by a white Brooklyn Dodgers teammate, Pee Wee Reese.

Goodman, Joan Elizabeth. 1994. *Songs from Home*. San Diego: Harcourt Brace.

Anna and her father sing in the streets of Rome for money. Little eleven-year-old Anna only dreams of a normal home and family life.

Gordon, Sheila. 1989. *Waiting for the Rain*. New York: Bantam.

Tengo, a black farm worker who later fights apartheid, and Frikkie, the white future owner of the farm and member of the army, have been friends since their youth. Now they are at odds—one seeking change and one trying to preserve the status quo—and so their friendship is severely tested.

Greene, Bette. 1993. *Summer of My German Soldier*. New York: Dell.

Patty Bergen is twelve, Jewish, and the victim of a dysfunctional family. Then her hometown becomes the site of a German prisoner of war camp during World War II. Patty engages in a dangerous friendship with Anton, an escaped prisoner. In the end, a horrible price is paid for the love the two friends are able to share.

Grifalconi, A. 1986. *The Village of Round and Square Houses*. Boston: Little, Brown.

The author blends folklore, fiction, and illustration in an African folktale of Tos, a remote village in Cameroon.

Gross, Judith. 1992. *Celebrate: A Book of Jewish Holidays*. New York: Grosset & Dunlap.

This book introduces young adults to the fasts and feasts of such Jewish holidays as Shabbat, Rosh Hashanah, Yom Kippur, Hanukkah, Passover, and more.

Grossman, Mort. 1975. *The Summer Ends Too Soon.*. Philadelphia: Westminster.

When a Jewish boy and a Protestant girl fall in love, they must deal with parental attitudes and their religions' differences.

Hahn, Mary Downing. 1991. *Stepping on the Cracks*. New York: Clarion Books.

Eleven-year-old Margaret and her best friend find that appearances are not always what they seem as they find the truth about what motivates a school bully. During World War II, they learn about loss and making difficult choices.

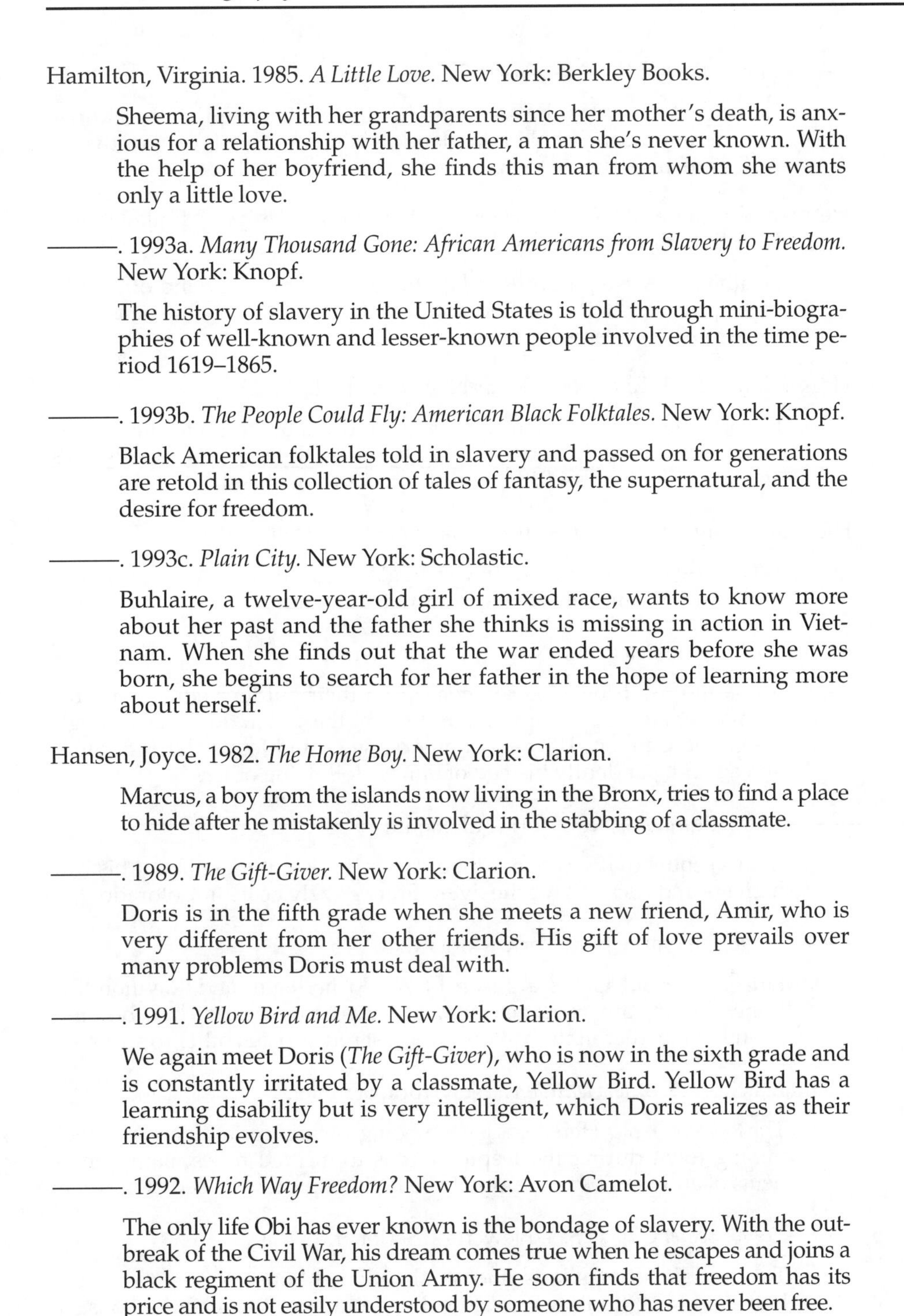

Hamilton, Virginia. 1985. *A Little Love.* New York: Berkley Books.

Sheema, living with her grandparents since her mother's death, is anxious for a relationship with her father, a man she's never known. With the help of her boyfriend, she finds this man from whom she wants only a little love.

———. 1993a. *Many Thousand Gone: African Americans from Slavery to Freedom.* New York: Knopf.

The history of slavery in the United States is told through mini-biographies of well-known and lesser-known people involved in the time period 1619–1865.

———. 1993b. *The People Could Fly: American Black Folktales.* New York: Knopf.

Black American folktales told in slavery and passed on for generations are retold in this collection of tales of fantasy, the supernatural, and the desire for freedom.

———. 1993c. *Plain City.* New York: Scholastic.

Buhlaire, a twelve-year-old girl of mixed race, wants to know more about her past and the father she thinks is missing in action in Vietnam. When she finds out that the war ended years before she was born, she begins to search for her father in the hope of learning more about herself.

Hansen, Joyce. 1982. *The Home Boy.* New York: Clarion.

Marcus, a boy from the islands now living in the Bronx, tries to find a place to hide after he mistakenly is involved in the stabbing of a classmate.

———. 1989. *The Gift-Giver.* New York: Clarion.

Doris is in the fifth grade when she meets a new friend, Amir, who is very different from her other friends. His gift of love prevails over many problems Doris must deal with.

———. 1991. *Yellow Bird and Me.* New York: Clarion.

We again meet Doris (*The Gift-Giver*), who is now in the sixth grade and is constantly irritated by a classmate, Yellow Bird. Yellow Bird has a learning disability but is very intelligent, which Doris realizes as their friendship evolves.

———. 1992. *Which Way Freedom?* New York: Avon Camelot.

The only life Obi has ever known is the bondage of slavery. With the outbreak of the Civil War, his dream comes true when he escapes and joins a black regiment of the Union Army. He soon finds that freedom has its price and is not easily understood by someone who has never been free.

———. 1995. *The Captive.* New York: Scholastic.

Life as he knows it in the Ashante Kingdom ends abruptly when Kofi is captured and sent to New England as a slave. This is a narrative of Kofi's life, his struggle to fit into a strange place.

Herman, Charlotte. 1994. *What Happened to Heather Hopkowitz?* Philadelphia: Jewish Publication Society.

Heather, a Jewish girl, must adapt to the stricter dietary and other religious practices of the Orthodox Jewish family with whom she is staying while her parents are away.

Hesse, Karen. 1992. *Letters from Rifka.* New York: Holt.

Rifka, a Jewish girl, is left in Warsaw and unable to go to the United States with her family after leaving Russia with them. The year is 1919 and, in her loneliness, Rifka writes letters to her cousin.

Hicyilmaz, Gaye. 1993. *Against the Storm.* New York: Dell.

A twelve-year-old Turkish boy struggles with his family's decision to move away from their village in search of a better life.

Hobbs, Will. 1991. *Downriver.* New York: Atheneum.

Jessie and her friends sneak away from their outdoor education program after stealing equipment and travel the Colorado River through the Grand Canyon. They encounter dangers, and Jessie learns to think and act independently instead of blindly following others.

———. 1993. *Beardance.* New York: Atheneum.

In this sequel to Bearstone, Cloyd Atcitty finds out more about his Ute heritage and tries to save the lives of rare grizzly bears in Colorado.

———. 1996. *Far North.* New York: Morrow.

Fifteen-year-old Gabe, a Texan of Anglo heritage, and Raymond, a Dene Indian, are roommates in a Canadian school. They become stranded together in the Yukon and must rely on each other to survive.

Holman, Felice. 1978. *The Murderer.* New York: Scribner.

Thirteen-year-old Hershy, a Jewish boy growing up in a Pennsylvania mining town during the Depression, is tormented by escalating incidents of anti-Semitism, eventually being wrongfully accused of murder.

———. 1990. *Secret City, U.S.A.* New York: Scribner.

Two middle schools kids find an abandoned house perfect to shelter homeless kids. It takes a great deal of endurance to make the house a home and finally achieve their dream.

Hughes, Monica. 1993. *The Crystal Drop.* New York: Simon & Schuster Books for Young Readers.

A futuristic story set in the summer of 2011, when Megan and her younger brother Ian, after the death of their mother, must journey across the wilderness of Canada plagued by drought and the devastation of a collapsing civilization.

Irwin, Hadley. 1987. *Kim-Kimi.* New York: McElderry.

Sixteen-year-old Kim Andrews/Kimi Yogushi tries to fit in but also investigates her Japanese roots. She discovers that Japanese Americans were imprisoned in their own country during World War II.

Johnson, Angela. 1994. *Toning the Sweep.* New York: Scholastic.

Long ago, when someone died, a relative would hit the sweep, a plow, with a hammer, to let everyone know. In this book, three generations of African American women share a truth about life, death, and themselves, however different that may be.

Karp, Naomie J. 1976. *The Turning Point.* New York: Harcourt Brace Jovanovich.

In 1938, twelve-year-old Hannah leaves the Bronx when her family moves to the suburbs, but she also leaves a Jewish neighborhood for a mostly Protestant area. Karp's book describes Hannah's experiences with anti-Semitism.

Kaufman, Stephen. 1985. *Does Anyone Here Know the Way to Thirteen?* Boston: Houghton Mifflin.

Myron fears his Bar Mitzvah and would prefer becoming a Little League star. As a result of his conflicted feelings, he learns a lot about his heritage and himself.

Kent, Deborah. 1992. *Why Me?* New York: Scholastic.

Not only does thirteen-year-old Rachel have to struggle with the difficulties of a life-threatening disease, she must also deal with the newly acquired knowledge that she was adopted.

Kerr, M. E. 1978. *Gentlehands.* New York: HarperCollins.

Buddy must confront his thoughts about the Holocaust when he learns that his grandfather is an escaped Nazi war criminal and that his girlfriend, the wealthy, college-bound Skye, is an anti-Semite.

Koningsburg, E. L. 1971. *About the B'nai Bagels.* New York: Atheneum.

Mark, a member of the Little League team called B'nai B'rith but nicknamed B'nai Bagels, deals with his preparation for his Bar Mitzvah, his achievement on the Little League team, his friendships, and practicing his religion. Many Jewish customs are described in this book.

Krisher, Trudy. 1994. *Spite Fences.* New York: Delacorte.

In the summer of 1960, thirteen-year-old Maggie of Georgia becomes more self-reliant and discovers a way to document events related to the civil rights movement.

Kyoko, Mori. 1993. *Shizuko's Daughter.* New York: Fawcett Juniper.

After the suicide of her mother, twelve-year-old Yuki must learn to make sense of her life growing up in Japan with a father who doesn't seem to love her and a stepmother who treats her badly.

Lasky, Kathryn. 1986. *Pageant.* Portland, OR: Four Winds Press.

Sarah, the only Jewish girl at an exclusive Catholic boarding school in the Midwest in the early 1960s, must confront pressures to conform in many areas—from dress codes to political thought. After many adventures and misadventures, Sarah rebels.

———. 1996. *Journey to the New World: The Diary of Remember Patience Whipple.* New York: Scholastic.

Mem—a twelve-year-old immigrating to Plymouth, Massachusetts, on the Mayflower—relates details of life in America in 1620 through a diary of her journey and settlement.

Lee, Marie G. 1994. *Finding My Voice.* New York: Dell.

Ellen, a high school senior, is the sole Korean American in her school. Although bright and popular she finds herself dealing with prejudice from both students and teachers.

Leighton, Maxinne. 1992. *An Ellis Island Christmas.* New York: Viking Children's Books.

A picture book about a young Polish girl's immigration to America.

Lester, Julius. 1968. *To Be A Slave.* New York: Dial.

A narrative of what it's like to be owned by another man, to be a "thing," a possession. Slavery is vividly described to the reader, who learns how the black slave used music and religion to fight against bondage.

———. 1994. *The Last Tales of Uncle Remus.* New York: Dial.

Inspired by black folk tradition, the tales of Brer Rabbit are told by a master story teller who makes these tales seem both contemporary and timeless in this children's picture book.

Levine, Ellen. 1995. *A Fence Away from Freedom.* New York: Putnam.

Recounts the evacuation and relocation of Japanese Americans 1942–1945.

Levitin, Sonia. 1987a. *Journey to America.* New York: Atheneum.

The thrilling description of a Jewish family's escape from Nazi Germany.

———. 1987b. *The Return.* New York: Atheneum.

Tells the drama and struggle of an unusual group of refugees, the "black Jews" of Ethiopia, who were smuggled by the Israeli government to their new homes in Israel in the mid-1980s.

Lichtman, Wendy. 1986. *Telling Secrets.* New York: Harper & Row.

Toby, a freshman in college, wrestles with the teachings of her religion and the family secret and shame of her father's imprisonment. She wonders whether she can or should confide in her roommate.

Lowry, Lois. 1989. *Number the Stars.* Boston: Houghton Mifflin.

This Newbery Award–winning book focuses on the friendship between two girls. Ten-year-old Annemarie and her family find the courage to help shelter Jewish friends from the Nazis during their occupation of Denmark.

Lyon, G. E. 1993. *Dreamplace.* Illus. P. Catalanotto. New York: Orchard.

The present meets the past in this supernatural story as visitors recount what they see during visits to pueblos which once were the homes of a group of Anasazi.

Lyons, Mary E. 1992. *Letters from a Slave Girl: The Story of Harriet Jacobs.* New York: Simon & Schuster.

In fictionalized letters, Harriet recounts her life and struggles as a slave and eventual escape to the North.

Maestro, Betsy. 1996. *Coming to America: The Story of Immigration.* New York: Scholastic.

A realistic look at immigration to America that excludes none of the hardships.

Matas, Carol. 1987. *Lisa's War.* New York: Scribner.

Lisa is a teenage girl in Nazi-occupied Denmark. When she and other Jews attempt to resist the Nazi occupation, they must flee for their lives.

———. 1990. *Code Name Kris.* New York: Scribner.

The sequel to *Lisa's War* finds seventeen-year-old Jesper continuing to resist the Nazi occupation of Denmark.

McKissack, Patricia. 1992. *The Dark Thirty: Southern Tales of the Supernatural.* New York: Knopf/Borzoi Books.

The thirty minutes before nightfall is the perfect time to tell suspense stories. Several African American tales make up this collection to be told in *the dark thirty.*

———. 1994. *Christmas in the Big House, Christmas in the Quarters.* New York: Scholastic.

This illustrated text tells of the preparation for celebrating Christmas—the customs, recipes, songs, and poems—both in the "big" plantation house and in the slave quarters. Happiness and sadness are part of this seasonal celebration, depicting the continuation of life.

McKissack, Patricia, and Frederick McKissack Jr. 1994. *Black Diamond: The Story of the Negro Baseball Leagues.* New York: Scholastic.

This book traces the history of black American leagues in baseball and includes stories of many great heroes such as Monte Irwin, Buck Leonard, and Cool Papa Bell.

Meyer, Carolyn. 1987. *Denny's Tapes.* New York: McElderry.

As the son of an interracial marriage, Denny finds the need to travel across the country to discover his black-white heritage from both sets of grandparents.

———. 1992. *Where the Broken Heart Still Beats: The Story of Cynthia Ann Parker.* San Diego: Harcourt Brace.

Although a captive of the Comanche Indians, Cynthia Ann Parker becomes a part of "The People," bearing several children, one of whom becomes a chieftain. When returned to her white family, she longs to be rescued by her Comanche people.

———, ed. 1994. *Rio Grande Stories.* San Diego: Harcourt Brace.

A multicultural seventh-grade class in New Mexico researches and creates a book, thus teaching and learning about their cultures—Native American, Hispanic, African American, Jewish, and Anglo.

Mohr, Nicholasa. 1986. *Going Home.* New York: Dutton/Dial.

After living in America, Felita finds it difficult to return to her homeland of Puerto Rico. She feels alienated, alone, and unable to fit in.

———. 1996. *Felita.* New York: Bantam Doubleday Dell.

This is the story of a Puerto Rican girl growing up in a close-knit family, as she tries to fit in in the United States.

Murphy, Jim. 1993. *Across America on an Emigrant Train.* Boston: Houghton Mifflin.

This book provides a historic look at America and its railroads through the eyes of an immigrant and is based on the journal memoirs of Robert Louis Stevenson.

Myers, Walter Dean. 1988. *Fallen Angels.* New York: Scholastic.

Unable to afford college but tired of the mean streets of the inner city, Richie enlists in the Army in the summer of 1967. He hopes to see light duty on his tour of Vietnam because of a physical injury; instead what he sees and lives for the next year changes his life forever.

———. 1990. *The Mouse Rap.* New York: HarperCollins.

Mouse and his friend Styx discover that someone they know was involved in a crime back in the days of Al Capone. The two begin a caper of their own when they try to find the treasure, supposedly hidden in an abandoned building in their inner-city neighborhood.

———. 1992. *Somewhere in the Darkness.* New York: Scholastic.

Jimmy Little's father returns home after nine years in prison. Jimmy struggles to accept his father as he tries to clear his name and get to know his son.

———. 1995. *Mop, Moondance and the Nagasaki Knights.* Boston: Houghton Mifflin.

The Little League baseball team called the Elks play in a special tournament with international teams in hope of winning a trip to Japan. Communication becomes a problem, not only with the international teams, but among the Elks team as well.

Naidoo, Beverly. 1984. *Journey to Jo'Burg: A South African Story.* New York: HarperCollins.

With their baby sister gravely ill, Naledi and her younger brother journey to Jo'Burg to retrieve their mother, who works as a live-in domestic in the suburbs. This book brings to light the harsh realities of the apartheid of South Africa.

———. 1990. *Chain of Fire.* New York: HarperCollins.

This story presents the challenges facing Naledi and her younger brother Tiro, as they join other demonstrators in an attempt to save both themselves and their village from certain destruction under the "homeland" policy of the apartheid.

Namioka, Lensey. 1994. *April and the Dragon Lady.* San Diego: Harcourt Brace.

April, a first-generation Chinese American, struggles to find her place in society. She doesn't feel a part of the American culture or the Chinese culture, but through the help of her American boyfriend and her Chinese grandmother she finds she can happily fit into both cultures.

Neville, Emily. 1991. *The China Year.* New York: HarperCollins.

A New York teenager spends a year in China when her father accepts a teaching position in Beijing.

Nixon, Joan Lowery. 1993. *Land of Hope.* New York: Dell.

Book one in Nixon's Ellis Island series tells the story of fifteen-year-old Rebekah, who leaves Russia and its pogroms for New York City in the early twentieth century. New York is very different from Rebekah's expectations.

———. 1994. *Land of Promise.* New York: Dell.

Book two in Nixon's Ellis Island series tells the story of fifteen-year-old Rose, who leaves Ireland for Chicago. She befriends Rebekah and Kristen on the journey to America.

———. 1995. *Land of Dreams.* New York: Dell.

Book three in Nixon's Ellis Island series tells the story of Kristen, who leaves Sweden for Minnesota. She finds a life similar to the one in Sweden and longs for some independence.

Nye, Naomi Shihab, ed. 1992. *This Same Sky: A Collection of Poems from Around the World.* Portland, OR: Four Winds Press.

Visit and learn about the world around you through an eloquent collection poems giving attention to our elders.

———. 1994. *Red Suitcase.* Brockport, NY: BOA Editions.

Powerful poems make up this collection about Palestinian life and the continuing search for peace.

———, ed. 1995a. *The Tree Is Older Than You Are.* New York: Simon & Schuster.

This multicultural collection of poems and short stories from Mexico aptly shows our similarities through the use of metaphor, simile, and personification.

———. 1995b. *Words under the Words: Selected Poems.* Portland, OR: Eighth Mountain Press.

In this collection of poems by an Arab American author, learn about Arabic coffee, the man in the village who makes brooms, the gypsies of the desert, and much more.

Oberman, Sheldon. 1997. *The Always Prayer Shawl.* New York: Viking Penguin.

A sentimental story about a young Jewish boy named Adam who experiences great changes in his life when hard times force his family to immigrate to America.

Okimoto, Jean Davies. 1993. *Molly by Any Other Name.* New York: Scholastic.

Molly was adopted as an infant by a white family and, although she knows she is of Asian descent, she is not sure which nationality. With the help of her Japanese American boyfriend and her adoptive parents, she begins searching for her birth mother.

Oppenheim, S. L. 1995. *The Lily Cupboard: A Story of the Holocaust.* Illus. R. Himler. New York: HarperCollins.

This story depicts, in both illustration and text, the Nazi occupation of Holland and how a Dutch farmer and his family safeguarded a young Jewish Dutch girl.

Palacios, Argentina. 1994. *Standing Tall: The Stories of Ten Hispanic Americans.* New York: Scholastic.

Recounts the lives of ten Hispanic Americans.

Paterson, Katherine. 1995. *Rebels of the Heavenly Kingdom.* New York: Puffin.

Story of rebellion in nineteenth-century China as a young boy and girl engage in activities to overthrow the Manchu government.

Paulsen, Gary. 1985. *Dogsong.* New York: Simon & Schuster.

In a story of the passage from youth to adulthood, a fourteen-year-old Eskimo boy embarks on a dogsled journey and must survive the frigid wastelands of the north.

———. 1990. *The Crossing.* New York: Bantam Doubleday Dell Books for Young Readers.

This story tells of two people who come together at the U.S.-Mexican border—both trying to escape. A young Mexican orphan desires to cross the border and escape his life of poverty, and a U.S. army sergeant, stationed at Ft. Bliss, attempts to escape into a bottle as a means of obliterating his memory of Vietnam.

———. 1994. *The Car.* San Diego: Harcourt Brace.

Terry, abandoned at fourteen by his parents, builds a car from a kit and travels from Ohio to try to find an uncle in Oregon. He is joined eventually by a Vietnam veteran and others on this journey of discovery.

———. 1995a. *Hatchet.* Boston: Houghton Mifflin.

Brian is on his way to see his father, but the pilot of the plane has a heart attack and dies. Suddenly, Brian finds himself on an adventure in the

Canadian wilderness; he must land the plane and try to survive with only the clothes on his back and a hatchet that his mother gave him.

———. 1995b. *Nightjohn.* New York: Dell.

In the 1850s, Sarny, a slave with a desire to learn to read, and Nightjohn, a slave returning from the North to teach other slaves to read, risk severe punishment to teach and learn.

Perera, Hilda. 1992. *Kiki: A Cuban Boy's Adventures in America.* New York: Pickering.

In the 1960s, Kiki, a Cuban boy, comes to America.

Pettit, Jayne. 1993. *A Place to Hide: True Stories of Holocaust Rescues.* New York: Scholastic.

Oskar Schindler and Miep Gies are among true life heroes introduced in this dramatic book. As rescuers, they saved Jewish lives at the peril of their own.

Pitts, Paul. 1988. *Racing the Sun.* New York: Avon.

A young Navajo boy learns to take pride in his heritage through the aid and guidance of his grandfather.

———. 1992. *The Shadowman's Way.* New York: Avon.

Nelson Sam is a Navajo Indian who lives on a reservation. Life had been pretty unremarkable until he made friends with the new white boy in town; he ends up making enemies at the reservation.

———. 1994. *Crossroads.* New York: Avon.

Young Hobart Slim discovers, through the aid of a new found friend, that once you learn to believe in yourself and stand up for yourself, problems can be overcome and anything can be accomplished.

Rana, Indi. 1994. *The Roller Birds of Rampur.* New York: Fawcett.

After spending much of her life in England, this Indian teen returns home to India to discover her identity.

Rinaldi, Ann. 1993. *Wolf by the Ears.* New York: Scholastic.

A light-skinned, reddish-haired slave begins to question who her father is, especially when neither she nor her siblings have been sold and all have received a good education. Could the master of Monticello, Thomas Jefferson, be her father?

Robert, Willo Davis. 1988. *Sugar Isn't Everything: A Support Book, in Fiction Form, for the Young Diabetic.* New York: Simon & Schuster.

A presentation for young adults focusing on the facts concerning diabetes.

Rosofsky, Iris. 1988. *Miriam.* New York: HarperCollins.

Miriam, growing up in an Orthodox Jewish family in Brooklyn, confronts and questions her faith when her ailing brother dies.

Salinger, J. D. 1945, 1984. *The Catcher in the Rye.* New York: Bantam.

This is the story of the internal struggle involved in the transition from childhood to youth and youth to adulthood. The sixteen-year-old protagonist, Holden, is searching for love, stability, and honesty—virtues he feels that individuals lose as they leave childhood. In childhood he had truth, genuineness, and innocence.

Salisbury, Graham. 1994. *Under the Blood Red Sun.* New York: Delacorte.

This story tells the experiences, thoughts, and emotions of several teenage boys living in Hawaii during the attack on Pearl Harbor.

———. 1997a. *Blue Skin of the Sea.* New York: Bantam Doubleday Dell Books for Young Readers.

A moving account of adolescent boys growing up in Hawaii through a series of interrelated stories.

———. 1997b. *Shark Bait.* New York: Delacorte.

An adolescent boy growing up in Hawaii is faced with a number of difficult choices and does not always make the right decision.

Say, Allen. 1993. *Grandfather's Journey.* Boston: Houghton Mifflin.

A young Japanese American tells of his grandfather's journey from Japan to America. The reader learns of the grandfather's struggles and his love for both countries.

Schami, Rafik. 1992. *A Hand Full of Stars.* New York: Puffin.

An aspiring young journalist begins to keep a daily journal of his life in the suppressed society of Damascus, Syria.

Scieszka, Jon, and Lane Smith. 1995. *Math Curse.* New York: Viking Children's Books.

A unique twist dealing with the frustrations and anxiety of math.

She, Colleen, ed. 1995. *Teenage Refugees from China Speak Out.* New York: Rosen.

Teenage refugees from China tell why and how they left home and how they have adjusted to life in the United States in this volume in a series of "In Their Own Voices" books.

Shoup, Barbara. 1994. *Wish You Were Here.* New York: Hyperion.

After his parents divorce, this high school senior's life seems to spin out of control when his best friend suddenly leaves, his mother remarries, and his father has a brush with death.

Soto, Gary. 1991. *Baseball in April and Other Stories.* San Diego: Harcourt Brace.

Although the flavor is Latino, the messages are universal in eleven short stories which feature young Hispanics growing up in a contemporary Mexican American neighborhood in Fresno, California.

———. 1994. *Jesse.* San Diego: Harcourt Brace.

Tired of his abusive home life, Jesse moves in with Abel, his older brother. The two young Mexican Americans struggle to live a happy life, making ends meet working migrant jobs, while fulfilling the dream of higher education to overcome a life of poverty.

———. 1995. *Chato's Kitchen.* Illus. S. Guevara. New York: Putnam.

The language and life of the barrio of East L.A. are presented with a twist in this colorfully illustrated story which places animals in human roles.

Spinelli, Jerry. 1996. *Maniac Magee.* New York: HarperCollins.

Jeffrey Lionel "Maniac" Magee, an orphaned white boy, is not only a star athlete; he is also something of a celebrity who helps dispel prejudice between the black East End and white West End of his town.

Staples, Donna. 1993. *Arena Beach.* Boston: Houghton Mifflin.

Tee, a seventeen-year-old, has spent her life fairly unconventionally, having been raised by a mother who is a former hippie. Her life becomes even more tumultuous as the father she's never known suddenly appears.

Staples, Suzanne Fisher. 1989. *Shabanu: Daughter of the Wild.* New York: Knopf.

Young Shabanu has liberal beliefs which are at odds with her nomadic Muslim culture. When she finds out she is to become the fourth wife of an old man, she must choose between her own identity and family honor.

———. 1995. *Haveli.* New York: Random House.

This is the story of a young Pakistani woman's struggle between her heart and the ancient traditions and values of her culture.

Stolz, Mary. 1992. *Stealing Home.* New York: HarperCollins.

Thomas and his grandfather enjoy a cozy life together, fishing and listening to baseball, until Aunt Lizzy moves in and tries to change the way they live, even the way they eat. Most of all, she hates the baseball that they so love, yet they somehow endure and thrive as a family.

Strasser, Todd. 1981. *The Wave.* New York: Laurel Leaf.

Based on a true story from 1969, *The Wave* is the story of a high school teacher's experiment that had a surprisingly powerful and destructive impact on the students. It demonstrates that any type of extremism, in the hands of charismatic leadership, can grip high school students today.

Tan, Amy. 1996. *The Joy Luck Club.* New York: Ivy.

In California, four American-born daughters of four women born in China learn of their mothers' struggles, hopes, and lives in China before 1949. In the discovery process the daughters learn about being Chinese, being American, and preserving memories and cultures.

Taylor, Mildred. 1990. *Mississippi Bridge.* New York: Dial.

A ten-year-old white boy in rural Mississippi describes the events which take place as black passengers are ordered off a bus to make room for late-arriving white passengers. The blacks must then forge the raging Rosa Lee River on foot.

———. 1976, 1997. *Roll of Thunder, Hear My Cry.* New York: Viking Penguin.

Cassie and her family struggle with courage and pride to keep their land, the source of some security, in Depression-era Mississippi in the face of extreme prejudice against African Americans.

Tekavec, Valerie, ed. 1995. *Teenage Refugees from Bosnia-Herzegovina Speak Out.* New York: Rosen.

Teenage refugees from Bosnia-Herzegovina tell why and how they left their country and how they have adjusted to life in the United States in this volume in a series of "In Their Own Voices" books.

———, ed. 1995. *Teenage Refugees from Haiti Speak Out.* New York: Rosen.

Teenage refugees from Haiti tell why and how they left home and how they have adjusted to life in the United States in this volume in a series of "In Their Own Voices" books.

Temple, Frances. 1992. *Taste of Salt: A Story of Modern Haiti.* New York: Orchard.

Seventeen-year-old Djo tells the story of his life in poverty and his work with social reformist Father Aristide, as they struggle in their fight against repression in Haiti.

Uchida, Yoshiko. 1971. *Journey to Topaz.* New York: Scribner.

Seen through the eyes of eleven-year-old Yuki, this story describes the disgrace and indignities suffered by Japanese Americans after Pearl Harbor.

Ure, Jean. 1993. *Plague.* New York: Puffin.

Fran had just survived a month-long camping expedition, but the true test of survival awaits her as she returns home and encounters a city of death and devastation, surrounded by barricades and barbed wire.

Vanasse, Deb. 1997. *A Distant Enemy.* New York: Dutton.

Young Joseph, a fourteen-year-old, struggles with the changes to his Yup'ik Eskimo village brought on by the white people. His struggle is intensified by the fact that he himself is half white, has been abandoned by his white father, and must find his identity between these two cultures.

Van Der Rol, Ruud, and Rian Verhoeven. 1995. *Anne Frank: Beyond the Diary: A Photographic Rememberance.* New York: Puffin.

This book provides insight into the life and death of Anne Frank. The book includes photos, diary excerpts, and a chronology of events.

Voight, Cynthia. 1982. *Dicey's Song.* New York: Atheneum.

In this sequel to *Homecoming,* the four children are adjusting to their new beginnings with their grandmother, but Dicey now faces the internal struggle dealing with the love, trust, and courage needed in this new relationship.

———. 1992. *David and Jonathan.* New York: Scholastic.

Henry and Jonathan's friendship is affected when Jonathan's cousin, David, a Holocaust survivor, moves in with Jonathan's family.

———. 1993. *Homecoming.* New York: Ballantine.

After having been abandoned by their mother (who simply walked away from the parked car in the shopping mall of a strange city), four young siblings are forced to survive on their own. Dicey, the eldest at thirteen, must now make all the decisions, feed them, find a place to sleep, and above all avoid the authorities who would split them up into separate foster homes.

Volavkova, Hana. 1994. *Never Saw Another Butterfly.* New York: Schocker.

This book is a stirring anthology of artwork and poetry by some of the 15,000 children held at Terezin concentration camp in German-occupied Bohemia.

Vos, Ida. 1993. *Anna Is Still Here.* Boston: Houghton Mifflin.

Hidden in an attic to survive Nazi atrocities, Anna struggles to adjust to home and school in a postwar Holland where the hate of Jews survived the end of World War II.

Walker, Alice. 1993. *To Hell with Dying.* Illus. Catherine Deeter. San Diego: Harcourt Brace.

Old Mr. Sweet has been on the verge of dying several times. It is the loving attention and affection of a young girl and boy that repeatedly revives him as he continues to cheat death.

Wallis, Velma. 1994. *Two Old Women.* New York: HarperCollins.

Abandoned by their tribe, two old women find the courage and skill to survive a bleak Alaskan winter. These two women become heroes as they teach others about survival and life.

Wapner, Kenneth, ed. 1995. *Teenage Refugees from Vietnam Speak Out.* New York: Rosen.

Teenage refugees from Vietnam tell why and how they left Vietnam and how they have adjusted to life in the United States in this volume in a series of "In Their Own Voices" books.

Wiesel, Elie. 1996. *Night, Dawn, Day.* Northvale, NJ: Aronson.

This trilogy includes the first three books written by the author. *Night* is Wiesel's Holocaust memoir. *Dawn* is a novel narrated by a man who is his family's sole survivor of Auschwitz. The man is then torn by becoming a paid murderer. And *Day* is about the struggle of a man who has seen too much evil.

Williams-Garcia, Rita. 1995. *Like Sisters on the Homefront.* New York: Dutton.

Gayle, a fourteen-year-old troubled youth, experiences a change in her life and the healing power of the family when she moves south to live with her aunt and uncle.

Wolff, Virginia Euwer. 1994. *Make Lemonade.* New York: Scholastic.

Verna LaVaughn has but one goal in her young life: to go to college and escape the poverty facing her in the inner city. Answering an ad for a babysitter, Verna finds herself working for a young single mother of two who is barely three years older than she is, and she soon finds her own goals challenged as she is drawn in to the lives of Jolly and the two children.

Woodson, Jacqueline. 1994. *I Hadn't Meant to Tell You This.* New York: Delacorte.

Twelve-year-old Marie, from a well-to-do black family, and Lena, from a low-income white family, befriend each other initially because each one has lost her mother. Lena shares a frightening secret with Marie, and their friendship is strengthened.

Wyeth, Sharon Dennis. 1994. *The World of Daughter McGuire.* New York: Delacorte.

With her parents' separation, eleven-year-old Daughter McGuire finds herself at a new school, where to make matters worse a member of the Avengers gang calls her a "zebra," referring to the fact that she's neither black nor white. A school project reveals that her ancestry isn't simply black and white, giving her a better sense of identity.

Yee, Paul. 1989. *Tales from Gold Mountain: Stories of the Chinese in the New World.* New York: Macmillan.

Short stories about the immigrants who built the transcontinental railroad, panned for gold, and settled the western United States

Yep, Laurence. 1975. *Dragonwings.* New York: HarperCollins.

Yep's historical novel relates eight-year-old Moon Shadow's experiences when he emigrates from China to join his father in early twentieth-century San Francisco.

———. 1993. *American Dragons: Twenty-five Asian American Voices.* New York: HarperCollins.

A collection of poems, short stories, and excerpts from plays dealing with some adolescent issues of Asian Americans. Identity, World War II, and love are a few of the themes found in this collection.

———. *Child of the Owl* (1990 HarperCollins), *Dragon's Gate* (1993 HarperCollins), *Mountain Light* (1997 HarperCollins), *The Serpent's Children* (1996 HarperCollins), *The Star Fisher* (1992 Puffin).

A variety of novels about China and Chinese immigrants to the United States.

Yolen, Jane. 1992. *Encounter*. Illus. D. Shannon. San Diego: Harcourt Brace.

The landing of Columbus and his men on the island of San Salvador is retold through the eyes of a young Taino Indian boy.

———. 1993. *Briar Rose.* New York: Tor.

Yolen intertwines the familiar German folktale of Briar Rose with an American's investigation of her grandmother's past in Poland during the Holocaust.

Zaslavsky, Claudia. 1995. *Africa Counts: Number and Pattern in African Culture.* New York: Lawrence Hill.

A biographical reference to the numbers, words, gestures, and symbols of ethnomathematics. Included are origins and background, as well as a regional study.

Zemenova, Tatyana. 1995. *Teenage Refugees from Russia Speak Out.* New York: Rosen.

Teenage refugees from Russia tell why and how they left Russia and how they have adjusted to life in the United States in this volume in a series of "In Their Own Voices" books.

Editors

Jean E. Brown and **Elaine C. Stephens**, professors of teacher education at Saginaw Valley State University (SVSU), have co-authored several books together, including *Toward Literacy: Theory and Applications for Teaching Writing in the Content Areas* (1993), *Teaching Young Adult Literature: Sharing the Connection* (1995), *Learning About the Holocaust . . . Literature and Other Resources* (1995), *Images from the Holocaust* (1996), and *Exploring Diversity: Literature, Themes, and Activities* (1996) . They also co-edited the resource books *Two Way Street: Integrating Reading and Writing in the Middle Schools* and *Two Way Street: Integrating Reading and Writing in the Secondary Schools*. Both have received distinguished faculty awards from the Michigan Association of Governing Boards of State Universities. In addition, **Jean Brown** has written over eighty-five articles and book chapters and is contributing editor of *Preserving Intellectual Freedom* (1994). She is a former high school English teacher and department chair, as well as past president of the Michigan Council of Teachers of English (MCTE) and former editor of its newsletter. She has served on NCTE's SLATE Steering Committee and chaired NCTE's Commission on Intellectual Freedom. Her honors include recognition by MCTE for service to the profession, by SVSU for research and scholarly achievement, and by the Saginaw chapter of Phi Delta Kappa for her research. **Elaine Stephens** is a former classroom teacher, reading consultant, and professional-development specialist. She has written more than fifty publications and is a frequent inservice speaker and conference presenter. She also serves as director of professional development for the Greater Saginaw Valley Regional Education Consortium and has served as president of the Michigan Association of Colleges for Teacher Education. Her honors include recognition by SVSU for excellence in teaching and by the Saginaw chapter of Phi Delta Kappa for leadership, as well as the PRAISE Award of Distinction for her work with the Michigan Reading Association.

Contributors

Joan Bauer recalls as one of her earliest and most sustaining memories her grandmother, a professional storyteller, telling her stories when she was a child. "More than any other person," Bauer says, "she influenced my writing style and my approach to humor. She knew how to bridge the seriousness of life with the absurd." Born in River Forest, Illinois, Bauer now lives in Darien, Connecticut, with her husband, daughter, and dapper dog. She has worked in advertising, radio, television, and film. Her books for young adults include *Squashed,* winner of the Delacorte Prize for a First Young Adult Novel, and *Thwonk,* an ALA Best Book for Young Adults. Bauer is also the author of *Sticks,* a novel for middle readers. Her new YA novel, *Rules of the Road,* will be published in 1998.

Janet Bode is an in-the-trenches researcher, chronicling the lives of kids around the country. Ultimately her books are collections of their stories. In their own words, in their own way, today's adolescents speak frankly about the reality of being caught in the crosshairs of social change and their strategies for succeeding. Many of Bode's titles have received awards from such organizations as the American Library Association, the National Council for the Social Studies, and the International Reading Association; and her book *Different Worlds: Interracial and Cross-Cultural Dating* inspired a CBS-TV Schoolbreak Special. She has also written two adult trade nonfiction books, as well as articles for various periodicals, including *The New York Times, Village Voice, Glamour,* and *Cosmopolitan.*

Eve Bunting is the author of more than 150 books for children and young people. Born and educated in Northern Ireland, she now lives in Pasadena, California, with her husband, Ed. Her first book, published in 1972, was a retold Irish tale. Although she has written over 150 books for a wide audience of readers, ranging from young children to young adults, she is best known for her picture books that address serious topics. Bunting's many honors include twenty-eight state awards, the Golden Kite, the Edgar Allan Poe Mystery Writers of America Award, and the Pen International Literary Award. She is the author of *Smoky Night,* a Caldecott Medal winner. Her most recent honor was the 1997 Regina Medal.

Kelly Chandler, a former high school teacher, is now a doctoral student in literacy education at the University of Maine, where she teaches courses in reading, children's literature, and teacher research. Her articles have appeared in *The ALAN Review, Teaching Tolerance, Journal of Maine Education, Teaching & Learning: The Journal of Natural Inquiry,* and *Teacher Research.* She contributed chapters to Joan Kaywell's *Adolescent Literature as a Complement to the Classics, Volume 3* (1996) and Stephen Tchudi's *Alternatives to Grading Student Writing* (1997). With Brenda

Power and Jeff Wilhelm, she edited *Reading Stephen King: Issues of Censorship, Student Choice, and the Place of Popular Literature* (1997).

Ruth Ann Lee Copp earned her B.A. in English and secondary education from Macalester College in St. Paul, Minnesota. She has taught English at Madison High School in New Jersey and currently lives in Midland, Michigan, where she is a substitute teacher in English, history, and foreign languages; has taught English at Northwood University; and has researched and written about environmental issues for Earth Generation. She currently supervises preservice field-experience students in middle school and secondary education for Saginaw Valley State University, where she will soon finish her M.A.T. in reading.

Christopher Paul Curtis has felt a burning desire to write ever since he realized he couldn't talk his way out of many of his problems. Born in Flint, Michigan, Curtis spent his first thirteen years after finishing high school on the assembly line of Flint's historic Fisher Body Plant #1. His job entailed hanging doors, and it left him with an aversion to getting into and out of large automobiles—particularly big Buicks. Curtis's writing—and his dedication to it—has been greatly influenced by his family members, particularly his wife, Kaysandra. It was she who told Curtis that he "better hurry up and start doing something constructive with his life or else start looking for a new place to live." And with those loving words of inspiration, a writing career was launched.

Denise R. Emery teaches eighth-grade English in an English/American History block at Northeast Middle School in Midland, Michigan. She is a member of the National Council of Teachers of English and Michigan Reading Association. In the summer of 1998, Denise and a team of teachers plan to return to the Cree Indian Reservation in Norway House, Manitoba, to continue their work with the children of the tribe. Besides Native American literature, her interests include the use of picture books in the middle school classroom, the development of young writers, the importance of reading and writing in all curricular areas, and the application of history for today's middle school student.

Dallas W. Fischer (M.A.T.— Reading, Saginaw Valley State University) is currently teaching language arts in an adult education program in St. Charles, Michigan, for both high school completion and G.E.D. He is an active member of both ALAN and M.C.T.E.

Christa Goldsmith has spent most of her elementary teaching career in both private and public school in southeast Michigan. Her passion for art led to further studies, and she designs pen and ink stationery and watercolor paintings in her spare time. This creative spirit enhances every aspect of her teaching as she develops thematic units to challenge all learning styles. This commitment is a direct result of her educational experience. According to Goldsmith, "In school, we raised our hand to give the right answer, but it was seldom discussed. I knew I would become a teacher because I firmly believed there had to be other ways in which to learn. My students would write their own stories, poems, and songs. They would read about other cultures in faraway lands. They would dream and discuss, compare and create." As she approaches retirement, Goldsmith can't imagine that even then she would not be working with children.

Amy Hackett teaches science, health, and physical education at Mott Middle School in Flint, Michigan. She has recently completed a Master's in Art degree with an emphasis in reading.

Joyce Hansen writes fiction and nonfiction for the middle-grade and young adult reader. For twenty-two years, until her retirement in 1995, she was a classroom teacher and staff developer in the New York City public school system. She also taught writing and literature at Empire State College (State University of New York). Hansen was born in New York City and lived and worked there until she retired. She presently lives with her husband in South Carolina and writes full time. She has seven published books and several others that are scheduled for publication. Her books have won various awards, among them the Coretta Scott King Honor Book Award, the Parents' Choice Award, and the Children's Book Award from the African Studies Association.

Mary R. Harmon, an award winning 7–12th grade English language arts teacher for twenty-three years, now teaches in the English Education Program at Saginaw Valley State University, where she is chair of the English Department. She has been active in the Michigan Council of Teachers of English and has served as college chair and as editor of *The Michigan English Teacher.* Especially interested in the issues surrounding language use, power, and classroom discourse, she drafted NCTE's Position Statement on English-Only Amendments and Laws and initiated SVSU's Language and Education course. The author of a variety of articles dealing with multicultural, gender, and sociolinguistic issues, she has been a frequent presenter at NCTE Conferences and many other regional, state, and national conferences.

Louise Garcia Harrison teaches creative writing, American literature, and composition classes at Heritage High School in Saginaw, Michigan. Her students regularly are recognized for excellence in creative writing in state and national competitions. She has been honored by the Michigan Youth Arts Festival as Creative Writing Teacher of the Year for Michigan. Additionally, the Saginaw Arts Council honored her in 1993 for her contributions to the arts. It was the only time that they have so recognized the contributions of an educator. She earned her BA from Purdue and her M.A.T. from Saginaw Valley State University.

Ted Hipple teaches English education, adolescent literature, and general curriculum courses at the University of Tennessee. He has served NCTE in a variety of ways over the years: chair of the Conference on English Education; chair of the Secondary Section; president of ALAN; and, since 1983, executive secretary of ALAN. He has written widely, with articles on young adult literature in *English Journal* and *The ALAN Review* and some fifteen authored or edited books.

Diane Hoffbauer, an associate professor at Alaska Pacific University, teaches graduate and undergraduate courses in children's literature and literacy/communication. Through structured practicums in the Anchorage public schools, students in APU's classes use a variety of books and strategies to reach students with a wide range of needs and ethnic backgrounds. Hoffbauer has published articles on literacy issues and has been a regular presenter at the International Reading Association and National Council of the Social Studies conferences.

Alyce Hunter is a supervisor of curriculum and teaching for the West Windsor–Plainsboro School District in New Jersey. She works with teachers to create interdisciplinary experiences that help learners connect facts and concepts from all subject areas. She believes that infusing multicultural ideas, facts, and images into the curriculum helps students understand the ways in which people are diverse and yet united by values, practices, and traditions. Hunter has received grants from the U.S. government and the Korean Society. She has a doctoral degree from Lehigh University and teaches at the Graduate School of Education of Wagner College, Staten Island, New York.

Jeffrey S. Kaplan is assistant professor of Educational Foundations at the University of Central Florida in Orlando and the area coordinator for the College of Education at the Daytona Beach campus. A 1996 recipient of the State of Florida Teaching Incentive Program Award for exemplary teaching, he is passionate about assisting preservice and practicing teachers in discovering new ways to improve their teaching. He is an active member of the NCTE, ALAN (NCTE Adolescent Literature Assembly), and the Florida Council of Teachers of English, where he serves on many committees. He is published in many academic journals, regularly reviews novels for *The ALAN Review,* and has contributed to these textbooks: *Adolescent Literature as a Complement to the Classics, Volumes III and IV* and *Helping Adolescents at Risk through Literature.* He is editing a volume in the Greenwood Publishing series on understanding adolescent literature, entitled *Identity Conflicts.*

Charlotte Valencia Lindahl, a native New Mexican, has taught primarily in the humanities for the last twelve years. Lindahl received her master's degree at the University of New Mexico as a James Madison Fellow. She is currently a professional development instructor for American Indian education in the Albuquerque New Mexico Public School system.

Diana Mitchell, an independent language arts consultant, is president of the Michigan Council of Teachers of English, co-editor of the *Language Arts Journal of Michigan,* and co-director of the Red Cedar Writing Project at Michigan State University. She was a middle school and high school teacher for twenty-nine years. Mitchell is on the Executive Board of NCTE's Conference on English Education, is actively involved in WILLA (Women in Literature and Life Assembly), and is past-president of the Assembly of Literature for Adolescents of NCTE. She is on the editorial review board of *The New Advocate* and is a reviewer for *English Education.* Her publications include *Explorations* *in the Teaching of English,* co-authored with Steve Tchudi; a chapter in *Adolescent Literature as a Complement to the Classics,* edited by Joan Kaywell; an essay in Scribner's *Writers for Young Adults* (forthcoming); a monthly column in *English Journal;* and articles in various journals.

Elizabeth Noll, a former middle school teacher, is assistant professor of Language, Literacy and Sociocultural Studies at the University of New Mexico. She teaches courses in multicultural literature, writing, and literacy methods.

Elizabeth A. Poe is associate professor of English at Radford University in Radford, Virginia, where she teaches undergraduate and graduate courses in young adult and children's literature. Previously she taught secondary English for thirteen years in Colorado. She currently serves on the IRA's Literature for Young Adults Committee and as editor of IRA's *SIGNAL Journal.* She is a past-president of NCTE's ALAN and the former book review editor for *The ALAN Review.* She has also chaired the Colorado Blue Spruce Young Adult Book Award Committee. Her publications include numerous journal articles, book chapters, scholarly essays, teaching guides, and book reviews. She is the author of *Presenting Barbara Wersba* and *Focus on Sexuality: A Reference Handbook;* and co-author of *Focus Relationships: A Reference Handbook.* She lives in Blacksburg, Virginia, with her husband and twin teenage sons.

David K. Pugalee is assistant professor of teacher education at the University of North Carolina at Charlotte. He holds Master's degrees from the University of Southern Mississippi and North Carolina Central University. He earned his Ph.D. at the University of North Carolina at Chapel Hill. He brings thirteen years of classroom teaching experience to the university level. His area of expertise is mathematics education. His research interests include mathematical literacy, particularly the impact of writing and reading on the learning of mathematics.

Debra Salazar recently finished student teaching and graduated from the University of New Mexico. Debra, who describes herself as a lifelong learner, is looking forward to a career in secondary English.

Graham Salisbury grew up in the Hawaiian Islands, where his family has lived since 1820. He graduated from California State University, Northridge, and received an M.F.A. degree from Vermont College of Norwich University. He now lives with his family in Portland, Oregon. His first novel, *Blue Skin of the Sea,* won the Bank Street Child Study Association Children's Book Award, the Judy Lopez Award, the Parents' Choice Award, and the Oregon Book Award, and was selected as an ALA Best Book of the Year. *Under the Blood Red Sun* won the Scott O'Dell Award for Historical Fiction, the Parents' Choice Honor Award, and the Oregon Book Award, and was also an ALA Best Book for Young Adults and *Booklist* Editor's Choice. Salisbury is the winner of the 1993 PEN/Norma Klein Award.

Gary M. Salvner is professor of English education at Youngstown State University, where he teaches courses in English methods, adolescent literature, and writing. Salvner is the 1996–97 president of the Assembly on Literature for Adolescents (ALAN) and has written extensively on English teaching and young adult literature. He is the author of *Presenting Gary Paulsen,* former editor of *The Ohio Journal of the English Language Arts,* co-editor of *Reading Their World: The Young Adult Novel in the Classroom,* and co-editor of the book review section of *The ALAN Review.* In 1993 Salvner was honored as Ohio's Outstanding College English Teacher by the Ohio Council of Teachers of English Language Arts.

Karen Selby is assistant professor of teacher education at Saginaw Valley State University. She teaches courses in social studies education, foundations of education, and multicultural education.

Ellen Shull grew up in Peoria, Illinois, a blue-collar town in the heart of farming country, where she knew little of diversity, her childhood being remarkable for its homogeneity. Moving to Japan, however, with her military husband and even writing poetry for the emperor's New Year celebration changed that. Thereafter, she tried to bring the world to her students across the academic spectrum from elementary school to college. Currently, she teaches at Palo Alto College in San Antonio, Texas, where she is associate professor of English. A proponent of diversity, she created and teaches multicultural American literature courses. She also co-edits *Palo Alto Review: A Journal of Ideas,* which celebrates diversity in print.

Kent Sikora is a first-year middle school teacher in the Trenton, Michigan, schools. He graduated from Saginaw Valley State University with a B.A. in Secondary English Education and was awarded recognition for outstanding accomplishments by the Department of Middle and Secondary Teacher Education.

Dee Storey is professor of Teacher Education at Saginaw Valley State University in Michigan specializing in children's literature and language arts. Storey is author of *Twins in Children's and Adolescent Literature: Annotated Bibliography* (1993). She also specializes in storytelling and perpetuation of traditional literature. She has told stories at young author conferences, libraries, and schools and teaches storytelling in the graduate Elementary Education program at SVSU. Storey has written articles and given presentations about censorship and about using children's/adolescent literature in the social studies curriculum. She was the co-initiator of the Nebraska Golden Sower Reading/Award Program in 1981. She received her doctorate from Michigan State University.

Erin Sullivan is a native of Bay City, Michigan. She is married and the mother of two beautiful girls. She is a 1991 graduate of Saginaw Valley State University. She recently gave up a long-time banking career to earn teacher certification in secondary education at SVSU, where she was recognized as an Outstanding Student in Secondary Education. She is founder of an Exchange Student Club at a local high school and recently coordinated a Shakespearean Festival with performances given by at-risk ninth- and tenth-graders. Sullivan is a published poet and is currently working on publishing a YA short story. She is currently teaching English and economics at Bay-Area Community High School in Bay City, Michigan.

Deborah Forster-Sulzer is a middle and high school language arts teacher, an undergraduate and graduate instructor at the University of Central Florida, and the Secondary Language Arts Program Director for Orange County Public Schools in Florida. Sulzer understands the demands and passions of teaching from all sides of the profession. She has presented locally and nationally to share ideas and methods for engaging students in relevant language arts learning. She is currently completing her doctoral degree in Curriculum and Instruction, with an emphasis on best practices in lifelong literacy. Her greatest desire is to write, share, reflect, and always continue to grow.

Deb Vanasse began her teaching career in 1979 in the Yup'ik Eskimo village of Nunapitchuk, Alaska, where she taught English and other subjects in a small high school, one of many which gradually replaced larger boarding schools for village students. She taught for eight years in the region, where she observed the clash between strong Yup'ik traditions and the forces of external change. She eventually wrote about this conflict in a short story that later became *A Distant Enemy*, her first young adult novel. She lives in Fairbanks, Alaska, with her husband and two teenage children. She teaches English at North Pole High School and continues to write for children and young adults.

Jeffrey D. Wilhelm is assistant professor of literacy education at the University of Maine, where he teaches courses in adolescent reading, drama, secondary methods, and research. He is the author of NCTE's *Standards in Practice: Grades 6–8*. He is also co-editor with Brenda Power and Kelly Chandler of *Reading Stephen King: Issues of Censorship, Student Choice, and Popular Literature* (1997).

Mitzi Witkin is consultant to North Middle School, Great Neck, New York. She says, "As a child of hard-working immigrant parents who never had much formal schooling, I am proud of achieving the highest academic degree from the City University of New York, part of the school system that continues to educate many immigrant students. The value my immigrant parents placed on education accounts for my vocational choice of teacher and for my emphasis in the classroom on the *unum* in *e pluribus unum*. This theme was affirmed in Witkin's article "The Universal Classroom: 'Locution' a la Lincoln," published in *American Educator* and winner of the 1992 Distinguished Achievement Award of the Educational Press Association of America. Witkin has also published articles in *English Journal* and contributed lesson plans to *American Women/American Lives* (1995), a resource book published by the New York Council for the Humanities.

Index